DRUIDS, DUDES AND BEAUTY QUEENS
The Changing Face of Irish Theatre

DRUIDS, DUDES AND BEAUTY QUEENS

BEAUTY QUEENS

The Changing Face of Irish Theatre

Edited by Dermot Bolger

**NEW
ISLAND**

49340320   6-3-02

DRUIDS, DUDES AND BEAUTY QUEENS
The Changing Face of Irish Theatre
First published November 2001 by
New Island, 2 Brookside
Dundrum Road, Dublin 14

ISBN: 1 902602 74 9

British Library Cataloguing in Publication Data
A catalogue record for this book is available from the British Library

New Island receives financial assistance from The Arts Council
(An Chomhairle Ealaíon), Dublin, Ireland.

Cover design: Slick Fish Design, Dublin
Cover image by Douglas Robertson,
from the Abbey Theatre production of Barbaric Comedies
Printed in Ireland by Colour Books Ltd.

CONTENTS

This Festschrift is published in honour of Phelim Donlon,
Drama Officer of the Arts Council of Ireland, 1984-2001,
for his work on behalf of Irish theatre.

DERMOT BOLGER

Introduction

Seventeen years ago — in a 1984 thankfully unrecognisable in the main from Orwell's novel, and long before his menacing concept of 'Big Brother' had been diluted into a new form of voyeuristic entertainment — Irish theatre was holding its own against a backdrop of high unemployment, increasing emigration and a teetering economy. Without the hidden human subsidy of long hours willingly put in for little or no money (often under the cloak of short-term Mickey Mouse Government employment schemes) most of Ireland's regional Arts Centres and theatre companies would have collapsed.

In the script department of the Abbey Theatre a new play with a peculiarly long title, *Observe the Sons of Ulster Marching Towards the Somme*, was being developed for the Peacock stage, on which Tom MacIntyre was continuing his series of experimental plays with *The Bearded Lady*. A new comedy by Bernard Farrell — *All The Way Back*, reflecting the economic straits of the middle-classes — was being pencilled in for next season on their main stage. Across the country in Galway the Druid Theatre Company was incubating a masterpiece that would shortly become Thomas Murphy's *Bailegangaire*. Field Day in Derry were touring *The Riot Act* (Tom Paulin's version of *Antigone*) along with Derek Mahon's *High Time* (based on Moliere's *School for Husbands*). In the SFX hall on Dublin's northside, The Passion Machine were launching into their stride with Paul Mercier's debut, *Drowning*, containing language that poor Saint FX certainly never dreamt of. Down in Waterford, T.V. Horan was hiring a dress suit in which to welcome patrons to productions mounted on makeshift stages in rooms above pubs by the new Red Kettle Theatre Company, which he was in the process of starting with Jim Nolan and others. Foreign visitors to Dublin's innovative Project Art Centre constantly mistook the various buckets that hung from the theatre ceiling for artistic installations rather than a means of coping with leaks in the roof. And over in 70 Merrion Square, Phelim Donlon was settling into his first days as Drama Officer in the Arts Council of Ireland, trying to bridge the virtually insurmountable gap between the growing needs of that burgeoning section and the meagre grants available at that time.

In the seventeen years since, Phelim has gone on to become one of the most popular figures in Irish theatre. In editing this festschrift, which marks his retirement, I felt it would be in keeping with Phelim's immense, but deliberately underplayed, contribution to Irish theatre to commission a series of essays that focused not on Phelim himself nor any of the initiatives he was directly involved with, but on the changing face of Irish theatre over that period.

Accordingly, *Druids, Dudes and Beauty Queens* deliberately does not set out to be a comprehensive survey of Irish drama. Such surveys are published elsewhere and are well worth reading. Instead my intention has been to provide a forum for a range of people from different perspectives (academics, critics, writers and theatre professionals) to express contrasting opinions. In commissioning each essay, I tried to nudge authors towards examining a particular aspect of theatre, but at the same time allowed them the option of digressing from (or totally disregarding) their brief if they felt they had something more immediate to say about another facet of Irish drama.

Often the impetus for an essay arose from an intriguing proposition — like, for example, wondering what John Waters (one of our foremost commentators on the reality of West of Ireland life) would make of Martin McDonagh's re-imagining of that province in his Leenane trilogy, or speculating on how Colm Tóibín (whose own fiction vividly captures his native Wexford) might respond to Billy Roche's plays which share in part the same location. (I say 'in part' because anyone underestimating the distance between Roche's Wexford Town and Tóibín's Enniscorthy should read the late Maeve Brennan's brilliant *The Springs of Affection* to witness the desolation of a Wexford Town mother whose son marries 'a foreigner' from the village of Oilgate, several miles distant.)

In each instance my sole agenda as an editor was curiosity. As it happens, both essayists responded positively to the re-imaginings of their native place, with Waters finding *The Lonesome West* 'a strange and beautiful achievement' and regarding McDonagh as engaging 'with something real and terrifying — the emotional palsy of a people trapped in their own unrealised dreams'. But this book is not about furthering any singularly exclusive view of Irish theatre; thus in the context of such discourse it appears equally valid for another contributor, Vic Merriman (in his essay on the politically challenging theatre of Donal O'Kelly), to consider McDonagh's plays to be a travesty of the experiences of the rural poor which 'offer a kind of voyeuristic aperture on the antics of white trash whose reference point is more closely aligned to the barbarous conjurings of Jerry Springer than to the continuities of an indigenous tradition of dramatic writing'.

Similarly Vic Merriman criticises Marina Carr's work for offering 'bourgeois audiences course after course of reassurance', while other contributors praise her plays highly, such as Anna McMullan who considers that Carr 'focuses on those who are marginalised from the success obsessed climate of the Celtic Tiger, and confronts us with female difference and deviance'.

Waters and Breandán Delap (in his study of Irish language drama) also take strongly contrasting views on Mícheál Ó Conghaile's translation — or seeming 're-translation' — of McDonagh's *The Beauty Queen of Leenane* (*Banríon Álainn an Líonáin*), which Waters reports as having fallen flat, whereas Delap considers that it 'stripped the play of its affectations, displaying a sensitive ear for the vernacular which ... [makes] ... it easier to sympathise with the characters rather than treating them with the comic derision favoured by McDonagh'.

My own proudest moment in the theatre occurred in a tiny venue one night watching the reaction of four young women at the end of a one-act play of mine. Two stood up to give the actors a standing ovation (I did check their seats afterwards to ensure nobody had placed a sharp object thereon) while their two companions resolutely sat with arms folded, disliking what they'd seen so much that they steadfastly refused to clap. That they likely had a blazing row afterwards struck me as the perfect response to any piece of theatre. In similar fashion, it would be hoped that some essays here may provoke readers as much as others may perfectly reflect their opinions.

Finding myself awkwardly wearing two hats as both a playwright and an editor, I gave no direction beyond asking contributors to avoid my own work unless genuinely necessary in the context of their theme. That they pop up more frequently than I had wished leads me to the observation that the trick is to either die or edit an anthology. But I assure readers that for every Owen Dudley Edwards who finds merit in my work, another critic exists with an opposing view and would happily match me with the photo-fit given by John Crowley — in Karen Fricker's essay — when claiming that he devised his *True Lines* show as 'a reaction against my mythic notion of an Irish theatre tradition, which was of a bearded playwright somewhere writing things I couldn't understand'.

A highly innovative theatre director, Crowley's brilliantly mould-breaking 1993 *True Lines* (devised in conjunction with his cast) was rooted in the realities of a pre-Celtic Tiger Ireland. However, Karen Fricker in her careful study of that production and of the challenges it threw down to Irish theatre, suggests that these challenges have not been taken up. In posing the question 'What happened to the energy and productivity of the early and mid-Nineties?' she wonders whether 'the "Celtic Tiger" could well be the worst possible thing to have happened to Ireland at this particular point in its artistic life'.

Money certainly wasn't flowing at the formation of Glasshouse Theatre Company. The difficulties that a band of idealistic (and quickly impoverished) people experienced when they attempted to fill a perceived gap in the arts is superbly captured in an essay co-written by four women instrumental in forming Glasshouse as a vehicle for women playwrights. The authorial quartet are actors Siân Quill and Clare Dowling (Clare was later company writer), director Katy Hayes and producer Caroline Williams. Their piece perfectly captures the wing-and-a-prayer nature of so many small production companies with tales of borrowed furniture for props; of the intensity of the creative process culminating in production meetings in the corridor of a maternity hospital; of the crazy events that can befall theatre companies (who could invent a newspaper headline like 'Man Shot at Lesbian Play'); and of the eventual burn-out that inevitably results from such idealism.

At the other end of the spectrum, Ben Barnes has been remarkably forthright in allowing the publication of extracts from his diary, detailing the pressures of being Artistic Director of the Abbey Theatre. The diary provides an insight into background details of plays opening at home, controversy at the Edinburgh Festival with *The Barbaric Comedies*, and trips to countries like Hungary in the company of Brian Friel.

It seems vital to a book like this to include such first hand experience of the creative process by actual participants like Ben Barnes and the Glasshouse Four. In this context, the innovative writer and director Johnny Hanrahan contributes a study of the dramatic representations of Cork as evidenced in the exciting new theatre being produced by himself and others in that same city.

However, it seems equally important to highlight outside perspectives on Irish drama. When Phelim Donlon was chancing his initial visits to the AGMs of impoverished theatre groups, the Hungarian Professor Csilla Bertha was taking far greater risks (with potentially grave consequences for her personal safety) as a smuggler of Hungarian language books (including copies of Brian Friel's plays) into Transylvania, then under the Ceausescu reign. Hungarians living there suffered a cultural apartheid with

Hungarian place-names and, often, personal surnames being forcefully changed. For a time even the mention of original Hungarian place-names in print was a crime. As Professor Bertha writes: 'Friel's *Translations* thus dramatised present reality for Hungarians as late as ten to fifteen years ago ... the haunting feeling of familiarity sometimes proved traumatic. The young woman acting Sarah often broke into tears while rehearsing her role. She was from Transylvania. The deprivation of a people of their language, the forceful changing of old place-names ... were not literature for that actress but living experience as they were for a great part of the audience.'

Professor Bertha and her friend and esteemed colleague Professor Mária Kurdi are two of Hungary's leading authorities on Irish writing. Between them they examine Brian Friel's work following his huge success with *Dancing at Lughnasa*, with a special emphasis on how his work is received in their native country and its parallels with Hungarian playwrights. Professor Kurdi provides both an introductory study of Friel's productions in Hungary and an examination of his adaptations from other writers, while Professor Bertha considers his original plays during this period.

Meanwhile, from a Gallic perspective, Emile Jean Dumay examines Irish plays that have recently been translated or staged in French, while nearer to home Owen Dudley Edwards provides an incisive, entertaining, provocative and knowledgeable survey of Irish plays and players that have graced the Edinburgh Festival.

I am grateful to Mic Moroney for undertaking an extensive and highly comprehensive tour-de-force excursion through the history of Irish theatre over this period: one which not only vividly recreates early productions by Conor McPherson, the heyday of the Project Arts Centre under the direction of the Sheridan brothers, and neglected representations of Dublin like James McKenna's *The Scatterin'* and Heno Magee's *Hatchet*, but which also highlights the emergence of newer voices like Eugene O'Brien and Mark O'Rowe.

Moroney's detailed description of so many productions in

Northern Ireland is complimented by Ronan McDonald's careful study of representations of the Northern Troubles in the work of such playwrights as Gary Mitchell, Seamus Heaney, Christina Reid, Anne Devlin as well as Bill Morrison with his 1992 trilogy, *A Love Song for Ulster*.

Devlin is among the many writers considered in Anna McMullan's extensive survey of Irish women playwrights, which looks back at two uncompromising mirrors held up to a conservative, hierarchical Ireland in Máiréad Ní Ghráda's *An Triail* (1964) /*On Trial* (1965) and Edna O'Brien's *A Pagan Place* (1972) before proceeding to study a range of new voices like Marina Carr, Paula Meehan and Gina Moxley.

Breandán Delap's aforementioned study of drama in the Irish language provides a frank assessment of both the writers and theatre companies most active in this sphere in recent years. It argues that: 'One of the underlying problems in recent years has been that everybody wants to write the great Irish play but nobody seems to want to produce accessible and entertaining material that doesn't affect literary pretensions. There are many Beckett wannabes in the Irish language scene, but few Bernard Farrell wannabes. The last twenty years have consequently seen an endless conveyor belt of plays that long to be taken seriously, being produced by companies hopelessly out of sync with the needs of the audience.'

A deliberate decision was taken not to impose any house style in this collection. Therefore academic contributors accustomed to using endnotes did so, whereas other writers whose natural tendency was to avoid the flow of their work being interrupted did not. Each contrasting voice was simply allowed to speak for itself in whatever way it wished.

In the early 1990s, I served nearly five years on the Arts Council of Ireland, at a time when armed robbers wouldn't serve half that sentence. (Indeed I note that Jeffrey Archer will only do four years for perjury.) The constant pressure of meetings was a culture shock to the solitary routine of the present writer, happiest alone at his desk. I quickly sensed that the Redemptionists of old would have enjoyed greater effect with their barnstorming sermons had they announced that hell consisted not of fire and brimstone but of an infinite labyrinth of sub-committees.

But at the same time I discovered the extraordinary dedication and passion which many arts officers brought to their respective portfolios. The late Lar Cassidy for example — literature officer for many years — was a true friend to Irish writers (as has been his successor, Sinéad Mac Aodha), one who quietly and steadfastly transformed the environment in which we worked. Paying my final visit to him — a walk along the coast when he was a gaunt man near death — Lar remained full of enthusiastic fight, talking of new initiatives needed to improve living conditions for certain writers, and still filled with his familiar concern for others.

Likewise in Phelim Donlon I encountered someone who fought with passionate conviction for Irish theatre — and who will continue to do so in new ways, I'm sure, in the years to come. To take the liberty of quoting from an e-mail by Karen Fricker concerning her essay: 'a book dedicated to him that is not overtly 'about' him is actually the best tribute to a man whose subtlety, grace, and modesty were hallmarks of his work.' Similarly I think Ben Barnes echoed the opinion of many in the theatre world in another e-mail: 'Phelim has been a wonderful and sympathetic support to a generation of theatre practitioners and there could be no more fitting dedication.'

The last seventeen years have seen their share of controversies as well as successes involving the arts organisation for which Phelim worked. However except where specifically linked to the thrust of an essay (as in Delap's criticism of certain funding policies) this book has not addressed the fortunes of the Arts Council. From what it has explored though it is certain that, looking back, Phelim Donlon can reflect with pride on a personal involvement in a host of initiatives. These include the emergence of professional theatre companies outside Dublin like Red Kettle, Island and Meridian; the many young companies expanding their repertoire like Loose Canon, Corn Exchange, Pan Pan and Barabbas; the emerging circuit of well-equipped, professionally managed venues enabling regional audiences to access the work of professional touring companies; the establishment of training schemes for actors and travel schemes for the theatre sector; the innovative and challenging work emerging from theatre projects schemes that help expand the potentialities of stage craft like mime, movement and physical theatre; the significant work of the Gate and Abbey Theatres, contributing to the status of Irish theatre overseas; the significant work produced by Northern Ireland based playwrights and companies; and exciting overseas theatre presented at the Dublin Theatre Festival and Galway Arts Festival, enabling audiences and practitioners alike to see international companies like Els Comediants, Footsbarn, Cheek by Jowl and Théâtre de Complicité.

Without doubt the landscape of seventeen years ago has been transformed. What remains to be seen is exactly what new theatre will now emerge from this new landscape? Back in 1984, with Conor McPherson still in primary school and the prospect of purpose built theatres in places like Longford and Carrackallen seeming as remote as Martians landing in Leitrim, who could have possibly sketched an accurate picture of Irish theatre at the start of the twenty-first century?

I have no intention of similarly trying to predict the state of Irish theatre in the year 2018, as our utterly changed society starts coming to terms with the new pressures and social tensions wrought by political and cultural changes both at home and abroad. *Druids, Dudes and Beauty Queens* is rather offered as a series of snapshots, an attempt to capture the moving object that is Irish theatre today, itself a perpetual transformation which simultaneously builds on and rejects tradition, a theatre which strives to re-examine our past, comprehend our present, and imagine our futures before they happen.

Dermot Bolger
October, 2001

COLM TÓIBÍN

The Talk of the Town: The Plays of Billy Roche

While staying at Coole in the summer of 1901, W.B. Yeats had a dream which became the play *Cathleen Ni Houlihan*. He dreamed a scene of domestic harmony being disrupted by a force that could not be resisted, that had the power of an oracle, and could destroy. That force arrived in the shape of an old woman, who represented Ireland, and who would become young again once Ireland had asserted its right to freedom. She would draw the young man out of the house, away from domestic harmony towards some higher, more noble aim.

Yeats could not write ordinary dialogue. Language for him was full of symbolic resonance; he wanted his words to be charged and electric rather than domestic or realistic. Thus in the days that followed, Lady Gregory wrote his play for him. She created a peasant family in a state of material comfort, she allowed them to plan a wedding and worry about getting more land. She kept the play short and simple; the audience could reasonably have expected the drama to arise from a jilted lover or a secret that had not been told. She resisted Yeats' efforts to have some intimation of the final scene earlier in the play. At her insistence, the arrival of the old woman seemed to have nothing strange about it, and thus her transformation was all the more shocking and dramatic and highly charged.

The play was performed in Clarendon Street in Dublin in 1902. Maud Gonne played the title role and the audience was full of zealous and serious young men who had found a drama that matched their own solemnity, lofty principles and anti-materialism. Thus Yeats and Lady Gregory had created the problem which would emerge again and again over the next twenty-five years. Their own essential impulses as dramatists was heroic and idealistic just as their political impulse was anti-materialist. A part of them was to remain in tune with the nationalist movement and its leaders. But the other part of them recognised the genius in the anti-heroic dramas of Synge and O'Casey, and in the few years after the production of *Cathleen Ni Houlihan*, they set about re-aligning their dramatic principles to include Synge. They were not, they insisted, a political theatre; their aim was to produce art, to enact on the stage the true and the beautiful.

Thus began the abiding tension in Irish drama in the twentieth century between a nation whose self-concept was idealistic and heroic and a set of dramatists who viewed this as a sour and elaborate joke, and who set about deflating it or creating an alternative world, which had been written out of Ireland's heroic history. The dramatists were lucky: they had not only Pearse's rhetoric to work against, but they also had the entire body of Yeats' and Lady Gregory's dramatic writings, so concerned with myth and symbol and heroism.

The founders of the Abbey Theatre offered Irish dramatists, then, an example not to follow, a powerful influence to evade and avoid and mock and destroy. But stylistically Yeats and Lady Gregory also offered them a powerful example, which was to maintain its spell for a hundred years. In the significant work produced in the Irish theatre in the last twenty years of the twentieth century, the writers have played with the sharply realistic and attempted to place around it a halo, or a shining from within, using a real voice but allowing a poetic force to build from within the voice. In these Irish plays there has been a sense of language as mysterious, a sense of speech moving into prayer, a sense of utterance having at its centre the rhythm and power of song. What Yeats and Lady Gregory attempted to do in *Cathleen Ni Houlihan* — move the ordinary into the miraculous — comes up many times in the plays written in Ireland between 1980 and 2000, at its most heightened and intense in Brian Friel's *Faith*

Healer and Tom Murphy's *The Gigli Concert*, but also in ways more hidden and mysterious, but just as powerfully, in the works of Frank McGuinness, Sebastian Barry, Dermot Bolger, Paul Mercier and Marina Carr. A speech in the work of these writers, or a snatch of dialogue, is produced to move the audience like a song, is poetic in the sense that it unsettles, it hits the nervous system, it works wonders.

In style and tone, then, there has been great continuity in the Irish theatre in the twentieth century. Also, the anti-heroic impulse, the insistence on working against the grain of the national narrative, has remained central. If the national narrative is the father, then each playwright from Synge onwards sought to kill the father. In *Riders to the Sea*, Synge refused to allow any consolation, except for the words themselves, against the harshness and brutality of western life in Ireland. In *The Playboy of the Western World*, Synge offered a version of Irish life at its most pagan and comic and anti-heroic. And once the struggle for Irish freedom became part of the heroic narrative, part of the terrible beauty, many young men from Sean O'Casey to Denis Johnston to Brendan Behan set about undermining the heroics, subverting the narrative. And once Irish freedom had been achieved, the playwrights set about establishing the terms of that freedom as tawdry and sad and restrictive and hopeless.

Between 1980 and 2000, a number of playwrights sought to bring the stage one step further by attempting to put a flag up over a narrative of their own, an aspect of the national narrative which had been pushed aside, or erased, or prevented from emerging. Thus the young volunteers in Frank McGuinness's *Observe the Sons of Ulster Marching Towards the Somme* came back into the Irish narrative from which southern Ireland had excluded them. Thus figures with Dublin accents, pushed towards violence and self-destruction, and lacking the music-hall humour of O'Casey and Behan's Dublin characters, appeared in the work of Paul Mercier and Dermot Bolger. And so too characters from the margins of history — religious sects, the old gentry, the soon-to-be-disbanded RIC — had a flag raised over them and they became central in the work of Sebastian Barry. And in the work of Marina Carr, there is an insistence on the old, dark, violent, atavistic forces — Cuchulain at home — just as the national narrative was moving towards a version of Ireland as bright and shiny.

Thus Irish dramatic writing at the end of the twentieth century set about destroying and subverting and replacing and indeed recreating national heroics and idealisations in *Cathleen Ni Houlihan*, but also adapted the tension between current speech, poetic rhythms and the possibility of transformation from which the play derived its power. In this context, the five plays by Billy Roche — the Wexford Trilogy (1988, 1989, 1991), *Amphibians* (1992, revised 1998) and *Cavalcaders* (1993) — remain pivotal in the Irish theatre of the period and should be placed at the very centre of contemporary Irish theatre.

Billy Roche's Wexford begins as a real place. The speech in his plays begins as a living speech, whose tones and colours and cadences belong to the streets of Wexford alone. There is not a single line in his plays which could not be spoken by real people in a real place. His urge towards transcendence is more muted and modest than most of his contemporaries, but the urge is there nonetheless, hovering at the edge of almost everything said and done in his work.

His Wexford is fading and faded. The port has silted up and the fishing industry is a thing of memory. But the Wexford Billy Roche was brought up in had all the characteristics of a metropolis and some of its energy. A long narrow main street snakes its way from Redmond Square to the Faythe, running parallel to the quays. Most of the shops are small with large plate glass windows. Half the town manages to walk along the main street at some time of the day or other, and everyone in the shops keeps an eye out, recognising the passers by. There is a great deal of mockery and warm, ebullient talk in Wexford, fellow citizens are sources of great amusement and interest, from their funny walks to certain other distinguishing characteristics. A great deal is known about everyone, from what you did last night to what your grandfather did forty years ago.

The town has a medieval shape and its cultural make-up is unusual in Ireland, being a mixture of Norman and Gaelic, with some English and Hugenot added. The two historical journals, for example, are not divided Catholic-Protestant, or new and old generations, but, in general, one of them has been run by people with Gaelic names and the other by people of Norman ancestry. (The Norman invasion, incidentally, happened in 1169.)

Competing with the quiet way in which these cultures merge and the quiet way the town watches itself is the heroic narrative of county Wexford, its glorious history. All over the county, there are monuments and plaques to the men of 1798; great ballads are dedicated to their memory. With Cromwell's attack on the town, the Rising of 1798 is Wexford's fundamental narrative, it puts everything else in the shade; what story can compete with it for grandeur and bravery and tragedy?

The flag which Billy Roche flies over the town, however, is also an act of rebellion. His flag insists that there is another story that must be told, a narrative which is not heroic, another reality which must be attended to. His flag comes in two colours, two tones. One half of his vision is political: the urge to represent the talk of the town, the disappointed lives, the sense of a haunting not by history, but by the doings of parents and by the parts of the self we seem powerless to control. But the other part of his vision, more than that of any of his contemporaries, is existential. He is prepared to dramatise his Wexford as a Trojan horse with no Troy in sight, no opening available. He is prepared to dramatise the business of existence as raw sadness, uneasy futility, masked by language and then, suddenly, unmasked and left bare by the same words.

He prefers public places. The plays are set in a snooker hall, a betting shop, a church, a factory and a shoemaker's shop. Only in a few scenes in *Amphibians* does he allow part of a play to be enacted in the classic cauldron of the Irish theatre — the kitchen or living room of a family house. He is especially skilled at dramatising that central moment in the public life of Wexford — the arrival of a talkative person into a shared space, full of opinions and gossip. Billy Roche's characters are defeated already, or will have their defeat re-enacted on the stage. No one will become a snooker champion or win money at the betting shop. The shoemaker's is about to be modernised, and the fishing has come to an end, and the old beliefs no longer hold. No one in Roche's work, with the exception of Jimmy in *A Handful of Stars* has huge ambitions, large desires. The plays are set among an artisan class to working class who were born in the town and will stay in the town. No one wants to go to Philadelphia or sing like Gigli; perhaps more important, no one mentions Ireland. Ireland is not a place in Roche's work, there is no nation to fight against or adhere to. And this gives him a freedom to work with his characters, to allow, in spite of his own modesty, his Wexford to stand for the world. It gives his best work, such as his masterpiece *Poor Beast in the Rain,* a strange timelessness and beauty. His lack of a governing myth — Catholicism means nothing in his work — gives the plays a raw power except when he is finally forced to invent one in *Amphibians.* It is then one most understands what it must have taken to free his characters in the other plays, to allow their own trapped longings and bursts of hope and hopelessness to become solid and dramatic enough that no myths or governing structures were required.

All of the plays have characters who are full of talk, funny, accusing, boastful, mocking. Within this talk, there are, in all the plays, moments of pure sadness, or vicious savagery. A line, or a piece of dialogue, without any extra flourish, can stun the audience into silence. This is done with immense subtlety and skill. In *A Handful of Stars*, it comes in Paddy's speech about Jimmy's parents:

> No God I remember when the two of them were only courtin'. She was dyin' alive about that fella. I often saw them up in the Town Hall and they waltzing the legs off one another. They were grand dancers too. He used to be all done up like a dog's dinner I'm not coddin' yeh — great suits on him

and all. And she'd be smilin' up into his face all the time. To look at her you'd swear she had just swallowed a handful of stars. Jaysus she was a lovely girl, so she was.

Paddy normally talks in monosyllables, and Jimmy's father, the dancer, is now in a place for the homeless, having beaten his wife and made her miserable for many years. Paddy has also spoken of Stapler leaving his wife: 'God and Stapler was married to a grand girl.' All the images of happiness here are presented as small half-remembered events that now seem all the more miraculous because of the misery and the treachery that came after. All eight sentences of Paddy's speech have an innocent beauty about them, a sense of wonder. The first seven of them begin with an iambic beat, the last is more muted in its beat and can be spoken wistfully and sadly and because of what the audience knows, it has the possibility of making everyone in the audience hold their breath. But it is not underlined, or specially marked out. Another actor could choose one of the other sentences to do the same work and let the last sentence carry less emotion.

Steven's speech at the end of *Poor Beast in the Rain* has the same power as Paddy's speech. Steven, too, has been mostly silent in the play and his longest speech ends:

> Your Mammy was the very same. She was always wondering what was over the next hill. She was always wonderin' about somethin'. Jukebox fellas and carnival boxes seem to fascinate her. A fancy scarf blowin' in the wind, a tattoo, anythin' the least bit outlandish at all and she was off. I never knew whether I was comin' or goin' with her. I never knew what way I was fixed with her at all to tell you the truth.

Although the last sentence is the plainest and the least

obviously poetic, it is the most expressive. It hits us like a line in a song that seems to have no obvious power. It seems to have a hidden nervous system of its own, all the stronger because you do not know where the emotion is coming from. Sometimes the same emotional weight is carried by a single line rather than a line within a speech. In *The Cavalcaders*, Nuala says 'It's a terrible lousy thing to do, yeh know Terry — to take someone's love and throw it back in their face like that.' While the second part of the line could be from a pop song, the first part has a directness about it. There is a sense of real hurt in those first few words that manages to rescue the second part of the sentence from cliché. In *Belfry*, Pat has a line with a similar power: 'This is a queer lonely auld life Artie yeh know.' Or Isaac in *Amphibians* when he says 'What are youse wantin'?'

What Steven's speech and Nuala's line and Pat's line and Isaac's line have in common, and this is central to Roche's work, is they use an understated speech as if to suggest that they themselves are not worth grander phrases than 'I never knew what way I was fixed with her at all to tell you the truth' or 'It's a terrible lousy thing to do, yeh know Terry.' But because the focus of the play has been entirely on them, rather than Irish society or class conflict or a national narrative, there is no distance between them and us, their suffering carries enormous weight, much greater because their language isn't up to it; how they speak is ostensibly as beaten down as they are, and this tension between the poverty of the language and its beauty brings with it a terrible pathos and helplessness.

Paddy in *A Handful of Stars* and Molly in *Poor Beast in the Rain* operate as a sort of chorus, as a warning to the young about hope. They are mostly stoical, but when their stoicism breaks into a narrative of sadness and regret, it takes on a different sort of power. Everyone is these plays is locked into a cycle of moments of hope and possibility followed by years of dull regret and despair. Class conflict is not in these plays to be resolved or even dramatised, it is simply part of the prison in which people are locked. Badness and weakness in *A Handful of Stars* are passed on from father to son. Love is something that may have happened in the past, or be celebrated in the songs which pepper the plays, but here it is to be enacted as longing and rejection as Linda rejects Jimmy in *A Handful of Stars*, as Eileen rejects Georgie in *Poor Beast in the Rain*, as Terry rejects Nuala in *The Cavalcaders*, as Sonia rejects Zak in *Amphibians*. The men who are rejected are the ones with most spirit, most hope. It is that very hope and spirit which makes them oddly unreliable and untrustworthy.

In all of his plays, Billy Roche takes the idea of love one step further. He dramatises adultery in his work as no other writer does. There is a long tradition of dealing with adultery on the stage. However, it is mostly comedy and it is often farce. In Pinter's play *Betrayal*, it comes in its full glory as treachery, it is presented as part of the treacherous nature of the society itself, or indeed as part of the treacherous nature of the very words being used to tell the tale. In Billy Roche, adultery is not comedy and not metaphor and not part of a social malaise. It is another way of making his characters sad, or leaving them sad. In *A Handful of Stars*, Stapler's going off with the hairdresser is reduced to treachery by Paddy's line about Stapler's wife as 'a grand girl'. In *Poor Beast in the Rain*, both Steven and his wife have been destroyed by his wife's departure with Danger Doyle. In *Belfry* Donal discovers that his wife Angela has been having an affair with the sacristan:

> I mean to say a man works hard, dreams hard for
> his wife and family only to come home one day and
> discover that she's whorin' around with a gobshite
> like you. A feckin' little mammy's boy, be Jaysus, I
> wouldn't mind but I gave her everything she ever
> wanted …

In *The Cavalcaders*, Terry's wife who was 'a queer good lookin' woman', now, having run away with his friend, has found only misery: 'They say she lives like a nun now. I believe she rarely goes out any more.'

The Cavalcaders has all the elements of a farce; it is full of exits and entrances and sparkling dialogue and funny songs. As in a classic farce, it is hard to keep tabs on who has been sleeping with whom. Terry's wife has run away with Rogan, the best man at their wedding; Ted is having an affair with Rory's wife; and Terry and Josie have had it off with Terry's uncle's wife. This event is twice described by Josie in the play: 'she was sort of cryin' when I went in though, like, yeh know.' Nuala commits suicide, driven to it by a number of savage scenes with Terry. Josie dies in hospital. Both come back from the dead. And yet despite the abiding sense of loss in the play, by the end Terry has found Breda whose love he has been resisting throughout the play, Rory's wife is expecting a baby with Ted, Rory and his mother are looking after his daughter. There is almost a sense of harmony in Wexford, the completion of a comedy in coupling and symmetry.

This playing with genre, this refusing to write either comedy or tragedy, is as crucial in the work of Billy Roche as his refusal to deal with the national narrative. Every Irish playwright writing during the last two decades of the century except Roche has attempted to write a tragedy, a play in which a hero is caught between conflicting epochs of belief, in which the hero is doomed because of a fundamental change in the forces at work in the world. Some of the plays merely allow tragedy as a possibility, others pursue it for all it is worth. Roche's characters, on the other hand, accept their fate. Jimmy in *A Handful of Stars* will wait for the cops to arrest him. Steven in *Poor Beast in the Rain* does nothing to prevent his daughter leaving. Both Nuala and Josie in *The Cavalcaders* are only too ready to die. No one shakes their fist at God; no one tries to kill their father. Roche's characters accept what is coming, they have no illusions. They live in an age when tragedy is no longer possible, nor comedy either, when drama is merely an acting out of the sadness which small hope brings. Those locked in the Trojan horse are no longer haunted by the possibility that Troy is in sight. They have only themselves to blame and one another to console or amuse or betray. And there is only a limited time.

Ritual for Billy Roche is the same as romance. The rite of passage for Tony in *A Handful of Stars* to the inner sanctum, which is so delicately handled in the play, will become impossible, just as Isaac's rite of passage in *Amphibians* will be rendered meaningless. So too will birthdays, weddings, New Year celebrations, hurling matches. All of these will end in misrule. Roche will allow his characters no consoling ceremonies.

His standing alone in Irish drama, refusing to dramatise the conflicts within identity and nation and history in Ireland, and his refusal to work within a genre, does not mean that Roche's plays are not fully alert to certain traditional themes and tropes. He may not have deliberately set out to make *Poor Beast in the Rain* a retelling of the Electra story, but the connections are there for the audience to make. Eileen has watched her mother kill her father by running away with Danger Doyle. Danger Doyle is both Aegisthus, who has married Electra's mother, and Orestes, her brother who has returned after many years to help her seek vengeance. Eileen, like Electra, is alone with no husband and no children. In Sophocles's play Orestes leaves a sign on the grave of his father to suggest that he has returned, including a lock of his hair. In *Poor Beast in the Rain*, the locket which Eileen receives from her mother has been bought in Wexford, thus suggesting the presence of her mother or her mother's emissary in the town. And what the emissary wants her to do is not to seek revenge as in *Electra* and punish her mother for her crime. He wants her to do something more savage and more disturbing. He wants her to kill her father again, repeat her mother's action rather than seek revenge for it. This is the stark, dramatic choice she is offered. Danger Doyle wants her to come back with him to London and leave her father behind in Wexford as her mother once did. 'It broke my heart,' Steven tells his daughter, 'when she ran off on me like that yeh know. It broke my bloody heart so it did.'

In an Afterword to the published version of the Wexford Trilogy, Billy Roche describes working on his second play called *Runaway* which eventually became *Poor Beast in the Rain*. It began as the story of Johnny Doran 'who refused to wrap himself up in the flag of his tribe' during the run-up to the All-Ireland Hurling Final. This is essentially what Billy Roche himself has done. His work is closer, in its integrity and its careful nuanced study of hope and hopelessness, to the early stories in Joyce's *Dubliners* or to certain themes and tones in Tenessee Williams and Arthur Miller than to anything in contemporary Irish theatre. In refusing to deal with national myths and insisting on placing his characters in the time after tragedy, he has bravely followed his own route and created a body of work which has an extraordinary emotional power and intensity.

JOHN WATERS

The Irish Mummy:
The Plays and Purpose of Martin McDonagh

My first response on reading the script of *The Beauty Queen of Leenane* was an exclamation of frustration that something so close to me had escaped my observation. It was the same reaction as towards the early songs of Shane McGowan and the Pogues: somewhere deep inside me, I *knew* this. Why hadn't I been able to articulate it? Who was this interloper McDonagh and what was he about?

The music of the Pogues was in one sense a formula: Irish traditional ballads given a punk treatment, a straightforward combination of incongruous elements, which carried also an element of the ambiguity with which we who grew up in Ireland had regarded the music growing up. Surrounded by the mythic balladry of our fathers, we had rushed into the embrace of Bruce Springsten or Johnny Rotten. The last thing we imagined was that the leaden, desperate ejaculations of our drunken uncles might one day be turned into gold.

It wasn't a case of recognising that Shane McGowan, the bastard, had had a keener eye for the main chance. There was nothing about this suggesting cynicism or opportunism. It was simply that he had *heard* and identified something that we, who grew up beside it, for whatever reason, could only *feel*. Our attitudes towards the ballad tradition had been dominated by both love — or at least a reluctant liking — and a tyranny born of the grim passion it excited in our elders. It was at once laughable and sacred. Our rebellion at its earnestness was countered by our awe at its undeniable dignity. This tradition had been road-tested under the most extreme of conditions, and it still travelled. We could not readily mock it, so we left it alone. And yet, simply by virtue of being a new generation, we felt some deepset call to rebel against it. We sneered at it behind our hands, but without total conviction. We possessed neither enough love nor enough hatred to do to the music what the Pogues did. We were detached, but in the wrong ways.

But here, notwithstanding, was a music which at once expressed our attachment to Irish balladry and our ironic repugnance of it, simultaneously a celebration and a refusal, a kick and a kiss — a soundtrack for our neurosis. In one sense, of course, it could be heard as a simple 'turn', a trick born perhaps of resourcefulness, like making turkey casserole the day after Christmas. But the music also demonstrated a passionate attachment to what it sought to deconstruct and conveyed this in both the intensity of the transformation and the energy of the result. The punk-inspired blurt of rage or mockery was itself ambiguous, conveying within the very energy of the sound a profound sense of nostalgia combined with a rage at once rooted in a possible disdain for the culture from which it derived, but also seeming to merge with the spirit of that music in attacking and rebelling against everything else. It had both loathing and pride, attachment and rejection, assault and embrace. It was not simply two things at once but two opposing things at once.

The preciousness with which music in Ireland had come to be regarded was largely a function of the exaggerated reverence towards the indigenous by virtue of its having appeared to survive oppression and still speak truly. In a healthy society, this kind of solemnity is constantly, publicly and roundly undermined by the scepticism and disdain of the rebellious and the young. But in a society where the issue of culture has become one of life or death, this necessary contempt is often absent or suppressed. You cannot laugh with conviction at the only life you've got.

The Pogues, by virtue of profound connections with Ireland had access to the culture without necessarily being hidebound by its various paralysing elements. Being mainly outsiders in the sense of being removed by a generation and a stretch of water, they achieved a detachment which enabled them to see something we all knew but could not speak. In a sense, their removal allowed them to participate in the organic growth of the culture in a more authentic manner than if they had fully 'belonged'.

So it is with Martin McDonagh. I have up until now had mixed feelings about him, and maybe that is the way it should be. Some of the mixed feelings are born of a profound jealousy — perhaps less of his talent than of his vision, although his talent is awesome and totally unconstitutional. The world he places before me is known to me, and yet remained invisible until he recreated it on page and stage. He says his stories are not about places, but are simply stories. That's easy for him to say: he didn't have to live here.

There has been, without doubt, an enormous over-the-top element to the reception accorded to Martin McDonagh. This is not to disparage him, since it is impossible to conceive of anything, never mind a newly arrived writer of theatre plays, which or who might conceivably deserve to be feted as he has. It would seem over-the-top if even Shakespeare, arriving with complete canon, was to be the recipient of such overwhelming praise and celebration. There is therefore a degree of difficulty in deciding what is great about McDonagh and what is merely good.

A complicating factor has been a certain reluctance in Ireland to have a good, old-fashioned argument about him. McDonagh himself has noted that his most vocal critics have been from outside Ireland, especially London, but this may be misleading. 'The only place I've had any grief is here in London from a few English punters going on about how I was taking the piss out of Irish people,' he told Sean O'Hagan in a March 2001 interview for *The Guardian*. My sense of it is that he is slightly wrong about this: there is a fair degree of resistance to him in Ireland, but like many such phenomena it is underground, ambivalent and slightly dishonest. The latter-day reluctance to be denounced as a 'begrudger' has meant that the willingness to criticise McDonagh has existed in inverse proportion to his success. Several leading Irish playwrights, for example, are known to be deeply traumatised by the arrival of Martin McDonagh and his drawer-full of sharply-minted plays, but their more critical responses emerge only under the influence of drink, or in off-the-record comments to journalists they hope will stick the boot in on their behalf. There is also a degree of negative feeling in the academic arena, where a certain amount of discussion has taken place, but little or nothing of this has appeared above ground. And finally, in the responses of ordinary theatre-goers, and even more so among non-theatre-goers, one can encounter occasional outbursts of anger at McDonagh for taking the piss.

The best — indeed, virtually the only — summary of the case against McDonagh was in an article by Ian Kilroy in *Magill* magazine in January 2000. It was a fair article, acknowledging both McDonagh's strengths and weaknesses, and extending space to his admirers and detractors. On the critical side, the case was made that McDonagh's work would have a short shelf-life; that it relied upon the exploitation of outrage and a few 'basic comic jokes'; that his work is shallow and superficial when compared to that of other Irish playwrights; that he perpetuates stereotypes of Irishness; that he lacks empathy with his characters and that his characters consequently lack personalities and are given no opportunity for moral development. Kilroy quoted one academic, Professor Kevin Barry of NUI Galway as follows: 'The work is posited on the idea of the cultural poverty of the people on stage. The relationship of the playwright to his material and his characters is most easily explained by a relationship of easy and lazy hatred. Contemptuous hatred. I can discover no relationship of sympathy or affection. The dominant emotion of the plays is bitterness. No. Contempt might be a better word.'

The other side of the argument is best represented by Fintan O'Toole, who has written several articles about McDonagh, including the Introduction to the published version of the *Leenane Trilogy*. O'Toole perceives McDonagh as a child of his own re-imagined Ireland, a place which never properly achieved modernity but in which the primitive and the postmodern exist side by side. McDonagh plays, O'Toole told Kilroy, relate to 'the idea of the West, of playing with a certain kind of Irishness, a certain kind of Irish construct that comes from a hundred years ago, of looking at that at its moment of decadence and playing with the remnants of it, the fragments of it'.

In a sense, what debate there has been about Martin McDonagh relates also to something else, providing yet another arena for a long-standing argument about the relative merits of tradition and modernity in Irish society and culture. Another way of saying this is to observe that it is another opportunity for a re-enactment of the collective neurosis of modern Ireland. In a sense, both sides are right and wrong, and in another, both are saying the same thing.

Much has been made by critics of the references in McDonagh's plays to the allegedly postmodern Ireland of Tayto crisps, Kimberley biscuits and Australian soap operas. It is as though the existence of this Ireland is celebrated for the offence it gives to what existed before. But there is nothing 'postmodern' about the Ireland emblemised by such things. Neither can it be said that there is anything virtuous about it. It is simply modern Irish reality. The interesting aspect, in McDonagh's work, is the manner in which this Ireland co-exists with one drawn from theatre mythicism, nostalgia and the organic fusion of past and present which is reality virtually everywhere.

*

Both admirers and detractors have gone to McDonagh in search of affirmation for the uppermost strain in their own neurotic relationship with Ireland and its past. Those who accuse McDonagh of showing disrespect for traditional Ireland and a lack of sympathy for its inhabitants, albeit imagined ones, are responding out of a deep sense of reverence for the survival of a people and a culture against extraordinary odds. Those who rejoice in what they perceive to be the mockery of McDonagh's work are expressing their own sense of anger at a culture they have felt oppressed by. One might easily be led to believe that this divide represents some intractable schism in the Irish mind, but in truth both sides are saying the same thing. I remember growing up seeing occasional BBC television plays in which there would be an Irish character. One of the things that puzzled me was what I perceived as the failure of English actors to capture the 'correct' accent — their efforts always seemed too broad, distorted, and pronounced to the point of caricature. It wasn't until much later that I recognised that these *were* real Irish accents — the accents English actors must have heard among the Irish in Britain. They were, in fact, the accents of an Ireland that had already been eroded in the reality of the homeland, but preserved, in fossil form, in the mouths of those whose sense of home had been arrested at the moment of departure. You might call it 'The Irish Mummy': by whatever quirk of longing or loneliness, the Ireland of 1950, or 1957, or 1962, had been preserved intact in the tongues of the ex-patriate community.

The Irish community in Britain, to the extent that it is or was a 'community' at all, existed not by reference to the society in which it existed, still less to the reality of the society it referred to across the Irish Sea, but to the Ireland existing at the frozen moment of parting. This had enormous, and mainly unrecognised, consequences for all concerned, but mostly for the ex-pat cast between two cultures, like a drunk who is constantly being thrown from one to another of two moving trains, moving approximately in parallel.

In *The Beauty Queen*, one such, Pato, talks about his inability to make up his mind or control his own destiny:

> I do ask meself, if there was good work in Leenane, would I stay in Leenane? I mean, there never will be good work, but hypothetically, I'm saying. Or even bad work. Any work. And when I'm over there in London and working in rain and it's more or less cattle I am, and the young fellas cursing over cards and drunk and sick, and the oul digs over there, all pee-stained mattresses and nothing to do but watch the clock ... when it's there I am, it's here I wish I was, of course. Who wouldn't? But when it's here I

am ... it isn't there I want to be, of course not. But I
know it isn't here I want to be either.

This is a variation on the themes of a speech in Tom
Murphy's play *A Crucial Week in the Life of a Grocer's Assistant*,
when John Joe says: 'It isn't a case of staying or going. Forced to
stay or forced to go. Never the freedom to decide and make the
choice for ourselves. And then we're half-men here, or half-men
away, and how can we hope ever to do anything?'

McDonagh, like Murphy, has inherited a profound sadness
from the forced dislocation of the generation just before him.
McDonagh was brought up in London, in a small enclave
comprising much of his extended family. He visited the West of
Ireland throughout his childhood. He says that, in starting out to
write his plays, he 'sort of remembered the way my uncles spoke
back in Galway, the structure of their sentences'. It is as though
the pain in his ancestry has been passed to him in the guise of
something else — in the rhythms of language, the absurdity of
humour and the phantom attachment to something that no
longer exists.

It is an extraordinary experience to be sitting in the living
room of such an Irish family in perhaps London, talking to a
married couple who left Ireland maybe forty or fifty years before,
and whose accents are more 'Irish' than your own. It is even more
extraordinary when the door opens to admit a young man or
woman who speaks like he or she has just walked off the set of
EastEnders, but who insists on calling the couple 'Mummy' and
'Dad'. The extent to which this phenomenon is merely a
superficial manifestation of a much deeper condition remains
culturally unexplored, but at face value at least it offers a startling
representation of the neurosis which is so much less visible on the
surface of the home territory. As countless studies have shown,
this neurosis erupted in the ex-pat population in the form of
alcoholism and mental illness; at 'home' it had an entirely
different manifestation.

Much of the debate about tradition and modernity now taking

place in Ireland has an invisible subtext relating to power. What irritates certain cultural commentators about the supposed traditional Ireland is not so much its iconography, or even as they might insist, its poverty, as the nature of its power structure. Much of such opposition derives from later-day ideologies such as liberalism and feminism towards what would be characterised as the oppressive hegemonies of, for example, Catholicism and patriarchy. But like the accents of the long-departed, these ideologies have little basis in the matured reality of the society: the church's power has long since waned and the patriarch is a phantom no one with good eyesight has ever seen. In this sense, there is an extraordinary similarity between the phenomena of the fossilised accents of the departed emigrants and the ideological beliefs of the children of those who remained: both, for different reasons, have preserved intact an element of Ireland that has, to the extent that it ever existed in the first place, long passed down the pipe of history.

This may be why Martin McDonagh has been embraced by those wishing to maintain their sense of oppression by the disturbing forces of an Ireland which no longer exists, since he, in his own way, would have grown up surrounded by a sense of disbelonging vaguely similar to theirs, his arising from the accents of his elders, theirs from the provocation represented by the iconography of alleged 'tradition'. In one instance the rejection is purely personal; in another it is deeply political. One represents rebellion against the Irish Mummy; the other against the Irish Mammy, the mist that does be on the bog, and the kitchen sink.

My fellow *Irish Times* columnist, Fintan O'Toole, a Dubliner, has written many times about such a sense of being oppressed by the mythic notion of the ideal Irishman emanating from the West, of the nationalism of post-independence Ireland and the cultural sense of Ireland as a rural society. Of course, such a sense is utterly truthful for those who feel it, but it is no more real than the constructs which it resists. It is a little like the proverbial itch felt in an amputated limb: very real to the sufferer but lacking external validation. There was no mythic West, no classic

Irishman, no pure nationalism, no rural ideal. To attack such notions is to attack ghosts of the rebel neurotic imagination. McDonagh's work is welcomed by such sufferers because it appears to validate such a sense of repression and rebellion, whereas in fact the whole point about it is that its author lacks precisely the political neurosis which would have made his plays impossible to write. To celebrate McDonagh for his alleged rage at the nature of Ireland Past is to see something that is not there. There is no rage, any more than there is contempt. There is simply a writer looking for something interesting to write about.

When Fintan O'Toole says that McDonagh's plays are about a place that does not exist he means that they are, in some sense, a product of a dislocated Ireland caught between fiction and reality. When McDonagh says, as he did to Sean O'Hagan, 'Though it may not seem like it, I never try to write about a place per se; it's always, first and last, about story,' he is speaking the literal truth. McDonagh is, like Synge, a creative tourist, a visiting dilettante, an intimate outsider.

It is somewhat fatuous, therefore, to attack McDonagh's plays on the same basis as, for example, Synge's plays were attacked in their day, on account of their 'stage-Irishness'. The accusation is often made that McDonagh is not doing Ireland any favours because he sets out to caricature rather than depict. It is alleged that his plays do not represent reality as it is lived in Ireland, that they are 'stage-Irish', and therefore damaging to the image of Ireland in the world and the self-confidence of the people at home. What popular criticism there has been of McDonagh had centred on what one letter to an Irish newspaper called his 'bogman stereotype'. This line has occurred also in reviews of McDonagh's work, especially in English newspapers. One theatre critic, Alastair Macaulay, writing in *The Financial Times* under the headline 'Manipulative Moonshine' did not put a tooth in it: 'Some of the laborious echoes and repetitions McDonagh keeps putting in the mouths of his characters belittle Ireland very determinedly.' This is unfair to McDonagh and an insult to Ireland's intelligence. But equally so is the assessment of *The Guardian's* Michael Billington, who described McDonagh's 'purpose' thusly: 'to explode the myth of rural Ireland as a place of whimsical gaiety and folksy charm. The reality, he suggests, is murder, self-slaughter, spite, ignorance and familial hatred.'

Luckily, Martin McDonagh is much too smart to suggest any such thing — he knows, I suspect, that murder, self-slaughter, spite, ignorance and familial hatred are as much the 'reality' of 'rural Ireland' as they are the 'reality' of anyplace else. And if the 'explosion' of myths about rural Ireland was indeed McDonagh's 'purpose' he would be a century or so too late. Irish writers had been exploding precisely such myths since they learned to write in English.

Instead, McDonagh is building on a style of Irish writing best represented in the works of Synge and Yeats, which caricatured such perceptions of Ireland as an act of rebellion against the externally imposed view. This was a form of exaggerated naturalism, and yet still remained within the bounds of the plausible. For reasons I have outlined, the natural, organic rejection of this vision did not occur, as it should have, from within. McDonagh is behaving in the manner of a true artist in a healthy culture, and answering back what came immediately before. He is our Deus ex Machina, sent to catapult us into the next phase.

This means, I believe, that McDonagh's works to date must be seen as on the side of the angels, acts of revolution rather than acquiescence. And yet, by virtue of engaging in this discussion McDonagh limits himself in precisely the manner of his 'targets'. Patrick Kavanagh, writing of the work of Frank O'Connor, asked: 'Has he a direction? His feet are too seldom on the earth for me to follow. Is he merely a high-flying entertainer? Does his work hold the mirror up to life? Does it mean anything?' The same questions might be asked about Martin McDonagh. And yet, such is the paradoxical nature of this process, that McDonagh also stands beside Kavanagh in the savage clarity of his implicit denunciation.

That is one way of seeing it. But what is remarkable also is the extent to which the world depicted in McDonagh's plays corresponds quite closely to the perceptions of real people. It is distorted reality, yes, but reality of a kind nonetheless. It's a bit like the sense of incongruity many Irish people get watching films made in Ireland which make much of the landscape and yet do not seem utterly truthful to the reality of Ireland. One example is the somewhat surreal movie *Hear My Song*, about the life of the singer Josef Locke, filmed mainly in the Wicklow mountains. The strange thing is that the pictures of the landscape, although naturalistic representations of what is 'there', manage to look beautiful in a way that does not gel with our sense of them. Perhaps it is because they seem out of tune with the lives being depicted within the landscape. Perhaps we never 'see' the landscape in this way in 'real' life, if indeed we in any meaningful sense see it at all.

The Irish landscape has a different visual meaning in reality to that depicted in the postcard or photographic movie, which are only an aspect of the truth. Similarly, what we call 'stage-Irish' is a theatrical representation of something we recognise as truthful, *but not completely truthful.* It is a capturing and commodification of an element of our cultural response which occurred in the first place as an intrinsic element of authentic life, but which has been extracted and given an artificial life in cultural iconography and artistic representations.

It is true, therefore, as some critics complain, that McDonagh's plays are not 'real' in the sense of being naturalistic representations of reality. Rather they are impressions of reality, from a certain angle or vantage-point. The difficulty is in pinpointing what that perspective is, or deciding rather, what elements combine to obtain it. Often, as I have outlined, it seems that McDonagh is looking at a dimension of Ireland from without, but it is perhaps more accurate to say that he is looking at it from within some distorted — often to the extent that it sometimes seems even drug- or alcohol-influenced — perspective. In the sense that these plays contain a 'commentary', it is in the nature of a reaction against an artistic rather than a sociological reality — the same phenomenon condemned by Patrick

Kavanagh as 'the myth and illusion of "Ireland"'. For Kavanagh, writers like Yeats, Synge and Lady Gregory had perpetrated a massive 'fraud' by inventing the Irish Literary Renaissance. Theirs was the Ireland of priests, peasants, old crones and whitewashed cottages. Kavanagh confessed to himself falling for the lie, which he says resulted in his autobiography *The Green Fool*. Some of those who have adopted McDonagh as a kind of cultural battering ram with which to promote their own denunciations, would say that Kavanagh was essentially saying the same things as they are. But Kavanagh's work was characterised, above all, by a deep attachment to both Catholicism and the land, both of which are central totems of the 'oppression' which McDonagh has been appropriated in resisting. There is, in other words, a subtle difference between the false and the true notes of Irish cultural experience, the distinction often residing in motive and intent rather than in the objective trappings, which may themselves be either benign, malignant or both at the same time. Kavanagh was not saying that priests, peasants, old crones and whitewashed cottages did not exist in Ireland. He was saying that they did not exist in the way in which they were being presented, and did not have the meanings ascribed to them. He observed the depiction of Ireland and its people by certain writers in terms of 'incidental local colour'. Strip their writings of this, he demanded, 'and see what remains'. Ireland, in this sense, he argued was the invention of Protestant writers, who 'doubting that their Irishness would ooze, have put it on from the outside'. On another occasion, he wrote: 'Their outlook is similar to the sentimental patriotism which takes pride — or pretends to take pride — in the Irishness of a horse that has won the Grand National — with the emphasis on the beast's Irishness instead of its horsiness.'

This is close to the sentiment expressed by Ray, in the final scene of *The Beauty Queen of Leenane*. He asks Maureen if she's 'not watching telly for yourself, no?'

> MAUREEN: I'm not. It's only Australian oul shite they do ever show on that thing.

RAY: (slightly bemused) Sure, that's why I do like it. Who wants to see Ireland on telly?

MAUREEN: *I* do.

RAY: All you have to do is look out your window to see Ireland. And it's soon bored you'd be. 'There goes a calf.'

This strikes me as an ironic comment upon a certain kind of Irish artistic depiction of reality, which imagines that presenting what is there, or what appears to be there, is sufficient for an artistic statement. Irish writers have lacked an ability to perceive in their own reality the quintessence of universal experience, and have instead oversold that reality as representing something elevated or sacred for its own sake. This condition has been exaggerated in Irish writing and culture by the phenomenon of sentiment attaching to Ireland on account of its historical experience and the massive dislocation of its populace. A culture thus truncated seeks to resuscitate itself by reference to artefact and iconography and the fossil of its previous self, rather than re-imagining itself back into existence. If McDonagh is rebelling against anything, he is, like Kavanagh, rebelling against this.

In this sense, those like Fintan OToole, who have adopted McDonagh as a voice vindicating their own perspectives on Ireland are as right as they are wrong. Yes, as O'Toole argues, McDonagh does depict an Ireland dislocated between worlds. But that is not his primary objective, however airtight the analysis might appear. If these plays could have been arrived at by a route developed from the neurosis of the generation to which both myself and Fintan O'Toole belong, one of us might have written these plays. The reason we couldn't is that we were aboard the ship, cast adrift on the cultural swell of a society seeking at once to relate to the new while reviving the old; but, like seasick passengers, we cast our eyes to the dry land of England and America, and thus were unable to correctly relate to what was happening around us. Only the outsider, watching from the shore, had the detachment and the sureness of foot by which to develop the correct perspective.

In his undoubtedly perceptive and fascinating interpretations of McDonagh's relationship to Ireland, O'Toole repeats the neurotic insistence on blaming and self-serving redefinition which prevented us being able to see straight in the first place. 'McDonagh's plays,' he wrote in *The Irish Times*, 'represent a final reversal of Romanicism. To the Romantics, the West was proof of the utopian belief that life was better and purer before the imposition of modern society. Here, the West, without a functioning society, proves the opposite.'

The problem is that, were it not for the fact that precisely the feelings of attachment decried by O'Toole formed an intrinsic element of Martin McDonagh's upbringing, these plays would never have been possible. It is precisely because he fundamentally believes in the world he depicts that he makes such extraordinary plays to recreate it. He wants to reconstruct, not destroy. The comfort gained by O'Toole from McDonagh's work appears to reside in his failure to achieve this reconstruction, which vindicates Fintan's ideological outlook.

In a certain light, McDonagh's work is artistically indistinguishable from the iconography he is allegedly railing against. These plays, were they not so brutal, would risk accusations of the kind of sentimentality which Fintan O'Toole would be the first to decry. Fintan, like many of us who grew up in Ireland in the second half of the twentieth century, wanted to tear apart that sentiment and crush it underfoot, which is why we could never see enough good in it to write truthfully about it. In other words, the neurosis was as much a block to the vision of those who decried as those who worshipped with a dewy-eyed nostalgia. Clarity emerged only in the uncritical and relatively uninvolved vision of the objective outsider. 'I'm not into any kind of definition, any kind of -ism, politically, socially, religiously all that stuff,' McDonagh told O'Toole in one interview they did together. 'It's not that I don't think about those things, but I've come to a place where the ambiguities are more interesting than choosing a strict path and following it.'

*

Garry Hynes, the director who first staged McDonagh's work with the Druid Theatre told Sean O'Hagan about a woman who came up to her in Galway after the premiere of *The Beauty Queen of Leenane*, wiping tears of laughter from her eyes, and said: 'I have a funny feeling that I shouldn't be laughing so hard.' This encapsulates the attitude of a lot of Irish people towards Martin McDonagh. They find his work funny, because they find themselves funny. But they also possess a degree of sentiment for themselves and their ancestors which he clearly, understandably, and probably happily, lacks. This is the neurosis at work, and it means that Irish people of any kind are perhaps worst placed to judge McDonagh and his work. To enjoy his plays, we have not simply to achieve intellectual distance, but also to withdraw sympathy from ourselves, to join in the laughter of the ages, created precisely to numb ourselves, or those who begat us, against the pain of reality. It seems somewhat indecent to voyeuristically enjoy that humour deprived of its catastrophic context.

The characters in McDonagh's plays are in a certain sense real. But it is equally true to say that they have had their feelings removed, or at least removed beyond a humorous pane. We watch them in their misery and meaninglessness and can only laugh. As children in the West of Ireland during the second half of the twentieth century, we saw, met and knew them well: bent men cycling into town in new caps, bearded ladies limping along windswept boreens, desiccated spinsters with their dreams behind them, unwashed drunks on their knees in public houses on dole day. These people exist all right: they were our neighbours, our grandparents, our uncles and aunts. They lived next door or on the edge of towns or in houses with the doors open from which the smell of life emanated as you passed. These were lives which *happened*, as opposed to being constructed in the mythological imaginations of cultural critics. These were lives which seemed to the gaze of the modern eye to be without meaning or architecture. Their existence is not the issue. The issue is why their lives now seem more funny than heart-breaking.

Partly it is because the world they inhabited, and which seemed to trap them, was also a world saturated with nostalgic meanings for those who had gone away. They remained in poverty, but occupied a place which, in the memories of the departed, had a connotation of paradise. Thus their poverty was reinvented as kitsch and their misery became indistinguishable from a picture postcard. Their imprisonment in it was partly as a result of a desire to retain the image which so pleased those who occasionally returned. I remember a returned Yank aunt once leaving a week earlier than planned, and being convinced that it was because we did not, at the time, have an indoor toilet. And yet, if we'd had one, she would have complained along the lines that we were losing our 'authenticity'. One of the problems with an arrested culture is that it has no way of growing organically, or even of imagining how this might have happened if the interruption to its growth had not occurred. And so there are only two cultural ways of responding, one being fossilisation, the other a process of lurching forward in jumps and starts, reacting neurotically to developments elsewhere, imitating, rejecting and trying to un-become what you have been given as a self-description.

Some cope with this condition better than others. Some simply throw their hats at the past, and move on to become its antithesis. It is a strange irony that virtually the entire audience of theatre in Dublin is made up of this type of citizen. Others remained stuck in the past, while the future happened all around them and infiltrated their lives by leaks and seepage. These, strangely — or perhaps not — tend to be the ones who end up on the stage for the others to look and laugh at.

It has been said that McDonagh has no compassion for his characters, and in a certain sense this seems to be true. But he neither laughs at his characters nor invites us to do so: the humour comes by virtue of his faithful observation of the characters and their language. It's the way those of our ancestors who inhabited the worlds from which McDonagh's plays spring forth, used to laugh at themselves.

Many of the jokes in McDonagh's plays relate to the imprisonment of his characters in one world while another seeks to encroach. The existence of familiar items of modern living, like Tayto crisps and Australian soaps, in the lives of people who are in some ways recognisable as our own aunts and uncles, creates a tremendous poignancy and pathos. We might well cry because this is all they got of the harvest of modernity; and also because the imagined purity of their previous existence had been sullied in this way. But perhaps we laugh instead because this is the only way of protecting ourselves and the choices we have made.

This is what we always did, in real life as well, to inure ourselves to the tragedies of others. You might conclude that perhaps the Irish have always been heartless, two-faced bastards, but the real reason is that, to protect ourselves from the psychic disintegration which would have followed from a genuine encounter with our own sense of the sadness and despair of our fellows, we turned them into comic figures. We laughed at what they said, not to mock them but to protect ourselves from what we imagined must be their griefs. That is really what humour is, a layer of gristle between bones which would otherwise grind into one another to the point of seizure. The Complan, porridge, pisspots and brutality in the plays of Martin McDonagh would be unbearable if they were not funny. In this dimension of reality, the absurd was simply the otherwise unbearable everyday.

The humour in McDonagh's plays, then, is not a literary humour, but an organic comedy harvested from real contact with the homeland of his work, and of course also its inhabitants. The stories Martin McDonagh creates, as tightly-sprung as rat-traps, are undeniably beautiful creations, but the clarity of the humour is not a product of his imagination but of his ear for the altered reality of the places in which he spent, by all accounts, a great deal of his childhood. He is, in a sense, a satirist. But his satire is beyond mere attack, having mutated into a kind of kiss of life.

The humour in his plays, being born of the most unimaginable kind of horror, is not the dried tinder of so much modern comedy, but the purest, hardest, blackest anthracite, mined at the deepest level of the human soul.

Martin McDonagh has mined and gathered well. In his plays, from the very first lines, the voice he has located sounds pure and true. He does not depict this world humorously; he recreates it and it acquires the humour which, though somewhat buried or diluted in the reality of the present, has been in the past so necessary for mere survival. This comedy is not an accident, not a technique, but a necessity.

Like Flann O'Brien, McDonagh looks at Ireland through a humourous gauze, a filter of irony which reduces its inhabitants to cartoons. But whereas in, say, *An Beal Bocht*, O'Brien's purpose is to mock and deride his own characters' attachment to misery, McDonagh in a strange kind of way does not do this. Instead, he creates a sense of their forlorn nature in the midst of their misery, the way in which they project onto one another the feelings of anger, rage and despair which their condition excites in them. This is deeply funny to begin with, but ultimately saddening in a way Flann O'Brien's writing is not.

I always think a great writer carries an emblem of his overall genius in the very first words of a piece, and McDonagh achieves this in the very first exchange between mother and daughter in *The Beauty Queen of Leenane*:

> MAG: Wet, Maureen?
>
> MAUREEN: Of course wet.

Maureen's answer is both fatalistic and angry: fatalistic towards the world and the weather, but angry towards her mother on account, perhaps, of it all.

Such humour is the gristle which protects us from the raw engagement of more abrasive forces. It is a kind of self-protection, a philosophical response born of the need to maintain a blinkered outlook in the face of calamity. In the bleakness of McDonagh's visions is a profound comedy, born of the necessity to protect ourselves from the abyss, which threatens these characters at every turn. Only by virtue of their being cartoons are we spared their despair. This is so awful that we laugh to protect ourselves from it.

But because in real life this humour is a matter of life and death rather than entertainment or diversion, we have but rarely seen it transposed faithfully onto a screen or stage or page. Writers who are too involved in the very survival of their people develop an unconscious fear that any objectification of the world will de-humanise it. Many of us lived in this world and nurtured ambitions to write something truthful about it. But we were too involved in its paradoxes and pathos. It took the intimate outsider to at once see this world and recognise its potential, to see the joke, understand it and not feel pain on account of the betrayal of retelling it.

*

Irish people understand the joke because it is second nature to them. But it is a little surprising that it has become, in McDonagh's hands, universal. His success in capturing the universal quintessence often missed by his predecessors has enabled his shift from artist to a kind of multinational industry.

One of the collateral benefits for McDonagh of observing this world so faithfully is that he has hit upon a world which is by its nature exotic. In this he exploits the very syndrome which in another sense he seems to attack: the kitschification of Ireland and its meanings in the modern world. As the planet becomes smaller and more homogenous, the prospect of discovering true strangeness within it becomes more remote. What is fascinating about the world McDonagh has evoked is that, while existing right beside the 'real' world, it has about it a strangeness which is conveniently comprehensible, at least in its superficial aspects. The language, a quirk of the combination of two opposing tongues, is itself peculiar. Its strangeness is simple, a mere matter of turning sentences back to front, but this simplicity creates a comedy all the more potent because it is predictable. (A friend of mine, incidentally, went to see the Irish-language version of *The*

Beauty Queen in Galway, and was struck by how much of the humour had been removed by the change back to the native tongue. The parody of the underlying syntax having been removed, the play functioned more on the level of 'naturalistic' melodrama, and was accordingly less surreal.)

There is another sense in which McDonagh's plays are neither rooted in reality nor intended to be. This is the sense in which they are rooted in the canon of Irish theatre, in which they engage with the world of the 'stage-Irish' in the literal, not to say the literary, sense. They speak to an audience in a knowing way about the things that audience, being expectant of watching an Irish play in a long line of Irish plays, expects to experience. McDonagh's plays emerge from the same vague source as Synge's, Friel's, Murphy's and Keane's, and seem to 'know' all these with an immense sense of irony and varying degrees of respect.

A short while after McDonagh had his massive success at the Tony Awards, I happened to be in the Tricycle theatre in Kilburn, London, to see John B. Keane's masterpiece *Sive*. At the interval, eavesdropping on the audience, I overheard several debates about whether Keane was 'influenced by McDonagh', and indeed 'as good as McDonagh'.

Some people feel offended by McDonagh because they feel he is laughing at them. But to the extent that he is laughing at all, he is laughing at those who have laughed at them in the past, who for all that they have written great plays have in some way desecrated the source of their inspiration by objectifying it and rendering it laughable. *A Skull in Connemara*, for example, strikes me as a parody of *The Playboy of the Western World*, an absurdly comic flirtation with murder and mayhem, which peters out in the banality of false assumption and slapstick violence. It is as if, in a certain sense, McDonagh is in agreement with those who attacked *The Playboy* for precisely the offences for which McDonagh himself is attacked today. If *The Playboy* had not been written, perhaps this play could never have been written either. But if it is possible to imagine this play existing without being preceded by *The Playboy*, we would rightly think of it as the most outrageous caricature of Irish life. Because *The Playboy* has been written, and iconised, it is more reasonable to see *The Lonesome West* as an outrageous caricature of *The Playboy*, with a postmodern nod in the direction of Sam Shepard. It is as though McDonagh, far from ridiculing the people he writes about, seeks to redeem them from some vague, perhaps imagined slight at the hands of a previous exploiter. McDonagh's characters appear to act and speak in a fashion which seeks to answer back against the calumnies which would have them as vicious murderers. Their very incompetence, combined with a certain knowingness in their humour and actions, seems to be taking the piss out of Synge. Our caricaturist's caricaturist must therefore be our friend.

How good, or great, a playwright is Martin McDonagh? In some ways it is an irrelevant question. There is no point in comparing him with those who have gone before, because he is not creating a new vision but an original take on an old one. Until he moves to the next coherent stage of his artistic life, he cannot be seen, or judged, in isolation.

McDonagh reworks and parodies and reinvents. He is a hugely skilled writer. He belongs to the television age, but seems also to be rooted deeply in myth and fairytale. His plays have the quality of fairytales, of cartoons, but also of TV sit-com. In a superficial, shorthand sense, they do, as has often been noted, come from the same place as the TV comedy Father Ted, turning on a generational response to certain iconic tyrannies.

There are serious limitations in his writing. For example, his characters do not have distinct personas or voices — all speak in the same patois of English words placed over the structure and syntax of the buried Irish. And yet, as characters they work, because although lacking distinctive personalities, they do have distinct souls. Their histories and antagonisms provide them with the motivations and directions. This works well because of the tightly-constructed, cartoon-like quality of the plots and situations; but it is deceptively superficial, which is perhaps why some critics have observed that McDonagh appears to lack compassion for his characters. The moral development usually seems to be within the piece rather than within the characters, all of whom seem equally damned. And yet, there are exceptions: Father Walsh, in *The Lonesome West*, is a brooding, self-accusing, incompetent priest who acquires the qualities of a creeping redeemer, and whose melodramatic self-sacrifice as a means of obtaining the reconciliation of Valene and Coleman is at once hilarious and deeply moving. It is a strange and beautiful achievement in what is without doubt McDonagh's best play to date.

Of course, in a certain sense, both McDonagh's critics and advocates are right in virtually everything they say. He *is* taking the piss. He *does* exploit the gap between the pre-modern and the postmodern. His plays *are* cartoons. But since the only objective of a playwright is to create plays which people will watch and engage with, the concerns expressed about his relationship to reality are spurious, irrelevant and often quite ludicrous.

And he *does* engage with something real and terrifying — the emotional palsy of a people trapped in their own unrealised dreams, marooned in a cultural wasteland from which the essence of normality has been extracted, unable to jump-start a manner of self-description which will sound plausible to themselves. They seek gratification, release, relief, in a fashion which their own way of describing already tells them is a doomed errand. They chase the dream not to attain it but in order to remind themselves of the correctness of their own fatalism. All are trapped by the iconography of a place which was as distorted by its own life bursting out as by the external world breaking in. Maureen, the beauty queen of Leenane, is held prisoner by the moral blackmail of her Complan-guzzling Irish Mammy; Valene Connor, in *The Lonesome West*, accumulates religious figurines as a way of attaining Heaven. Father Walsh, whose spectre invades each play of the trilogy until he emerges fully-formed in *The Lonesome West*, is — literally — a failed priest, trapped by the demands of a calling to which, unable to prevent the dissolution of his community into murder and mayhem, he is clearly unsuited. All are broken spirits, living between paradise and limbo, whose relentless chatter is as though to drown out the voice from within which tells them they were born to absurdity and meaninglessness. All McDonagh's characters have either passed the point where their spiritual pilot-light has been extinguished, or reach that point in the course of the plays. They are the dead unburied, traversing a landscape which they are told is home but which means little or nothing to them in the terms they have been led to believe it should.

McDonagh's success therefore poses questions about the direction of theatre. For all the hit-and-miss qualities of modern theatre, the form retains its sense of mystique and, to a degree, artistic elitism. A play in the theatre, even a bad play, is still regarded as culturally superior to a television programme or a pantomime. There remains this sense that people still go to the theatre to be stretched and uplifted, rather than simply entertained. And yet, if you look at the kinds of plays which are generally successful in the theatre, you will see that their most obvious quality is entertainment value. There is still a type of play which is generally regarded as worthwhile-but-boring, and this will always bring people to the theatre who wish to make a statement about themselves. But the ideal play, for a producer's standpoint, is one which combines the notion of artistic profundity with pure entertainment.

It is as though Martin McDonagh has figured this out, and created the perfect vehicles for its exploitation. In one interview, he said that writing stage plays was for him a 'last resort'. He had tried radio plays, TV plays, films and short stories, all without a breakthrough. 'I always thought theatre was the least interesting of the art forms,' he told Fintan O'Toole in an interview for *The Irish Times*. 'I'd much rather sit at home and watch a good TV play or series than go to the theatre. I only used to go to see plays with film stars in them ... To be in this position is strange because I'm coming to theatre with disrespect for it. I'm coming from a film fan's perspective on theatre.'

The social status aspect of theatre-going creates a chronic problem for the integrity of the theatre, challenging it to produce works which are participative rather than voyeuristic, to subvert the contentment and complacency of its audience while not turning them away. As we sit through a play which attempts to deal with one aspect or other of the national psychology or personality, how well disposed can we be to the truth about what darkness it may contain? Are we willing to allow it seep into ourselves and release the griefs and pains which have been handed to us by our parents, who got them from their own parents? Are we willing to swim in the deep end of cultural experience? The temptation is to do otherwise. If we are to survive in the shadows of tomorrow morning, we need to maintain to some degree the defences of self-delusion which allow us to landscape out the uncomfortable realities. Is it, in such circumstances, possible for a play to transcend the cultural cohesion that binds the audience with the recreated reality of society outside the theatre? And what chance, then, of its seeping into those parts where its healing powers are most urgently required?

One thing modern audiences tend to seek from theatre is a form of anti-nostalgia, the experience of relief that, thanks be to God, we are not like that anymore. In a sense, this appetite corresponds precisely to the ideological objectives expressed by cultural neurotics who seek to deconstruct the past. Emerging into the theatre foyer from some devastating portrayal of ourselves, we affect a contented smile and congratulate ourselves on how far we have travelled down the thoroughly modern motorway. And isn't it great that we are able to laugh about the way we were before civilisation descended upon us?

Good theatre has a responsibility to interrogate the ways we protect ourselves. But drama is also entertainment and so most of us who go to the theatre happen to be the kind of people who feel they have, through background, opportunity or good fortune, escaped the realities which playwrights seek to explore. To deal in the things which a society seeks to conceal or avoid, while not alienating that society entirely, is one of the many paradoxical demands of writing for the theatre. Challenging impenetrably cosy delusions and flawless feats of landscaping, our best playwrights continue to present us with unsettlingly truthful versions of ourselves. The irony is that these versions must be coated in the taste and colour of our delusion. They must tell us what we need to know while allowing us the option of denying it in public. The laughs generated by Martin McDonagh's plays achieve this almost perfectly.

Merely to observe such things opens one to accusations of attributing 'sociological' or 'political' relevance to artistic statement. This is a cop-out, motivated by the same self-delusion. All art which continues to mean anything has relevance by definition; whether it be social, political or otherwise doesn't make all that much difference. Great artists catch such things in their nets without knowing. The only worthwhile question is whether the work serves the appetite for delusion or the search for truth. This is why, although I remain deeply jealous, I have to admit that Martin McDonagh is on the side of the angels.

VIC MERRIMAN

Settling for More: Excess and Success in Contemporary Irish Drama

Irish drama's claim to social significance rests on the pledge that in acts of theatre something more than box office, or the reputation of an individual artist, is at stake. Theatre is part of a broader cultural conversation about who we are, how we are in the world and who and how we would like to be. Theatre is a powerful means of constituting and invigorating community. The questioning stance of dramatic artists is essential to the development of critical citizenship, without which no social order can remain healthy. Such views informed the discussions of those active in the foundation of the cultural movements of the late nineteenth and early twentieth centuries, which created the cultural conditions for the establishment of the Abbey Theatre as a national theatre. From the point of view of the nationalist movement, a National Theatre made sense insofar as it consolidated the anti-colonial feeling which was approaching critical mass in the country, and among Irish groups in Britain, the USA and Australia. Many plays current in the early twentieth century clearly drew on and embodied anti-colonial desires crystallising in the collective consciousness of an emergent independent citizenry.

The Abbey, however, set out to exceed its particularity as an organ of national consciousness, specifically when such a role was circumscribed by pressure to evangelise on behalf of a nation 'free, Gaelic and Catholic'. In some respects, the early Abbey is better understood as a theatre of the nation, claiming the right to continue to dream dreams, rather than a building based monolith, dedicated to promulgating the pieties of a new order. As W. B. Yeats was later to declare to government, when arguing for subsidy for the theatre, 'What you get will not be what you want, but what we want.' This statement is often taken simply as evidence that Yeats remained an aesthete of sorts, a man seeking to transcend 'the greasy till' and 'the filthy modern tide'. In view of his commitment to the new state, continuing not only to live and work in a social order, which had swept his own people away, but sitting as a senator in its upper house of parliament, this explanation is plainly inadequate. Hence my use of the idea of 'excess' rather than 'transcendence' at the beginning of this paragraph. Drama is the art form with people in it, and Yeats, Gregory and Synge created stage worlds populated by *dramatis personae* drawn from people actually existing in Ireland at the time. One of nationalism's principle cultural goals is to communicate to its own people their homogeneity. In the plays written for the early Abbey, that goal is critiqued. Synge notably staged people who exceeded in their lived experiences the limitations of anti-colonial myth-making — especially in respect of the idealised peasantry of the western world.

The significance of early Abbey plays is thus underpinned by uneasy relationships with propagandist narratives. Even a play like *Cathleen Ni Houlihan*, which appeared to Shaw to contain a powerful distillation of fervour for the (Catholic) nationalist cause, contains within its first scene a critical stance which places it otherwise in relation to the emergent hegemonic 'we' of Irish nationalism. In so doing, Gregory and Yeats enact the role of dramatic artist as critical cultural interlocutor. In this way, the play earns its right to public attention. When J. M. Synge produced his 'playboy' to inhabit civic space opened up by the national theatre, he demonstrated the critical vigour of performative images themselves. Far from demanding space to express or enunciate a rarefied 'aesthetic' position, the theatre of Yeats, Gregory and Synge inaugurates a conversation with 'Ireland'. These early twentieth-century works critique triumphant nationalism with oppositional, or more tellingly, 'ambivalent' narratives and images of community. In so doing, they establish an ethical practice of staging autocritical social worlds and experiences which exemplifies the interrogative power of artists in society.

Such an oppositional role was not always welcome within the Abbey itself as it developed institutional norms. The fate of O'Casey, and of Denis Johnston has been well documented elsewhere. Many popular, and critical playwrights and artists of the theatre were to find the Abbey an inhospitable space for public challenge, especially after Yeats' day. Nonetheless, theatre persisted throughout the twentieth century as a vital form of public conversation. And when the Abbey proved averse to disturbing nationalistic pieties, playwrights such as M. J. Molloy and John B. Keane provided significant works for production by amateur groups local to them. Even under the watchful eye of reactionary priests and public representatives, figures such as Sanbatch Daly and Big Maggie appeared in rural halls to demonstrate that when public conversation is fully engaged, the apparently inevitable contradictions between the popular and the critical are destabilised. The foundation of Druid Theatre Company in Galway city in 1975 marked a moment of emergence of a more diverse account of who 'we Irish' might be. Arguably, Druid set in train a cultural momentum which, in tandem with the development in Derry city of Field Day Productions, set the scene for new arrangements on the island of Ireland which flowered briefly in the 1990s. In this respect, it was entirely appropriate that the guests of honour at Druid's 21st anniversary celebrations in the new Town Hall Theatre in Galway in 1996 were Mary Robinson, President of Ireland and Michael D. Higgins, whose Department of Arts, Culture and Gaeltacht had made provision for EU funds to develop the building itself. Something had taken its course.

During the 1900s, Gregory, Yeats, Synge, and Shaw (in *John Bull's Other Island*) used dramatic poetry to struggle with the predictable limits of an Ireland yet to come. In the latter decades of that century, Tom Murphy, Dermot Bolger, Billy Roche, Jim Nolan and Johnny Hanrahan have recognised ample dramatic material in the social wastelands of 'the Ireland we have settled for'. Twentieth-century Irish drama relentlessly exposes how the matter of lived lives exceeds accounts of living generated by received narratives. In other words, Irish drama operates as an allegory of acts of performance themselves: content is critically exceeded because it is represented in embodied actions. Murphy, Bolger and Roche address the collisions of social class, emigration, exile and desire unfulfilled in plays such as *Famine*, *The Lament for Arthur Cleary* and *Poor Beast in the Rain*. Nolan stages the collapse of social radicalism among the faded furnishings of *The Guernica Hotel*. Hanrahan stages the memorialisation of radical nationalism as a source of cultural and political inertia in *The Art of Waiting*. These two plays, both dramatically uneven, locate in the Robinson era the stirrings of that which was mobilising to replace it — a rough beast slouching toward the International Financial Services Centre to be born.

While such plays were being written, performed and revived, something else began to happen in the Republic of Ireland which, almost overnight, rendered the wistful cadences of Roche's *The Cavalcaders* and his *Wexford Trilogy* barely audible: the Celtic Tiger Economy began to roar. A rapidly established public consensus presented the sudden economic upturn as a logical outcome of the coincidence of maturing benefits of EU membership, and of a nation-state prudently refigured as a node in the network of new global capitalism. In a stunning fulfilment of the impossible 1950s aspiration 'We'll have America at home', this combination had delivered prematurely in the present a future of amplitude beyond our dreams. Since 1959, the dominant political force, Fianna Fáil, had begun aligning in its rhetoric the pursuit of economic goals with the achievement of a republic as co-terminus patriotic projects. With the advent of the Tiger Economy, populist political leaders no longer courted legitimacy by wearing the inherited anti-colonial mantle of the founders of the nation-state. The rhetorical alignment of the welfare of nations, many with the comfort of capital's few was, in the form of the Celtic Tiger, manifestly justified and ostentatiously successful. Where elites had heretofore been the focus of suspicion and hostility, now 'everyone' began claiming elite status for themselves. And such a sea-change found its cultural logic in the emergence of new kinds of Irish play, specifically in the works of its avatars, Marina Carr and Martin McDonagh, two of the most celebrated Irish playwrights of the late 1990s.

In an apparently bold oppositional stance, Carr's and McDonagh's successes have been built around plays which stage Ireland as a benighted dystopia. At a time of unprecedented affluence, Carr and McDonagh elaborate a world of the poorly educated, coarse and unrefined. The focus is tight, the performances of violence inhering in the people themselves, grotesque, unrelenting and calibrated to the tastes of an aggressive bourgeois palate. Carr's *By the Bog of Cats* and *Portia Coughlan* take as their point of departure the condition of being poor in contemporary Ireland. Both plays travesty the experiences of the poor, urban and rural. Introducing a category of internal outsider known in the United States of America as 'white trash', they posit worlds in which material poverty and moral bankruptcy map on to one another, eerie partners in a dance of death. In McDonagh's case, *The Beauty Queen of Leenane*, *A Skull in Connemara*, *The Lonesome West* and *The Cripple of Inishmaan* stage a sustained dystopic vision of a land of gratuitous violence, craven money-grubbing and crass amorality. No loyalty, whether communal, personal or familial can survive in this arid landscape. Death, affection, responsibility appear as meaningless intrusions in the self-obsessed orbits of child-adults.

Dystopic visions of Ireland are nothing new in theatre. The love scene in Tom Murphy's *Famine* is perhaps the most fully realised, and Johnny Hanrahan's and John Browne's *Craving* forges metaphors for Celtic Tiger Ireland from the collisions between commodity, desire unfulfilled and cultural collapse. McDonagh's work comes from a different place, and has different consequences. The decision to populate the stage with violent child-adults repeats the angriest colonial stereotypes as a form of communal self-loathing. The dramatis personae of these plays specifically mark out figures of the poor which are over-determined in their Irishry. Gross caricatures with no purchase on the experiences of today's audiences, their appeal to the new consumer-Irish consensus lies in their appearance as ludicrous manichaean opposites — the colonised simian reborn. In each belly laugh which greets the preposterous malevolence of its actions there is a huge cathartic roar of relief that all of this is past — 'we' have left it all behind. The entirety of the Leenane Trilogy stages not one moral voice, save that of the ludicrous Father 'Walsh' … 'Welsh', referred to in the first two plays and finally encountered in *The Lonesome West*. His contribution ends in a suicidal walk into the fjord at Leenane, leaving the fictional world of the West of Ireland with nothing to counter the craven barbarity of its inhabitants, except the strong possibility that they will one day wipe each other out. No Syngean anthem to robust paganism this. These plays offer a kind of voyeuristic aperture on the antics of white trash whose reference point is more closely aligned to the barbarous conjurings of Jerry Springer than to the continuities of an indigenous tradition of dramatic writing. Importantly, the repellent figures presented turn out to be representations of those most fully betrayed by indigenous self-rule: emigrants, under-educated peasants, bachelor smallholders, women abandoned in rural isolation by economic collapse.

Critics who confine themselves to accounts of performance which privilege categories such as sense of place, ear for dialogue, fine observation, quality of star acting/ensemble performances, appropriateness of design and technical precision, do a good job in recording the high production standards of the plays as originally performed. Criticism that goes no further than documenting the quality of the spectacle, is wholly inadequate to critique what these plays amount to as cultural interventions. The resources of the most successful of Irish theatre companies have been deployed in the service of deeply problematic work, to the extent that their theatricality — their ability to operate as spectacle — overpowers engagement with their significance as dramatic art. What is at issue here is the meaning of these representations as constitutory events in the evolution of civil society. What is being played — about whom, to whom and in whose interests? What are its meanings, and their consequences?

The cultural tone of Tiger Ireland is structured around a notion that the past is best forgotten, as its hopes and struggles have lost their relevance. Success is evident everywhere. This is not the whole story, however and the successes of Carr and McDonagh have little to do with the loss of relevance of older worlds and their inhabitants. *Portia Coughlan*, *By the Bog of Cats*, *The Cripple of Inishmaan* and the Leenane Trilogy come from, and perform something else. The argument that the apparent ironic playfulness of McDonagh's work marks an ability on the part of the nation to laugh at itself, claims cultural significance for the plays as manifestations of a coming of age, a type of post-colonial[1] maturation. In reality, the comfortable echelon of a nakedly divided society is confirmed in its complacency, as it simultaneously enjoys and erases the fact that 'our' laughter is at the expense of 'them'. The movement of the dramatis personae of *By the Bog of Cats* and the Leenane Trilogy to central positions in Irish theatre enables such figures to occupy and redefine the co-ordinates of cultural space. In celebrating the new Irishness of the audience for such spectacles, they simultaneously negate the interrogation of the conditions in which such images are produced and have points of reference. In this way, they point to a turn away from public inquiry, a willingness to settle for a divided society, a fatal refusal of the difficult process of decolonisation itself. A spurious post-coloniality of chronological severance institutes a lesser public role for theatre itself, in which its credentials as spectacle overpower its ethical obligation to critique and thus renew the social order.

Carr's *By The Bog Of Cats* specifically grounds her protagonist's predilections for violence, deceit and unnatural urges in her identity as a traveller. Hester Swayne, traveller, is beyond the pale, a constant figure in a mutating social order desperate for points of otherness against which to imagine its own impossible consistency. By othering representations of their near-selves, and scorching them in the heat of their derision, McDonagh and Carr offer bourgeois audiences course after course of reassurance, of the kind offered to the upwardly mobile when 1980s neo-liberal economics provided them with the prone form of the homeless to step over on their way to the stock exchange. In staging peasant life, Synge unambiguously confronted the ideological project to which it had been co-opted: a travesty serving the need felt by a resurgent nationalist bourgeoisie for a foundational myth. The journey from Synge to McDonagh takes us all the way from images which challenge the submerged ideological positions of an emergent neo-colonial elite to those which collude in reinforcing them.

Carr's and McDonagh's misrecognition as practitioners of the historical role of dramatic artists in twentieth-century Ireland testifies to the ways in which form eclipses content in the multiple circulations of late capitalism. If one is Irish and a playwright, the logic goes, then one must be an Irish playwright. If one is an Irish playwright, then one must continue or re-invigorate an Irish dramatic tradition. If one does that, one will succeed. If one has succeeded, then one has reinvigorated Irish theatre, and one's roots in tradition need only be exposed in order to be fully appreciated. Equally, it is self-evident that to be a playwright is to be a dissenting voice, an outsider. Carr's outsider status is suggested by the apparent mismatch between a midlands childhood and a devotion to 'Shakespeare and the Greeks'. McDonagh's persona plays more into Hollywood outsider iconography of the 'brooding', misunderstood malcontent. While neither persona is useful as a way of knowing either writer, they are hugely significant in relation to how they structure ways of seeing, not only the particular persons themselves, but Irish playwrights in general. To be oppositional is to expose the persistence of gender inequality and its attendant brutalities. To be oppositional is to 'have the courage to stage unflattering images of Irishness'. When Irish audiences 'laugh at themselves' the play unites the playwright's outsider project with the improbable proposition that mainstream theatre audiences are composed of courageous radicals. One thing such accounts of oppositionality refuse is any explanation of, for example, gender oppression or moral ugliness inherent in Western peasants. This is predominantly due to the tendency of both playwrights to work toward spectacle at the expense of interrogation. It is also a function of the strongly held prejudice that explanatory voices are didactic voices, and as such are not artistic. Donal O'Kelly's work for Calypso Productions provides a case study of the application of such 'aesthetic criteria' to a censorious — and censoring — purpose. His *The Business of Blood* attracted the following comment from the drama critic of *The Irish Times*:

> … it has been said, inter alia, that drama is comprised of conflict and change, yet within this work there is no dramatic conflict and there has been no significant change at its conclusion. This is theatre being used to make a point rather than a point being used to create drama.[2]

Recognisably drawing on the aesthetic forms of 1930s workers' theatre, O'Kelly's collaboration with Kenneth Glenaan went unrecognised as theatre at all in 1990s Dublin.

Donal O'Kelly is from Dublin. He is a writer, director and performer, well known for his solo performances of his plays *Bat the Father, Rabbit the Son* and *Catalpa*. Both plays have toured nationally and internationally to great acclaim. O'Kelly is also a founder member of Calypso Productions, for whom he co-wrote *The Business of Blood*. Calypso's didactic project is their raison d'etre. Their ethical position is explicit:

> Too often art and artists travel a journey where the landscapes they move through and the people they encounter become mere observations, ideas to be

used. Other artists travel as participants in their
landscapes. Their work is about, and comes from
their interaction with their fellow world citizens ...
Our landscape covers the planet. Our family is
global. Our creativity is a critical one.[3]

Description and discussion of O'Kelly's involvement as writer
and performer with Rough Magic, Red Kettle and the Abbey and
Peacock theatres would fill a full volume. This essay will confine
itself to *The Business of Blood, Asylum! Asylum!* and *Farawayan*. In
all of these works, Donal O'Kelly sets out to justify, develop and
exploit a publicly critical role for the artistic voice. O'Kelly's
theatre is a storyteller's theatre. Narrative-driven, all three
performances draw on montage, music and movement in the
service of critical statements. Yeats insisted that Irish drama serve
'a high ambition'. In specifically addressing the common
citizenship of artists, people represented in *dramatis personae* and
audiences for theatre, O'Kelly revisits concepts and principles
fundamental to the purposes of theatre as it emerged in Ireland at
the beginning of the twentieth century.

The Business of Blood, by O'Kelly and Kenneth Glenaan, stages
the story of Chris Cole, a Christian pacifist who broke into British
Aerospace Stevenage and destroyed components of the nosecones
of Hawk jetfighters. He acted in order to draw attention both to
their use against civilian populations in East Timor, and to what
he saw as the hypocrisy of a British government who publicly
announces that it does not sell arms to regimes known to be
involved in human rights abuses. The company addresses First
World audiences who have multiple positions on Third World
issues. The status of Ireland and Scotland as countries colonised by
England is re-affirmed in the visit to London, where the company
speaks in solidarity with the struggle of those colonised by Indonesia
in East Timor. The reality of the implication of Ireland and Scotland
in the oppressions of a colonial past, and of their membership of
power blocs of wealthy and belligerent nation-states is raised by
performances in Dublin, Glasgow and on tour.

The illustrated booklet, *Information and Action on Arms*, which accompanied the play includes the following transcript of a conversation between the journalist John Pilger and Alan Clark MP:

Flying the Flag

Alan Clark, former minister in the Thatcher government was responsible for the sale of the latest batch of Hawk aircraft to Indonesia.

John Pilger: In East Timor it (Indonesia) has killed more people proportionately than Pol Pot killed in Cambodia. By all credible accounts it's killed one third of the population. Isn't that ever a consideration for the British government?

Alan Clark: It's not something that often enters my ... thinking, I must admit.

JP: Why is that?

AC: My responsibility is to my own people. I don't really fill my mind much with what one set of foreigners is doing to another.

The link between the arms industry and the fate of subject populations is clearly made. What is also suggested in this carefully selected sequence is that moral blindness and amnesia are now constitutive aspects of governance in the civilised western world, and not a function of ministerial idiosyncrasy. The consequences of such gaps in western consciousness are stark and final for peoples of other worlds. It is O'Kelly's and Glenaan's particular concern to expose the extent to which strategic blindness and amnesia at government level have immediate and long-term consequences within western democratic regimes themselves.

The deliberate, uncompromising selection of incidents which illustrate lethal double standards in high places and in the population at large characterises the episodes dramatised in *The Business of Blood*. Following the play's dismissal in David Nowlan's review as something less than dramatic art, Fintan O'Toole responded:

> There is a strong tendency to patronise such writing, to see it as at best a lesser form of art, at worst a corruption of aesthetic purity ... The question posed by *The Business of Blood* — whether civilisation can be said to exist at all while complicity with mass murder is treated as a legitimate business — is a question that addresses the very possibility of art itself.[4]

As W. B. Yeats and J. M. Synge discovered in the 1900s, oppositional texts and their constitutive practices are unlikely to be widely distributed in bourgeois culture, either emergent or dominant. If the plays of the Celtic Revival staged dreams of possible worlds, the dramas of the Celtic Tiger are expected to appear as entertainment commodities organised around visual spectacle and narrative closure. The worlds depicted in such entertainments are spaces which exist to ratify existing social relations. They stage the life experiences of marginal persons and groups as departures from the norm. Such departures exist only to facilitate the triumphant return of that norm in the plenitude of narrative closure. Audiences are invited to question, only to the extent of exercising curiosity about situations, which the narrative is structured to disclose. Dramatic situations, and the people within them, appear as puzzling or threatening disturbances of an otherwise stable norm. The world, the people in it and their inter-relationships, are known quantities. They are not depicted as subjects for human inquiry, let alone transformative action. The transformative potential of any cultural practice depends crucially on the extent to which it structures the world as a question. *Farawayan*, a performance in eight scenes written and directed by Donal O'Kelly, applies this principle in its depiction of experiences of refugees and asylum seekers in late 1990s Ireland.

Farawayan uses the spectacular potential of theatre form to shift the rigid framing of the text's Refugee, Immigrant and Asylum Seeker. The reader might bear in mind the kinds of editorial perspectives and journalistic tropes which were current in print and broadcast media in the racially-charged atmosphere of 1997/8: a front-page editorial in *The Wexford People* spoke of dubious Romanians who could be found wearing designer clothing and basking on the balconies of brand new apartments while local people went without medical care and adequate housing. Specifically, it alleged that young Romanian men were lurking at the gates of local convent schools for the express purpose of enticing young girls to bear the children who would deliver Irish citizenship to the unscrupulous father. Radio phone-ins and evening paper headlines in Dublin were equally, if not more aggressively committed to demonising the arrivals in terms drawn from the worst excesses of British and American racism. The race card had been played — successfully — in more than one Dublin constituency during the close-run general election of June 1997.

Farawayan was staged at the Olympic Ballroom, off Camden Street, Dublin in autumn 1998. The play's genesis in opposition to the emergence and proliferation of racist discourse in Ireland fits the Calypso profile precisely. So too does the coalition of funders assembled to bring the project to fruition, and the accompanying resource file, *Information and Action on Racism*. In its genesis as a public project, *Farawayan* affirms and lays claim to the role of dramatic artist as critical cultural interlocutor, and asserts its right to public attention: the play inaugurates a conversation with 'Ireland'. *Farawayan* locates familiar content — experiences of emigration, dislocation and despair — among multiplying narratives and provocative images of community. Irish experiences are staged contrapuntally with the biographies of contemporary exiles from the east and from the south in pursuit of an ethical, historicised critique of emergent Irish society. In his programme note for the production, Andy Storey names the focus of the project in uncompromising language:

> Despite Ireland's relatively small numbers of asylum
> seekers, it seems to be beyond the capacity of this
> state to deal with them in a decent manner ...
> Asylum seekers and immigrants are not burdens to
> be borne or invaders to be repulsed. They are
> human beings with life stories and human rights,
> with abilities and energies, and with a range of
> contributions to make. They are to be welcomed.

The kind of Ireland that emerges from this theatre is stark and clear, as are the questions this piece of work poses to those who live and work within it. This is no mean achievement, and is central to Donal O'Kelly's purposes in developing this play. It is important also to reflect on this play's contribution to developments in contemporary Irish theatre. Specifically, its social questioning inaugurates an exploration of the languages of theatre itself.

In an article in the inaugural issue of *Irish Theatre Magazine*, Donal O'Kelly addressed theatre's uniqueness as communal experience, and referred to its capacities to forge connections between people, practices and life histories atomised in an increasingly distanced, privatised and mediated interaction with others. *Farawayan* is above all an audience experience. Queuing outside the Olympic Ballroom, people receive a programme on admission which is a replica of an Irish/EU passport. This document is stamped, and will be demanded throughout the evening by unpleasant masked figures who control admission to the balcony from where the first two episodes will be viewed, and the ground level — vantage point for episodes three to eight. Faraya is discovered by audience members, held in a dimly lit cubicle off the balcony, guarded by the functionaries, Belt and Buckle. The play stages her escape from the hell of Farawaya through a long sea voyage on a makeshift raft, arrival in Ireland, participation in Maud's glittering ball, unmasking as an outsider, bureaucratic assessment, terrified flight and disorientation, physical brutalisation and enforced return from whence she came. Throughout the experience, *Farawayan* explores the sensual immediacy of live theatre, the suggestive powers of dynamics of light/darkness, sound/silence, music/cacophony, stillness/movement. Crucially — in terms of its formal innovations and adaptations — *Farawayan* addresses the dynamic actual/virtual. It does this on a number of levels, including its embodiment of the horrors of contemporary warfare, exile and wandering: horrors available only through virtual contact to most of the people in the audiences for *Farawayan*. Equally, the traumatic disorientations of enforced exile, which completely defeat and are reduced by theatrical realism, are given form in Faraya's experiences at 'Maud's glittering ball' (Episode four), in 'The Forest of Hatches and Flares' (Episode five) and during 'The Assessment' (Episode six). Episode six finds an unmasked Faraya in flight from Maud's dogs, Costas and Airgead, lost and wandering in the forest of hatches and flares. The audience, at ground level, witness Faraya's encounter with animate trees containing hatches which open to reveal terrifying flare explosions. We are in the terrain of folk-tale and dreamscape in this episode, where ghastly references to the mutilating power of landmines and the psychic wounds of oppression and enforced migration proliferate. Faraya's youth, innocence and exhaustion are vividly staged in a theatre of spectacle and physicality that implicates the audience in her disorientation.

This search for implication over explication marks a remarkable artistic journey for Donal O'Kelly. In 1994, he wrote *Asylum! Asylum!* for the National Theatre. The play imagines the plight of a Ugandan petty criminal who arrives at Dublin Airport seeking asylum. In an affront to the received image of Ireland of the Welcomes, it will end with his being bound, beaten and deported by Irish officials acting in the interests of Fortress Europe. *Asylum! Asylum!* was staged at the Peacock Theatre, in a proscenium format, where the pull of the conventions of theatrical realism diluted its impact as a cautionary statement to a social order beginning to awake to the pleasures of flirting with full-blown consumer capitalism. My own production (Granary Theatre, Cork, 1997) of *Asylum! Asylum!* read the play as the story of the Dublin family into which Joseph Omara is inserted after arriving in Ireland. It also attempted to draw on Patrick Murray's in-the-round design in order to open up the theatrical playfulness of the script's African/Irish encounters, and to enable the magic realist ending to emerge more fully. This second production played directly into the kind of society it had anticipated only four years earlier. If the typical comment which greeted the premiere of *Asylum! Asylum!* was 'Interesting play ... couldn't happen here', the later version evoked similar objections from bourgeois audiences as did *The Business of Blood*: 'I don't like being told what to think.'

Following that production, the playwright felt that the content, having become more urgently visible in Irish experience needed not so much to be rewritten as rewrought. In what is probably a unique artistic revisitation in a culture dedicated to the idea of the play as completed literary text, he committed himself to a new engagement with theme, space, actors, exiles, musicians and dancers. Reflecting on the need to interrogate received forms when faced with the task of representing unprecedented realities, he wrote:

> *Farawayan* is about the feeling of being far-away and unwelcome. In it, I want to use a non-Irish form of theatre. Or be part by proxy of generating a new Irish form of theatre. We want to celebrate our barely-happening-but-there-nevertheless multi-cultural diversity. So I want to use Farawayan theatre techniques. And even if I didn't have that excuse, I just find naturalistic theatre ... well, boring a lot of the time ... the form is a bit musty at this stage. It's had its century. Now is the time to shake it off. Maybe. Leave it to the close-up focus-pullers.[5]

It is not the purpose of this essay to speak a final word on the extent to which Donal O'Kelly's *Farawayan* succeeds in 'generating a new form of Irish theatre'. What is of interest here is the commitment of the artist to an ethical vision, and his identification of theatre as a site of public conversation on the type of social order emerging in contemporary Ireland. Such a stance toward theatre-making is avowedly utopian. It is also critical, and practical. In marked contrast to contemporary productions emanating from Galway or Dublin, but with both eyes set on commercial success on Broadway or in London's West End, it embraces Irish drama's historical responsibility to critique who we are, how we are in the world, and how we would like to be. Donal O'Kelly's work reminds us that, notwithstanding the tone of the times, choices remain to be made in these areas. It is equally clear that ethical considerations around justice and equality will either inform the choices made, or will return to judge them. This is a significant public intervention, and provokes interrogation of the ways we have come to understand drama in Ireland since a group of artists, in an utopian act, critical and practical, first announced a high ambition to a national theatre.

ANNA MCMULLAN

Unhomely Stages: Women Taking (a) Place in Irish Theatre

'Home' in Irish theatre never seems to be a place, but a past memory or a future possibility. In Yeats and Lady Gregory's *Cathleen Ni Houlihan*, Tom Murphy's *Bailegangaire* or Marina Carr's *On Raftery's Hill* the traumas of personal and national history have ruptured any secure sense of home as a place of stability, refuge or restoration. Women, in their traditional roles as mothers and home-makers, are central to the concept of home. In Irish iconography, women have been associated both with the homeland, as Mother Ireland, and with the domestic space, particularly the kitchen. In the Irish theatrical canon women often figure a lost, damaged or barren home/land/womb — the Mother in Murphy's *Famine* or Sarah in Friel's *Translations*. The male literary artist has frequently spoken through female voices or created female bodies in order to explore alternative languages, desires or corporealities. However, if women have represented home, the loss of home or the space of the 'other' within the cultural imaginary, how do we define for ourselves our own place? What place is allotted to women's cultural production in the public spaces of print, media and the stage? The exclusion of most female writers from any place within the Irish theatre canon motivates this emphasis on a selection of female authored plays that have received relatively little critical attention.

These questions are complicated by the extraordinary rate of cultural and economic change in Ireland over the last decade. Since the election of two female Presidents, Mary Robinson and

Mary McAleese, more women are visible in public positions of authority. Irish theatre is going through a vibrant and expansive period; more women are now writing for the stage, and some are gaining an international profile (Marina Carr, Marie Jones). Yet growing economic and technological opportunities and increased cultural confidence for some does not mean that gender constraints and anxieties for both men and women have disappeared. Theatre remains a forum where social codes and roles can be scrutinised. Murphy, Friel and many playwrights of the Irish theatre tradition have linked their critique of familial, social or political *mores* to inadequate or oppressive models of masculine authority and identity. There is an increasing awareness of a history of women's theatre in Ireland which, until recently, existed mainly as footnotes and fragments, and which both complements and challenges the gender and dramatic conventions of the Irish literary theatre tradition.

Any history may be questioned from the perspective of those it has failed to accommodate. Popular theatre and performance, politically aligned theatre, directors, companies, performers, new and rediscovered playwrights, policy makers, regional and community based theatre, these and others are queuing up for their place in the reconstruction of Irish theatre histories. These histories are likely to restore to visibility women's creative contribution to Irish theatre. Yet because of the perception that 'There Are No Irish Women Playwrights', a perception which Glasshouse Productions challenged in 1992/3 with their two seasons of extracts from women's plays, *There Are No Irish Women Playwrights* I and II, a number of female authored texts are in danger of remaining outside history. The selected texts I will be considering range from 1964 to 2000, and I have focused on the ways in which these plays use and adapt available dramatic conventions in order to explore the complexities and contradictions of home, identity and location from a variety of female perspectives.

In *Staging Place: The Geography of Modern Drama,* Una Chaudhuri sees the tension between the individual and their place (meaning both location and position) as the central feature of dramatic realism since Ibsen. The definition of realist theatre, its mutations and boundaries are a matter of debate[6], and there are other dramatic genealogies to be traced in Irish theatre, but realism's recurrent concern with the pressures of place and home, as well as the familiarity of audiences with the conventions of realism may account for its adaptation within the Irish context. Chaudhuri argues that in realism home is both 'the condition for and the obstacle to psychological coherence'.[7] Realism stages the conflict between the possibilities imagined by an individual, and the limitations on the possible imposed by the individual's environment and actual location. In its focus on the domestic interior, realism can investigate the impact of larger public events or policies on individual everyday lives. Esther Beth Sullivan argues that 'Realism … is the strategy par excellence for making the 'quotidian' significant enough to garner focus and to underscore its "historical" dimensions'.[8] While many Irish playwrights as diverse as Yeats, Beckett, later O'Casey, Tom MacIntyre or Margaretta D'Arcy (collaborating with John Arden) radically rejected traditional realism[9], it has often been used by playwrights, including women playwrights, in post-independence Ireland, as a means of voicing frustration and anger with the unhomely conditions produced by the new State.

In order to present the space-time experience of the individual, realism has often been combined with more self-consciously theatrical conventions, as in Friel's *Philadelphia Here I Come!* (1964), which presents a double protagonist in Private and Public Gar, yet still maintains the realist frame of location. While some of the following plays adapt elements of theatrical realism in order to critique the constraints of the society they represent, the traditional forms of realism are often at odds with the perspectives, identities and relationships they offer. Many go beyond realism in their staging of female dis-location.

Displaced Lives and Unhomely Homes

Friel, Murphy and the generation of the Sixties launched a critique of the conservative, hierarchical, atrophied society and culture which the New State had produced. Máiréad Ní Ghráda's *An Triail* (1964) /*On Trial* (1965) and Edna O'Brien's *A Pagan Place* (1972) focus on exposing the Ireland of the time as a particularly unhomely place for young women. Born in 1896, Máiréad Ní Ghráda was a prominent figure in Irish theatrical, cultural and political life. A member of Cumann na mBan, she was imprisoned for collecting money for the Gaelic League in Dublin in 1920. She was a broadcaster with Radio Éireann, and wrote short stories, children's books and edited books in Irish as well as producing a body of plays in Irish. Her plays were produced at both the Gate and the Abbey Theatres, though her later work, particularly *An Trial* and *Breithiuntas* (1968)[10], was produced at the independent Damer Theatre, Dublin, under the auspices of Gael-Linn. Innovative in subject matter and form, *An Triail* / *On Trial* provoked both praise and controversy[11].

On Trial uses the framework of a trial to raise questions about who was responsible for the double deaths of Maire Cassidy and her illegitimate baby daughter. *On Trial* rejects the traditional realist focus on coherence of setting. The setting as indicated in the script shows a stark multi-levelled arrangement of stage rostra, with little evidence of realist scenery, enabling a rapid succession of scenes. The structure of the play juxtaposes trial sequences where members of Maire's family and community are questioned about their failure to help and support her, with episodic flashback scenes. These show Maire's increasingly desperate journey, as she is constantly displaced from one location to another, after she becomes pregnant by a local schoolteacher with an invalid wife. With very limited options, Maire nevertheless fights for survival for herself and her daughter. Banished from her home, she briefly enters into domestic service before being persuaded by Social Services to take refuge in a Home for Unmarried Mothers. On realising they will take her baby away from her, she leaves, against all advice, and finds a job in a factory where she cleans the toilets until the tenement lodging where she lives and leaves her baby in care, literally falls down. She is given shelter in a brothel, where she does some cleaning work, and where the prostitutes show her more compassion than her own family. Finally, she encounters the schoolteacher again there, who has come to the brothel, not, as she initially thinks, to see her. He has now married again, and has no interest in Maire or his daughter. At this point, Maire gives up, and death appears to her to be the only place of freedom for both of them:

> MAIRE: I killed my child because she was a girl. Every girl grows up to be a woman ... But my child is free.[12]

On Trial gives little space to the exploration of the inner psyche of the main character, Maire. While her plight elicits sympathy, the focus is mainly on the trial of a community which failed to accommodate Maire and her child. Maire's constant displacement turns her struggle to find any kind of socially or communally acceptable place into a fight for survival which in the end she loses. The identities of many of the female protagonists in the plays discussed below are bound up with other identities, either loved ones or other female characters, mothers, sisters, or, in Maire's case, her daughter. We will see the turning to suicide when no other habitable place can be found in the later theatre of Marina Carr.

Fiction and poetry have proved to be more accommodating media for women's writing than the Irish theatre, but several women, including Jennifer Johnston, Anne Hartigan and Edna O'Brien have also written for the stage. O'Brien's *A Pagan Place* premiered at the Royal Court Theatre, London, and not in Ireland. The play was adapted from her novel of the same title, and features a young girl, Creena, who escapes from her rural home and from Ireland through joining a missionary order. Male figures dominate the space and the bodies of the women. The scenery for each scene is rearranged by the male actors who are constantly on stage. In the first scene a local vagabond attempts to molest Creena. She is seduced by the young priest and beaten by her father, Con. When Josie, Creena's mother, resists Con's demands for sex, he remonstrates:

> CON: What are you talking about, not now! When
> the urge takes one, fire away, the gun is your own.[13]

Like Maura, Creena is not seen in any single location, but is
constantly out of place, even in her own home. The other female
characters fare little better — Creena's teacher drowns herself in
the lake, her friend dies, her sister leaves for the city but returns
when she becomes pregnant. The authority figures in the play,
including the sleazy doctor, are abusive and predatory. The more
sympathetic men in the play are those who are also marginalised,
like Creena's friend, Ambie, who is referred to by Josie as a
'yahoo'.

A Pagan Place disrupts realism quite radically in its refusal of
spatial, narrative or psychological coherence. The dominant
impression the play gives is one of splintered fragments: it exposes
the incoherence of the adult world around Creena, and her efforts
to piece together an identity and a refuge for herself that will not
be constantly threatened. The figure of the mad schoolteacher
whose narrative of Irish history disintegrates into a surreal
explosion of dates, facts, and fantasy embodies this fragmentation:

> MISS DAVITT: That's where Bally James Duff was
> before it went bust. (*She is laughing now.*) Forgive
> me if I seem bonkers. Ah bold Robert Emmet, till
> my country takes her place among the nations of
> the earth, till then and not till then shall my epitaph
> be written. Fight the foe, Hail light, sweetness and
> hope to thee do we pray poor banished children of
> Lir, Heaven, hell and shingles, Ulster Munster
> Leinster and Connaught, asses and gennets, when
> the cat is out the mouse can play and the Red
> Branch Knights doffing their pants in a quiet
> watered land.
>
> *Turning her back to the classroom, Miss DAVITT
> proceeds to undress herself. First of all she unties her*

suspenders. Then she takes off one stocking, holds it by
the thigh so that it has the shape of her leg, and laughs
at it derisively.[14]

A Pagan Place deploys derisive laughter as a response to the
rural world which is a brutal parody of De Valera's dreamed-of
Ireland with its 'cosy homesteads' and the 'laughter of comely
maidens, whose firesides would be the forums of the wisdom of
serene old age'.[15]

We are given no one dominant view of events, but different
and competing versions. Creena's letter to her friend after a
disastrous seaside picnic transforms the experience into a 'spiffing
day'.[16] Her departure at the end is an attempt to find some
alternative home, as many have done, in exile, though she does so
in the context of a religious order. Nevertheless, Creena's
departure emphasises her break from a family/community/island
which has allowed her no place. Josie has the last words of the
play: 'We're not her people any more.'[17]

Rather than constant displacement, Patricia Burke Brogan's
Eclipsed (1992) is set in a Magdalen Laundry, an institution
attached to a convent, where unmarried mothers and other
women who deviated from the mould of virtuous maidens or
pious mothers were incarcerated. The main scenes of the play take
place in the 1960s, framed by the present time story of Rosa, who
is searching for Brigit, the mother she has never known. All of the
scenes take place in the interior of the Laundry, defined through
'purple muslin drapes/cobwebs/washing' which dominate the space,
hanging from the top of the set, suggesting a forgotten, shrouded
suffocating space. As Rosa searches through the meagre
belongings left by the inmates after the institution was closed, the
claustrophobic world of the Laundry comes to life. The women's
lack of freedom is constantly emphasised. When Cathy, one of the
inmates, escapes, she is brought back the first time, but dies
through suffocation on her second attempt. The surveillance of
the women is contrasted with the freedom and travel of the priests
whose laundry the women take care of. The Bishop is off to

Rome, and some of the priests go to 'the Far East. Others to the States. Some to Africa.'[18] Burke Brogan refers to the laundry as an island, a microcosm of the lack of place in Ireland for women who do not conform to the national ideal of virtue and propriety. The title refers to the expectations of 'blind obedience' on the part of women in the holy orders, and the ways in which this renders impossible any critique of the status quo:

> MOTHER VICTORIA: Try to remember that We Are Eclipsed! But that deep inside there is a Shining that is Immortal — a part of us, which is outside Time. Hold on to that thought! Do not question the system![19]

It is also of course the women of the laundry who are eclipsed, hidden away from a society that tries to deny their existence:

> BRIGIT: Saint Paul's Home for Penitent Women! Home for the unwanted. The outcasts! Saint Paul's Home for the women nobody wants![20]

The young sympathetic novice, Sister Virginia, does question the system. Eventually, after Cathy's death has been discovered, she hands Brigit the keys and her freedom so that she can go and look for her daughter — the same Rosa who has come to the Laundry several decades later looking for her. In one of the monologues, which chart her journey towards individual resistance, Sister Virginia also draws attention to the erasure of female presence and authority not only in pre-Vatican II Ireland, but in biblical history:

> SISTER VIRGINIA: [...] Why are there changes in Our Holy Father's Book? Was early Christian History rewritten too? Women's witness sub-merged?[21]

Even for the not-so-penitent women, there are spaces of escape or rebellion. Performance and mimicry introduce possibilities of play, irreverence and comic deflation. Brigit dresses up as the bishop:

> BRIGIT: So, Brigit here will be Prince of the Church too! Get me my crozier.

> MANDY: The mop! Quick!

> *(Brigit puts on surplice. Mandy doesn't move.)*

> NELLIE-NORA: Ah, Brigit! Be careful!

> BRIGIT: I'll get it myself!

> *(Nellie-Nora and Mandy watch Brigit. Brigit uses an upside down mop as crozier.)*

> BRIGIT: Gawd bless you, my scrubbers! Don't squint at me, Nellie Nora! Stand up straight all of you! Knees together! Say 'Good awfternoon, my Lord'.

> [...]

> *(Mandy finds an underpants. Nellie-Nora lights a cigarette butt.)*

> MANDY: My lord! Your underpants! Freshly starched and trimmed with Carrickmacross lace!

> *(Brigit takes underpants and pulls it over Mandy's head.)*

> BRIGIT: I told you, Mandy, that the handling of my underpants is a Mortal Sin!

> *(Enter Sister Virginia. Her white veil is pinned back.)*

SISTER VIRGINIA: Brigit! Stop! Stop immediately![22]

Brigit does escape, and the laundry is closed down after the
events of the play, so resistance is shown finally to have some
impact on the system. However, institutionalisation takes its toll,
and Nellie Nora, who has shown Rosa into the disused laundry,
nervously tells her: 'I-I-I don't go out much.'[23] Theatre, however,
renders these hidden lives corporeally and publicly visible, and
provides a provisional cultural home for the accommodation of
their stories.

In all of these plays, the lack of a homely place to nurture self-
formation for women is compounded by the constant corporeal
threats of abuse, seduction, physical violence, or incarceration.
These plays also question the ideal of the autonomous individual.
Many of the women suffer not only through lack of freedom, but
through separation from their child, parents, friends, lovers. The
quest for home is for a space that will both nurture the individual
and support her connections with her loved ones, yet the borders
between self and other can also be a source of anxiety, even
dislocation.

Escape v Survival

Marina Carr's latest plays have created some controversy: three of
them, *The Mai* (1994), *Portia Coughlan* (1996), and *By the Bog of
Cats* (1998), depict the suicide of the central female character. In
On Raftery's Hill (2000), Raftery's two daughters are sexually
abused by their father. This presents an extremely pessimistic view
of Irish womanhood. Alternative futures are stifled, at a time
when Ireland seems never to have had it so good. Carr focuses on
those who are marginalised from the success obsessed climate of
the Celtic tiger, and confronts us with female difference and
deviance. Portia tells the story of the naming of Belmont river in
Portia Coughlan, which involved the outcasting of a woman from
the local community who branded her as a witch:

> PORTIA: She wasn't a mad hoor of a witch! And
> she wasn't evil! Just different is all, and the people
> round here impaled her on a stake and left her to
> die. And Bel heard her cries and came down the
> Belmont valley and taken her away from here and
> the river was born.[24]

Carr's women are out of place in the traditional domestic positions of wife and mother, and in the interior spaces of the kitchen or living room. Even the Mai, who has built her own house in the hope that her husband will return, is drawn to Owl Lake, which seems increasingly to invade the interior space, until we see her drowned body framed in the doorway at the end of Act One. Portia Coughlan moves between the spaces of her living room, the bar and the Belmont river, and Hester is seen almost always outside any interior, in the yard of her house, outside her Mother's caravan, and briefly in Xavier Cassidy's house, which Patrick Mason's premiere production, on the main stage of the Abbey, set on the bog. Carr's female characters are linked to rivers, lakes or bogs, which figure a more fluid, untamed space.[25]

In *On Raftery's Hill*, however, the confines of the house reassert themselves with a vengeance. All resistance is crushed, all escape blocked. While the mother is long dead, the father, Raftery, maintains the internal hegemony of the family by abusing both his daughters. All difference and heterogeneity are excluded: the raving grandmother is confined to the house, while constantly trying to escape to Kinneygar and her own daddy. The son is confined to the cowshed, and the neighbouring young man who courts the youngest daughter, Sorrel, is rejected by her, as she resigns herself to the tightening incestuous pattern of the Raftery family. However, many of these characters, particularly Portia, Hester and the unruly grandmothers, Blaize Scully and Grandma Fraochlán, make a provisional home for themselves in language which they fling against their world in defiance:

> HESTER: And as for me tinker blood, I'm proud of

it. It gives me an edge over all of yees around here, allows me see yees for the inbred, underbred, bog-brained shower yees are.[26]

The incorporation of myth and such uncanny characters as the Catwoman in *By the Bog of Cats*, who, like Hester, converses with ghosts, juxtaposes the regulated space-time-location of realism with other ways of imagining the boundaries of self and world. However, when their world fails to accommodate them, the Mai, Portia and Hester turn to the otherworld of death.

Paula Meehan's play, *Mrs Sweeney* focuses on those who survive. Set in Dublin corporation flats based on the Fatima Mansions where Paula Meehan lived in the 1980's, it draws on the Sweeney myth of the pagan king who was exiled after a clash with a powerful Christian abbot, who condemned him to madness and flight. Mad Sweeney has often been used as an image of poetic exile and creative inspiration. Meehan wrote a poem inspired by the figure of Sweeney and what it might be like to 'be his woman'. In an Author's Note following the published text of the play, she continues: 'Immediately after I'd finished the poem the thought flashed — *get a grip woman, it wouldn't be songs cast on water at all, at all. Scraping the shite off the mantelpiece you'd be.* The whole shape and smell of the play came immediately to mind.' [27] The frame of the play is realist, with the sense of the flat as both refuge and prison. Throughout the play, images of flight, sky and birds are contrasted with the limits and lack of space of the flat. Myth is placed in this everyday context to emphasise the narrow confines of the world of the play and to give significance to the quotidian struggle for survival. The Sweeneys' flat is a fragile refuge, whose borders are constantly invaded. The flat is ransacked and the window broken at the start of the play by young local lads — another in a long pattern of burglaries. Lil, the eponymous Mrs Sweeney, boards up the window and there is an increasing '*sense of entombment*' in Act II.

Sweeney cannot deal with the realities of his world, neither the death of his daughter, Chrissie, from AIDS, nor the slaughter of his beloved pigeons. His wits go astray and he adopts bird-like behaviour, but instead of flight, he retreats spatially further and further, nesting under the table. Lil briefly finds moments of respite under his 'wings'. However, it is up to Mrs Sweeney to 'put Humpty Dumpy together again'[28] and it is her voice and memory which are the focus of the play. The spaces she conjures beyond the walls of the flats include her memory of growing up in a ballroom where the entire family lived:

> LIL: I was born in a ballroom. The whole eight of us were born there. Would you credit that? One room. My Ma was delighted to move here. See, these flats really were mansions then. Long before your time. The ceiling in that ballroom. Dripping with fruit and angels and these long trumpets and scrolls of paper with musical notes writ on them. One of the angels fell down into the baby's pram once in the middle of the night. Me Ma thought it was a sign Git was going to be a bishop at least. The pram was one of those big black ones — like a shaggin tank it was. Me Ma used be wrecked from lugging it up and down the stairs. Funny I remember that ceiling as clear as day. I used dress up in me Ma's old dance dress and spin round and round. Then I'd stop and the ceiling would go on spinning. It was a blue yoke with sequins. She'd turn in her grave if she could see us now.[29]

Meehan focuses on the struggle for survival of a community as well as the individuals within it. References to Beckett's pub and to Doctor Joyce are to individual artists who left to follow their own creative quest in exile, like the mythical Sweeney. The pub and the doctor are no use to Lil — she must stitch together her own survival strategies, as materialised in the banners that the women make for the Halloween carnival at the end of the play:

> *Then from the largest, sturdiest black plastic bag she*
> *produces the decorations for the washing lines. These*
> *are an extraordinary assortment of colourful buntings*
> *recalling juggernaut adornments, ships pennants, flags*
> *of undreamt republics, textless banners for libertar-*
> *ians.*[30]

Lil's banner, the most magnificent one, is made from
fragments of her daughter Chrissie's clothes, creating an image of
gathering and integrating the fragments of a lost life as a survival
mechanism in the present. For the Halloween carnival, the
women transform themselves into exotic birds, and the banners
seem almost to peel back the boundaries of the flats:

> *Where possible a pulley system [should be used] so that*
> *when all is arranged a rope can be pulled and the*
> *whole thing can be hoisted like a ship getting ready to*
> *sail. It should be like the ceiling of the flat opens up to*
> *the sky.*[31]

In spite of the lack of prospects — Lil can see into the past but
not into her own future — the inhabitants of the flats survive as
best they can and establish support networks and spaces of
celebration and escape. The community do attempt to change
using available structures — Mariah applies for the job of Leader
of the women's project, but it is given to someone outside the
flats. Meehan uses the spatial confines of realism to highlight
social and economic injustice, which is creating hardship for those
who don't have the means to escape, and her focus on survival
suggests that individual self-formation and upward mobility are
the preserve of the privileged, within the existing order. If realism
reveals the confines of place and indeed the crisis at the heart of
our concept of home, the contemporary experience of dislocation
through emigration and immigration calls for different
representational strategies.

Migratory Homes

Anne Devlin's *After Easter* focuses on the tension between the allotted spaces of the 'literal' world, and the times and spaces of the imagination and story. The first scene of *After Easter* emphasises the fluidity of its spatial boundaries. Greta is seen initially only in spotlight, sharing her inner thoughts through monologue, after which the lights brighten and the outer location is clarified: a mental institution in England. We learn that Greta has been committed by her English husband who deems her unfit to look after their eleven-year-old twins and their newborn baby. *After Easter* is an attempt to piece together the fragments of a personal and cultural past, as Greta undertakes not only the literal journey charted by the play, from England to Belfast and back to London, but a quest to reclaim her own voice. While employing aspects of realism such as character or place, *After Easter* questions their status as the only way of representing reality, and explores alternative visions, perceptions and stories. Towards the end of the play, Greta's sister Helen speaks of 'grasping the possibilities before the walls and the rooms I'm supposed to see assert themselves'.[32] Through her refusal of the dominant narratives of place and identity and through several symbolic births, deaths and rebirths, Greta finds her home not in walls and a room, but in her own story.

On leaving Ireland to go to England, Greta lost her sense of her own voice, her place and her identity. She is haunted by visions, which are identified variously as a banshee, the Virgin Mary or Mary Magdalen. Alternative worlds inhabit the realistic world through visions, hauntings, stories and myths. Pentecostal images of tongues of fire are threaded through the play, as Greta confronts her familial, religious and cultural past. The Easter of the title is both the Christian festival of the death and resurrection of Christ, and the nationalist uprising of Easter 1916. The play insists on different perspectives and interpretations of events or signs. As Greta points out to the psychiatrist in Scene 1: 'Look, if I sat down on the road with twenty people I'd have been arrested.

Because I sat down on the road on my own it was a suicide attempt. Confirms what I've always suspected — the difference between insanity and politics is only a matter of numbers!'[33] When Greta has a vision of seven stars, Helen interprets these as 'the Pleiades. The seven sisters' while Greta's other sister, Aoife insists that they are 'The Plough! You saw the symbol of the Irish Citizen Army!'[34]

Coherence of place or character are abandoned, as marginal characters move in and out of focus, and supposedly secure spaces, like the hospital or the family home become scenes of violence and invasion. British soldiers force entry into the back yard of Greta's home mistaking her brother Manus, carrying a box of Communion veils back to his mother's drapery shop, for a terrorist. After her father's death, Greta and Helen return to London to scatter the remains of their father's ashes into the Thames. Tempted to throw herself off Westminster Bridge, Greta is persuaded to step down by Helen, who has undertaken her own journey away from a lucrative and capitalist career as a commercial artist, which was a rejection of her father's socialism. Identity is not self-begotten, but is negotiated with and against others. Helen suggests that 'very sensitive people are composed by the people around them'.[35] Both Greta and Helen have protean identities, and at the end of the play they both make new starts. Helen decides to sell her London flat, and Greta returns to her child. The last scene of the play tells us that '*Greta is at home, rocking a baby, telling it a story. The traditional empty chair is placed near the storyteller*'.[36] The scope of spatial and temporal planes of Greta's story go far beyond the literal walls and rooms of realism:

> GRETA: After Easter we came to the place. It was snowing in the forest and very cold into the fifth month. My mother and I were hunting. But because of the cold we couldn't feel anything or find anything to eat. So we sat down by the stream. I looked up and saw it suddenly, a stag, antlered and black, profiled against the sky. It stood on a ridge.

This stag was from the cold north. It leapt off the
ridge and down into the stream. It leapt through
hundreds of years to reach us. [...] So I got on the
stag's back and flew with it to the top of the world.
And he took me to the place where the rivers come
from, where you come from … and he took me to
the place where the rivers come from, where you
come from … and this is my own story.'[37]

The story is told to the child, and of course, to the audience.
As Benson states: 'the stories we construct about ourselves are also
of fundamental importance for locating ourselves across
representations of time and in relation to other self-worlds.'[38] *After
Easter* also suggests that however individual each quest may be,
reality and identity are shared, negotiated spaces. Home is not a
stable container, but a place which is subject to a continual
process of dislocation and relocation.[39]

Una Chaudhuri refers to theatre which 'posits a new kind of
placement, not in any one circumscribed and clearly defined place
but in the crossroads, pathways and junctions between places. At
the same time it advocates a new kind of placelessness not as the
absence or erasure of place but as the combination and layering
one on top of the other of many different places, many distinct
orders of spatiality'.[40]

Treehouses by Liz Kuti, an English born playwright of English
Hungarian background, now based in Ireland, explores the
dilemma of those whose identity is formed between places.
Treehouses interweaves three stories, which unfold simultaneously
in three space-time planes. The story of Old Magda is set in the
present time, in a nursing home and the language rhythms of her
care assistant who says she has rarely travelled from her home
would suggest Ireland. Secondly, the story of Eva, also set in the
present, in a garden on the day of her father's funeral. Thirdly,
there is the story of young Magda, as filtered through Old
Magda's memory, set in the past, on Magda's father's farm in a
remote rural area of middle Europe during World War Two. The

reality of what is happening to the Jews in the concentration camps gradually impinges on the self-contained routine of the community, with the arrival of a young Jewish boy.

Several distinct places and times are juxtaposed, and the apparently distinct stories of Eva and Magda connect and contrast with each other. The issue of boundaries and borders are foregrounded. In each story, a close relationship, whether between lovers, or between father and daughter (since Eva's mother has left the home), is disturbed by the arrival of another, a stranger, who disturbs the comfortable boundaries of the world into which he or she enters. Eva retreats into the treehouse constructed for her by her father in protest at his falling in love with their neighbour whom he marries:

> I was twelve that summer when everything I saw
> from my nest in the tree belonged to us, to me and
> to him, before it all ended, before I had to share it,
> before I stopped being the one and only, and
> became one of three and everything stopped being
> mine and his, and became something he shared with
> someone else and I was no longer queen but minion
> in some occupied territory.[41]

Magda is faced with the choice of accompanying the boy on his flight across Europe, or staying at home and marrying her local boyfriend. In the end she chooses to stay, but ends up leaving with her husband anyway, and remains tormented by her failure to 'save' the boy, although she gave him refuge and tended him at her father's farm. At the very close of the play, we recognise that he has remade his life as Eva's father, and again, with his second wife.

The interconnected symbols of the ark and the treehouse point to the ambiguity of borders and refuges. A recurring refrain in Magda's reflections is a passage from the Bible from Exodus about the Hebrew child, Moses, hidden by his mother for three months from persecution by the Egyptians. 'And when she could no longer hide him, she took for him an ark of bulrushes, and daubed it with slime and with pitch, and put the child therein; and she laid it in the flags by the river's brink', for some Pharoah's daughter to find. The ark here is a temporary shelter, provided by others and trusted to fate. The treehouse is a refuge too — Eva refers to it as 'this ark, this nest, this safe place' — but she seeks to keep the stranger out, and her poetic monologues focus on the boundaries of her own childhood world.

The stage world of the play in the premiere production at the Peacock Theatre, was bounded by the skeleton of a house, perhaps a treehouse, marking the limits of the playing area which was split into three zones, the treehouse, the barn and the nursing home. But when does the safety zone shelter and protect, and when does it exclude? The juxtaposition of these zones and images confronts us with the borders around our own worlds and discursive practices — the kind of language we use, the stories we tell and listen to, our construction of boundaries and of the stranger, not only on the big stages of history, but in our everyday lives. As Irish society becomes more diverse and new stories, traditions and histories are introduced into the fabric of our culture, the traditional boundaries of the realist room can no longer accommodate the layered and complex experiences of home and identity that inhabit contemporary Ireland.

The playwrights whose work has been discussed above have articulated fragmented, splintered identities, which must be patched together if agency is to be recovered, but whose visions and voices offer alternative perspectives and identities questioning the concept of a homogenous, shared world or audience which traditional realism assumes. Increasingly, women are occupying the stage in order to make, unmake and remake identities and invent their own stories and places.

JOHNNY HANRAHAN

Theatre in Cork/Cork in Theatre
An Exercise in Perspective

I attended a conference last year on 'The City and the Sublime' during which a very young and rather courageous American student presented a paper to a roomful of academic predators on the grid system of New York. At the heart of his paper were a few facts and ideas that were complete news to me. I had always assumed that New York was the product of a utilitarian mindset. The shortest distance between two points is a street. The shortest distance between two other points at right angles is an avenue. Clear, functional, easily understood. A system that worked for those more numerate than literate. A four-square universe where logic banished doubt. And to a certain extent my pre-conception was correct. The planners had indeed been driven by triumphalist rationalism. Hills, woods, ponds, marshes were subjugated by geometry. No natural feature was allowed to stand in the way of the grand design. With the interesting exception of Greenwich Village where curves survived, the world's most famous cityscape was forged according to a plan, which ignored the difference between earth and graph paper. Ever since the vertical indices of the buildings were added to the plan and the concrete canyons went up the physical experience of millions of New Yorkers has been defined by this fundamental commitment to straight lines. So far, so obvious. What was new to me in the paper, though, was the fact that this plan had not been drawn up as a response to massive immigration. Contrary to what I had thought, there had been no practical imperative to straighten the kinks in the place to facilitate the movement of teeming millions. When the plan was made there were no teeming millions; they hadn't been born and their ancestors lived elsewhere. The grid system of New York was the product of a visionary imagination that projected a metropolis onto wood and farmland. The city was willed into being as an embodiment of a particular world view.

Underpinning the epic building project was the ancient belief in the power of geometry to promote concord, to stabilise social relations by reference to a legible architecture. The supreme virtue of the grid system of New York as intended by its makers is that you always know where you are. Whether this literal fact can be given a metaphorical load to carry is a matter of debate. What is certain though is that the architecture of New York bodies forth a particular set of human aspirations, a specific vision of human relations as surely as it fulfils its obvious utilitarian functions. The very fabric of the city is a system of symbols, which exerts enormous power over all those who encounter it and creates an archetypal context for interpersonal events.

Many other towns and cities are planners' fantasies; the heartless geometry of Brazilia, the surreal green tunnels and endless roundabouts of Milton Keynes; the modern era is littered with formalist wet dreams masquerading as buildings and streets for real people to live in. Whether because of its sheer scale and political significance or because it's been around long enough or, as I suspect, because there is in New York a natural confluence between the visionary and the pragmatic, it seems to me to be infinitely more real and fit for human habitation than most of these more recent civic dreams of ideal proportion.

Most cities (thank God) were not conceived according to a grand plan. Some, like Naples or Cork look like nobody bothered to plan the growth of what is clearly an organism, sprouting naturally, putting out new growth, shedding and renovating its fabric over centuries till it has taken on its convoluted, corrugated, idiosyncratic mature form. Others have been semi-planned; the centre of Paris was destroyed and re-created in the service of the regal fantasy that gave us the Champs Elysee, the Place de

L'Etoile, the Place de Concorde and a great deal more of what we consider the essential Paris. However, the fact that large, more architecturally chaotic areas surround this formal centre is arguably of equal significance in determining the real character of that city.

The examples and variations are endless, the pattern clear; cities emerge either organically or according to a presiding vision or usually on the basis of some changing relation between these two primary engines of growth. The key point, though, is that cities only come to symbolic life if at some point in their history they are regarded and transformed by a visionary imagination.

> And now he approached the great city, which lay outstretched before him like a dark shadow on the ground, reddening the sluggish air with a deep, dull light, that told of labyrinths of public ways and shops, and swarms of busy people ... long lines of poorly lighted streets might be faintly traced, with here or there, a lighter spot ... then sounds arose — the striking of church clocks, the distant bark of dogs, the hum of traffic in the streets; then outlines might be traced. Tall steeples looming in the air, and piles of unequal roofs oppressed by chimneys.

This is a passage from *Our Mutual Friend* in which Dickens re-creates the London where he grew up. It's no casual chronicle. In his hands the city is invested with dark power. With 'sluggish', 'labyrinths', 'looming', 'unequal roofs', 'oppressed'; he is creating an ominous music that helps to charge the cityscape with an archetype of the underworld. This, as his biographer, Peter Ackroyd, says, 'is the London he saw as a child ... the London of 1775 in which his imagination continued to live. And with it, too, we can put the other constituents of his vision. Uncertainty. Poverty. Dirt. Squalor. Interconnectedness, the rich living beside the poor. Fog. Mist. Fever. Madness. A place of crime and of punishment. Prisons. Executions. Monsters created out of the mud, and crawling out of the mud.' Underlying Dickens' work, in all its comedy, charm, sentimentality and moral vigour is a sense of the city as a locale where violence and death preside. He has created London just as surely as London has created him. For all the jolly carriages rushing through gleaming snow or ruddy-faced beef eaters dismounting at cosy inns, which he has bequeathed to the greeting card industry and to symbolically bankrupt generations of Christmas revellers, his real legacy is a sense of London and, by extension, of the city per se, as a malign, monstrous growth sucking the suffering individual into its all-devouring maw.

London has had many other laureates of whom Ackroyd is probably the most exciting contemporary example. Think of any city and a writer will probably come to mind. But it's only when the writer is of sufficient brilliance and works in sufficiently dynamic relation to the place that the city is 'changed, changed utterly' and a new kind of common consciousness is forged.

Bloomsday is a bit of a farce in my book. All that dressing up and wearying bonhomie, all those kidneys and ostentatious competitiveness are a monumental pain in the ass. The whole thing is only redeemed by the fact that the day provides the best excuse for an epic piss-up ever devised. And who am I to be sneering at the legions of garrulous drunks world-wide who achieve heights of inebriation by the time the Angelus rings that ordinary men can only dream of matching at four o'clock in the morning?

It's a triumph for drink and talk and as such must be hailed as an important agent of civilisation. But at a more important level it's the bible as panto. Every day is Bloomsday in Dublin. Through the greatest imagination of the century the place, in all its vulgarity and grey beauty is elevated from the realms of the miscellaneous to a level of being where it becomes a holy city bathed in the light of forgiveness. Joyce's immensely humane treatment of human frailty has given Dublin a worldwide symbolic significance in this time. While brute fact may contradict this vision constantly, it is there as an embodiment of the finest common values, as a beacon of moral honesty, as a possible city in which the brutality of everyday experience can be transformed imaginatively.

The greatest of greats, primus inter pares, Joyce led his contemporaries in creating a symbolic Dublin, which has provided the foundation for all contemporary imaginings wedded to this place. They have created an imaginative vocabulary, a way of thinking and feeling; a mental landscape in which it's possible to be at home or at least to identify landmarks. That is equally true of Synge and the great M.J. Molloy who at different times and in different ways have converted the West of Ireland and Galway in particular into a totally compelling symbolic locale. Billy Roche has done the same for Wexford. Nobody who has ever lived imaginatively inside the cobblers shop of *The Cavalcaders* where the trivia of townie existence is treated with such loving reverence that it becomes a thing of aching beauty can deny that Billy Roche hasn't shown another Wexford, a mythic negative of the grimy, everyday place they might otherwise take for granted. Sebastian Barry in his tales of exile from Sligo, *White Woman Street* and *The Adventures of Aeneas McNulty* has similarly re-created that town, bathing it in a kind of paradisical lyricism.

The central fact of theatre in Cork is that no one at any time has succeeded in working this magic on the 'beautiful city'. The most interesting aspect of its current development is the struggle undertaken in different ways by two different experimental companies to create a symbolic vision of Cork adequate to its everyday complexity. I refer to Corcadorca and my own company Meridian who are both, for better or for worse, consciously engaged in a tortuous, long-term dialogue with our native place. This generation has no symbolic map of Cork to look at. The well-known Cork novelists of the past are minor figures compared to the Titans of the capital and the West and their dated work is interesting rather than inspiring. Notwithstanding the fact that Cork has excellent venues, a normal quota of talent, a strong amateur and pro-am tradition, professional companies since the courageous establishment of CTC in the early Eighties and arguably the leading TIE company in the country in Graffiti, there is still in my view a felt deficit in the level of theatrical achievement here. This sense of underachievement is usually expressed as a frustration with poor audience numbers (a complete myth as thousands go nightly to the numerous Cork venues) or as weary mystification with the city's failure to produce a 'Druid' or a 'Red Kettle'. In my view the problem is alive at a deeper level. Shaw, in one of his virtuoso introductions, talks about the fact that nobody thinks about their bones until they're sore. They just take them for granted. The fact that two adventurous companies, with different aesthetics and distinct declared aims circle constantly (obsessively?) around themes and images of our home by the Lee suggest that there is a commonly felt need to make the place live symbolically. Until that is achieved any structural developments such as the growth of a Kettle-style rep company are of secondary importance.

Enda Walsh has come closest to the necessary alchemy. In fact with *Disco Pigs* he represented Cork in a way that brings it more fully alive than anything else ever written about it. Everybody who saw it felt the power of Walsh's scalding poetry, the harsh beauty of his autistic characters' rage. In their furious rejection of the available life, in their gleeful contempt for the nonsense of normality they carry the anguish of a whole generation not just here but internationally viz the incessant productions of this piece in Germany and the success of look-alikes such as Fireface. But I actually think that much of the power of *Disco Pigs* derives from its bodying forth of the full complexities of life and language in Pork Sity.

> PIG: Jesus Runt! Dat be impossivle! A half hour, fuck! (Pause.) I wanna a huge space ship rocket la, take it up to da cosmos shiny stars all twinkle twinkle an I shit in my saucer an have a good look down on da big big blue. Derd be a button named Lazer dat blast all da shitty bits dat ya'd see, yeah. I press dat button an Lazer would fireball all below an

den back down I fly to Crossheaven happy dat all
das left a Pork Sity is my roam your roam an da
Palace Disco cause das all dat matters, Runt ... ress
is jus weekday stuff.

I always blank out a bit when people mention Foucault or
Lacan because basically life is too short to be trying to pick up the
lingo. But I've always been fascinated by their notions about the
way reality is constructed through language. In this rough poetry
it seems to me that Walsh has embodied a Cork, physically,
politically, romantically and in so doing has created an electric
city, which releases the pent-up energies of the place in his
characters and in his Cork audiences. I saw the piece on its
opening night in Triskel and everyone instantly knew that
something remarkable had happened.

PIG: Not big no but manky. Not big Runt bud a
big black barrel a black dat only do pause purr da
pissy grey rain. Bud ya know, ol girl, even a great
big poo poo has its diamonds an dis great big great
marbly monstrosity which you did righly call da size
of da Pork ferry, dis is Pork's own liddle gem!

Disco Pigs is the outstanding experiment in the long-term
adventure whereby Cork is symbolised.

Corcadorca was dominated for several years by Enda's
partnership with Pat Kiernan. During that phase Enda's writing
combined with Pat's direction to embody Corcadorca's stated
artistic policy — to electrify audiences and to represent the city
authentically. Not every production was equally successful but
through the mid and late Nineties a succession of productions —
The Ginger Ale Boy, A Christmas Carol, Disco Pigs and *Misterman*
all by Enda forged a distinctive Corcadorca style which continues
to flourish. Most interestingly for this discussion are *A Christmas
Carol*, performed at Cork Gaol and Burgess' *A Clockwork Orange*
— their first major success with site-specific work. Sir Henry's,

Cork's palace of grunge, was transformed for a week into a promenade performance space. Kiernan gave us a determinedly rough, raucous treatment of the classic of juvenile rebellion. Young audiences thronged to see their regular site of debauch charged with different violence and savage poetry. A perfect congruence of content and setting was the principal achievement of this production. With it, the company began a process that is now central to their aesthetic, whereby the very fabric of the city has become a key performer in the pieces they create.

Anyone who has had to climb Patrick's Hill on a hot day might indeed regard it as a Via Dolorosa but it took a major leap of imagination on Pat Kiernan's part to transform it into the site of a passion play. Cork chauvinism knows no bounds and there are many here who regard Patrick Street as the main street of heaven. Pat decided to turn the hill, which sweeps so majestically upwards from the bridge at its northern tip, into the road to Golgotha. Thus, on Good Friday night 2000, hundreds of us stood listening to the Trial of Jesus, as scripted by Conal Creedon at the base of the hill and then in ragged order we climbed slowly behind the labouring, burdened actor who carried the cross on our behalf. There were inevitable absurdities, friends greeting, touches of heritage centre performance here and there from some of the volunteer prostitutes and legionaries. People were hanging out windows, making phone calls, having a bit of a laugh as the Messiah was condemned to Death. But as the multitude moved onwards and upwards towards the site of crucifixion the miscellaneous amusements fell away and a sense of awe and reverence passed through the crowd in the same way as the arrival of the Eucharist used to move the Corpus Christi crowds of my childhood. We were, for a few moments, true participants in the symbolic mystery being re-enacted. Bell's Field was Golgotha, Braziers blazed beside the three crosses and laid out before us was the most beautiful urban panorama in Ireland. The whole city was visible from there and the whole vista became a major part of the experience of community which we all shared. Pat had planned that the steeples of churches in the city would light up at an appropriate moment. This didn't work out but I don't think that it mattered. The city was embraced and shown to its citizens in a wholly new way and as such given new symbolic life.

The company has just had another success with *A Midsummer Night's Dream* in Fitzgerald's Park and Fota Island and here again carefully chosen and highly significant parts of the city were transformed. In this highly inventive and paradoxically literal way Corcadorca forge onward in their unwavering desire to reveal the symbolic city.

The significance of their project is pointed up by the success of various productions but most tellingly by the critical response to their production of Ger Burke's *Banshee Makers* last year. *Banshee Makers* won their playwright competition in 1999. Set in a Carrick–on-Suir coalyard, it tells a Billy Roche-like story of titanic passions in small-town lives. It was a first play with obvious flaws but contained some truly beautiful writing by a playwright of such sensitivity and poetic grace that I'm certain a far greater play will come from him in years to come. The critics savaged it. Tina Neylon and the normally benign Gerry McCarthy tore it to pieces in an astonishing display of intolerance for new work. Their various criticisms can be accepted or dismissed but at the heart of both attacks was a sense of betrayal. Corcadorca have defined their ground so clearly that a perfectly acceptable new play was rubbished as a trivial diversion from the important business of the company's other work. The critics' vehemence was actually a perverse compliment to a company which continues to create a theatre in Cork as dynamic as any in the country.

In the case of Meridian the engagement with home-place is less overt but equally crucial. A whole succession of productions has grappled with the Cork experience in a variety of direct and indirect ways. From *Headroom* in 1987, to *Lear* and *The Overcoat* in 1989, to *Adios Amigos* in 1991 through a range of our more recent productions including *Craving** and *The River**, the city of Cork has loomed large in much of the work. Cork has been represented as a post-imperial dream space, as a futuristic war zone, as the inevitable place for those who flee it, as an Andean mountain village, as an organism, as St Petersburg of the West. Primarily through the content of the work the range of symbolic meanings the place affords have been mercilessly interrogated for over a decade.

A strange irony of this exploration is that the two productions which most consciously attempted to bring the city into the foreground of the imagery were easily the least successful. *Adios Amigos* turned Cork into an Andean village where Gogol's Government Inspector became a bizarre hybrid of samba music and intense local satire. The somnambulant bourgeoisie were berated, the ghettoes of Knocknaheeny and Gurranabraher represented as Indian reservations, the extraordinary musical qualities of our accent combined with a form of mock Portuguese. The whole was driven by Samba music written and played by John Browne and The Royal Cork Latin Band. The aim was exuberant satire both attacking and celebrating the complexities of the place. The sweep of the piece, its comic energy, its delightful music seemed to us ingredients for a funny and meaningful comment on our home. The result was a dispiriting shadow of what we had set out to make. Uncertain of its real nature, constructed rather than imagined, the whole ended up far less than the sum of its potentially excellent parts.

Last year we mounted a dark piece called *The River** in which again we sought to make the city a main player in our drama. Centring on a conceptual artist and a couple of his young acolytes, the play grappled with the complete alienation felt by people of a certain age and disposition in the face of the vulgar affluence surrounding them. The play included a film of the city and from the first imagery of a drowned wino floating in the Lee to the final shot of his illegal burial in the harbour, the river and the city at large played a dynamic and vital element in the story. The world outside the wall of the theatre was visible, the tension between the real and the fictional palpable. The young lovers walk through a magic city at one point and gaze down at their grubby home-place.

TOM: You see. You see. What did I tell you?

ROSE: It's beautiful.

TOM: A birds-eye view. This must be what the carrier pigeons see when they're flying home to Blackpool.

ROSE: It's like Toytown. A model of itself.

TOM: Yea. Isn't it like you could just reach out your hand and pick up the cathedral? Plonk it down on Blackrock?

ROSE: Or fall on the city like an avenging angel. Tear Pana to pieces. Flatten the County Hall.

Throughout the piece there is a consistent correlation between the atmospheres and symbolic locales afforded by the city and the experiences of the protagonists. Tearing Pana (Cork's main street) to pieces or flattening the County Hall is in this case an image of the suicide, which haunts the play. For the city is represented as a kind of second skin, an essential part of their being. Fine in theory but actually it didn't work as a play because the symbolic design was too clear and too constricting of the natural life of the characters. The result was a painful creative process and a show that left audiences unmoved.

The difficulties experienced with these shows are in marked contrast to the joys of shows where we have forged an appropriate role for the city in the fabric of the play. In *Lear* the contrast between the everyday somnolence of the place and the frenzied conflict of an imaginary war created massive energy in a piece that provoked everything from adulation to outright contempt. More recently with *Craving** the city was again filmed and integrated seamlessly by Alan Gilsenan into a story that U2 might call All You Can't Leave Behind. In this show our pre-occupation was not with the city itself but with the politics of advertising and with no effort at all the city's symbolic power was released and provided an epic charge to the narrative.

This is one of the central lessons we've learnt on the long march of the company's development. In relating to our home it seems to be imperative to forget about it in order to release its subtle energies. The need to create a symbolic city can only be met by making no conscious effort to construct it.

Robert Bly in *The Sibling Society* points out that the word symbol comes from the Greek word *symbolon*, which means one half of an object deliberately broken in two. A messenger from one merchant to his faraway colleague was trusted if the piece of pottery or shard of bone he carried fitted the symbolon in the possession of the man he sought out. While the city surrounding you may suggest an appropriate shape for the city of your imagination, only true messengers (i.e. genuine imaginative impulses) will fit the actual and the mythic cities together in genuine relationship.

In this regard I will finish by quoting from our current production; a new work combining one of our first adaptations — Gogol's *The Overcoat* with Dostoyevsky's *The Double*. The latter is a mirror of the first story, a cracked and shifting image of the original; one play haunts the other. The setting is St Petersburg, the language florid pastiche Victorian, the era vanished.

FRED: And what a skyline!

OTHERS: That's right.

FRED: Domes of burnished gold ablaze in brightness.

OTHERS: Those domes!

FYODOR: A garden of gourds I've heard them called.

OTHERS: And the cupola of St Isaac's.

FRED: Mere house-tops are compared to gigantic turbaned Turks.

OTHERS: They say it burns in bright noon like the sun burning on a mountain-top.

FYODOR: It's a whole city floating fire-balloons or bright coloured lanterns.

ALL: Petersburg! City of Dreams. Petersburg! In this place a man can truly live. Certainly!

When the *Irish Examiner's* ever-perceptive Declan Hassett saw this first performed, his only comment was that it could have been Pana. And that's right. By indirections we will perhaps continue to find directions out.

Note: Unless otherwise attributed all Meridian productions mentioned are original plays or adaptations by Johnny Hanrahan. Those marked with an asterisk were written with John Browne.

KAREN FRICKER

Travelling Without Moving:
True Lines and Contemporary Irish Theatre
Practice

The Irish are justly proud of their theatre. Because theatre and theatre artists were closely tied to the articulation of the Irish nation in the early part of the last century, the presence of a vibrant, distinctively Irish theatrical life is seen to reflect the nation's own viability, its own vibrancy. But this close association between theatre and national identity has also served to restrict the genre, to make it slow to accommodate change. To challenge the 'givens' of Irish theatre can be seen as challenging the larger systems in which it functions. Because of its difficult history of colonial intrusion, and because the country has been occupied with the processes of nation-building throughout the last century, Ireland has been, until relatively recently, an isolated and inward-looking country, and this too has kept Irish theatre relatively insular.

This insularity manifests itself both in content and in form; or rather, because Irish plays so often concern national issues — 'where we come from, where we are now, and where we are headed,'[42] in Christopher Murray's words — content remains the central focus, and potential innovations in the relationship between content and form have remained relatively unexamined. Single-authored, plot-and-character-driven plays in which the unities of time, space, and action are observed remain the norm. Language is foregrounded; text remains the central way of communicating to audiences.

But formal innovation and new ideas are necessary to keep expression alive and growing; without new ideas and new energy, art forms stagnate and lose their currency. One of the primary challenges facing Irish theatre is its need to find a way to foster and accommodate change, to expand its expressive forms, while not devaluing the existing canon. In a rapidly modernising, diversifying, and internationalising Ireland, there is a need for a multiplicity of modes through which Irish theatre can communicate.

In this essay I will discuss a theatre piece which successfully challenged the boundaries of theatrical communication in the Irish context. *True Lines* was created by director John Crowley and a company of four actors, Cathy Belton, Gwynne McElveen, Tom Murphy, and Stuart Townsend, for Kilkenny-based Bickerstaffe Theatre Company in 1994. The production told the parallel stories of four young people living and working in different parts of the world in the present day; when it played at London's Bush Theatre in 1995 it was hailed by Carol Woddis in *The Guardian* as 'the sound of a new generation of Irish drama'.[43]

Crowley says that the piece was created out of a frustration with the 'status quo':

> The piece was a reaction against my mythic notion of an Irish theatre tradition, which was of a bearded playwright somewhere writing things I couldn't understand … I wanted to put something on stage that I wanted to see. I didn't have a man-the-barricades attitude, but I did want to gently turn stuff on its head and do something which was unique, which did not have a precedent in Irish theatre.[44]

In many ways, *True Lines* bore little resemblance to anything traditionally identified as Irish drama. Its very reticence to identify its content as Irish is striking; other than one brief mention of Ireland in the show itself, the only thing that obviously marked it out as Irish was the fact that the actors spoke in Irish accents and that it was created by an Irish company. The usual anchors of Irish society — land, family, Catholicism, the national question — are mentioned nowhere.

Formally, as well, *True Lines* challenged convention in many significant ways, starting with the very notion of theatrical writing. This production had no one author, but rather was created through a process of collaborative devising by its director and cast. The text did not precede the staging; both were developed together, and stagecraft, scenography, and performance functioned alongside language in the way the production conveyed meaning. The piece contested traditional ways of configuring theatrical space and time; the play 'took place' simultaneously at the four corners of the globe over an indeterminate span of weeks, while continually drawing attention to its own theatricality — to the fact that it, of course, was actually taking place in a theatre over the course of less than two hours.

For all its inventiveness, however, *True Lines* did not break free from the traditional boundaries of theatrical representation completely. Its ultimate refusal to challenge the notion of unified character is striking, and marks a specific place in the articulation of a post-colonial Irish identity on stage. Its preoccupation with the notion of self-realisation — its foregrounding of its characters' search for a unified self — both placed it in a continuum of Irish theatrical writing, and pushed that continuum forward.

Or did it? *True Lines* threw down a gauntlet of innovation that has not been picked up in any consistent way since. It was created at a time of considerable excitement and productivity in Irish theatre, which now only six years later seems to have dissipated considerably. To investigate in depth the reasons for this loss of energy is the project of a different (but necessary) study; but I will suggest some hypotheses at the end of this essay, after having argued in full for the special place I feel *True Lines* holds in the recent history of Irish theatre.

*After I graduated from university, my whole gang
scattered. People went to Australia, France, Germany;
I went to Chicago for the summer. Being in touch with
people in different time zones, getting letters on
different kinds of paper — the whole experience, the
whole paraphernalia of keeping in contact was so
different, so new … it was the experience of doing that
bit of travelling that made me want to make a show
about it. — John Crowley*

True Lines was the first full-length theatre piece that John
Crowley directed after he graduated from University College Cork
in 1993. He had distinguished himself as 'one to watch' at UCC
with a devised play called *Alice or Walking and Falling*, which won
an Irish Student Drama Festival Award as the best production of
the year in 1991.[45] *Alice* caught the eye of Richard Cook, who was
in the process of setting up a new theatre company called
Bickerstaffe in Kilkenny. Cook offered Crowley the opportunity
to direct a production for the company. 'He said do anything,'
reports Crowley, 'just as long as it wasn't boring.'

Crowley assembled his cast not through traditional auditions
but through informal chats. 'I wanted to know where they were at
culturally, what books they read and what their record collection
was like. I needed to know what they were bringing to the table
and what references we shared,' says Crowley. The only 'givens'
when the company started their creative process were the way the
production was going to be created — through devising — and
the idea that it was going to investigate the experience of
characters who were living far away from home.

Through research, brainstorming, improvisation, and
structuring the company developed four interweaving stories,
which never intersected on a plot level, but were linked through
theme and image; each of the characters was engaged in a similar
search for answers to existential questions or for solace from past

pain. Each character was associated with a different part of the body — brain, lungs, heart, eye — and each had his or her own musical 'theme'; images of different kinds of lines ran through the production.

After a five and a half week rehearsal process, *True Lines* premiered at Cleere's Theatre (the converted back room of a pub) in Kilkenny in March of that year. The show had only really come together in the final days before it opened, and was still at a rough state when it first faced an audience: 'It was a mess,' says Crowley, 'but not an inept mess.' The company continued to work on the production throughout the run. Even the earliest reviews, however, were receptive and positive; on the back of strong critical and audience response, the company reassembled to work again on the production later that year, and embarked on an Irish tour which ended with a week-long run at the City Arts Centre, Dublin, as part of the Dublin Theatre Festival in October. The following May, it also played at the Bush in London.

True Lines was awarded the 1994 Stewart Parker Award for the best piece of new Irish playwriting by a first-time writer/s, a remarkable honour given its unconventional form and authorship. Writing credit for the show was shared between Crowley and his cast, and because the content often changed from performance to performance, each of the actors was responsible for remembering his or her own lines or cues as they changed. A script was finally assembled after the production closed, for the Stewart Parker judges, but it was never published.

Because there is no published record of *True Lines*, it's necessary to describe the production here in some detail. I saw the production live at City Arts Centre as part of the Dublin Theatre Festival, and have subsequently viewed a videotape of a July 1994 performance of the show. It is to the detail of that videotaped version that I refer here.

The set of *True Lines* was a simple square of dark blue side walls and a partial inset wall (part of which served as a screen for projections and silhouette effects) in front of the actual back wall. The floor was painted a striking burnt umber colour; the only furniture pieces were several bent-wood chairs, and there were a few simple props — a suitcase, a telephone.

The show was constructed in a series of vignettes, which progressed each character's story in turn, with the characters almost always appearing in the same order. The actors most often addressed the audience directly, as if speaking a monologue; occasionally, the action would shift to enacted scenes, with the other actors stepping in to take on different characters in each others' stories.

The first character to appear is Emmet (Murphy), who's working for a mining company in Australia — his musical accompaniment is the digiridoo. He's prone to blackouts: 'I cease to exist for a few minutes,' he explains, 'it's as if God decides to unplug me.' Emmet becomes increasingly preoccupied with the songlines — the invisible lines that the Aboriginal people in Australia believe connect everyone in the world and everyone who's ever lived: 'Perhaps the most perfect mental creation I've ever heard of. One big natural database.' The songlines for him become an image of completeness: '60,000 years of memory, one continuous song. Like consciousness.' Emmet is something of a social outcast; on a work trip to Alice Springs, his colleagues ditch him and he is left carrying a suitcase around a deserted part of Australia, totally on his own.

Aisling (Belton) is hitchhiking in the American West along near-deserted highways; we slowly deduce (though it's never stated outright) that she has had an abortion and is preoccupied by thoughts of her dead baby. Her story is accompanied by Joni Mitchell songs and shot through with allusions to *The Wizard of Oz*: 'The sound of cars going over the cat's eyes in the road is like a heartbeat,' she says, 'one big massive artery going all the way to San Francisco … back to New York … under the Atlantic Ocean … Dublin … London … and all the way to Oz!' She is given a lift by a hilariously laconic truck driver called Jim (Murphy), who asks her uncannily prescient questions about her boyfriend and her child. She waitresses for a while to earn money to continue on her journey. At one stage a phone box along the deserted highway rings, and when Aisling answers it, the caller asks for Dorothy.

McElveen plays Síobhra, an archeologist who, when we meet her, is sitting on a plane about to take off for Africa, where she's going to work on a dig. 'At least I'll be able to breathe away from my parents,' she says. 'And they're not even my real parents. I only ever talked to my birth mother through six feet of soil.' When it's time for take-off, Townsend comes on stage and leans over, and McElveen climbs on his back and stretches out her arms and legs: she becomes the plane itself, taking off to a soundtrack of Peter Gabriel. After a sweet, casual romantic encounter with an American she meets on a train (Townsend again), who seduces her by reading the lines on her palm, she gets down to the business of the dig. She dusts down a body (Belton) and begins to speak to it as if it's her mother, and the body responds: 'Who was my father?' 'Just a man.' 'Why did you give me away?' 'Because. Just because.' The sound of Síobhra's loud, anxious breathing lasts into the next blackout.

Townsend is Bill, who has just finished his architecture finals and is spending time in Berlin. Unlike the other three, who search for answers in the land, Bill is preoccupied with buildings — or with bodies that always seem to be falling from them. Bill's first three appearances on stage are preceded by the action of Murphy standing in the middle of the stage, then running backwards into the back wall, cueing a blast of David Bowie's 'Sound and Vision'; Bill then draws a line around Murphy's still form, and it 'becomes' a body splayed on the pavement. Bill's suffering from anxiety and insomnia, but is lying to his friends back home that he's having a great time. He illustrates his ideas by doodling them on the back wall; at one point when he draws straight lines down the back wall he talks about lines in the Peruvian desert: 'Maybe aliens used them for runways and landing pads? Yeah, right. Something was being said about being somewhere between the earth and the sky and I'm fucked if I know what it is.'

While *True Lines* was a show ostensibly about travelling, the main movement in the play is internal, within each of the characters. All are struggling to understand themselves and their lives, and by the end each reaches some kind of resolution, a new kind of peace with the world. 'The ancestors put a foot forward and said I am and began to sing the world alive. The only thing I know is that I am,' says Emmet. Síobhra says she's 'going to stop digging for answers. My mother is just a pile of bones. But I'm a pile of bones that can breathe. So I guess I'll just breathe.' 'I'm not going on to San Francisco,' declares Aisling, 'I'm going back the road I travelled. My little girl, she's sound asleep in her grave, but me, I'm wide awake.'

In the videotaped version, Bill appears on stage with a bucket and sponge and washes the chalk outline of the body off the back wall: 'The one thing I know,' he says, 'is that you've got to jump daily and not be afraid of hitting the ground … and while you're on the way down, enjoy the view.' Bill's story changed in the show's final version; unable to find peace, he jumps off a building and kills himself.[46]

*

True Lines functioned through an aesthetic of association and shorthand; what information was communicated to the audience came primarily through implication rather than direct statement. We were never told directly why these four young people were living away from home — in fact only in one instance were we told where home was. 'So you're from Ireland, huh?' Jim asks Aisling, 'I suppose your name is Theresa? Or is it Maureen, Maureen O'Hara? Deirdre … of the Sorrows?'

The truck driver's playful attempt to 'name' Aisling through obvious Irish clichés reflected the interest of the show's creators in working with, rather than shying away from, the notion of experiencing other cultures from the outside in. One of the basic tenets of the creation of the show, according to Crowley, was that the actors set their stories in places they had never been: 'I wanted what they were talking about to be purely from cultural impressions — not a travelogue. It was influenced by Baudrillard's notion of America as a virtual place, a state of mind. I liked that idea, being a tourist in your armchair.'

Travelogue or not, there was something striking about the

piece's complete ease with its characters' mobility. How many other Irish plays can you think of that never set foot on Irish soil? Nothing special was made of the fact that these four young Irish people (for we must assume their Irishness, even if just from the sound of their voices and the origin of the production) were living and working at every edge of the globe. Irish drama had come a long way since the prospect of leaving Ireland caused Brian Friel's *Gar* to literally split in two in *Philadelphia Here I Come!* exactly thirty years before.

The play marked a significant move forward in the way that the Irish represent themselves on stage. Displacement and outsiderism are recurrent themes in the Irish dramatic canon, as they are in all post-colonial literatures, but the central place that travelling held in *True Lines* is something quite new. It was one of the first and only theatre pieces that depicted the Irish outside of Ireland coping with life without referring to, relying on, or being helped or hindered by the usual defining aspects of Irish life.

In *Inventing Ireland* Declan Kiberd explores the symbolic power of the migrant or traveller figure in the writings of, among others, Yeats and Salman Rushdie: '[such a figure] is adaptive, one who moulds the new places that serve to mould him … the search is for a mode of expression, a fuller articulation, and this quest becomes its own point for the writer.'[47] Kiberd goes on to quote Rushdie about the sense that the writer of such works '[feels] obliged to bring his [sic] world into being by an act of pure will, the sense that if the world is not described into existence … then it won't be there'.[48]

The excitement of discovery, of 'describing a new world into existence' practically emanated from *True Lines*. And the freshness of the production came through not just in the kind of people and experience it represented, but through the formal means by which it expressed itself.

Where, to begin with, did it take place? We've ruled out Ireland. We could answer 'Berlin, Ethiopia, Kansas, and Alice Springs' but the best response is one borrowed from Conor McPherson's stage direction for his recent play *Port Authority*:

'This play takes place in a theatre.' *True Lines* revelled in its own theatricality; it made no attempt to hide the mechanics of how it worked as a piece of stagecraft from its audience. Scenography and staging, in fact, were a significant part of how the production created meaning; the constant transformation — of objects into other objects, people into other people, people into objects — added to the show's overall exploration of the things and ideas, seen and hidden, that connect experience and individuals.

Shifts between scenes were most often played in dim light so that the audience could see the actors moving props and switching from one character to another. The show had great fun playing with changes of perspective, as with the shifting use of the back wall in Bill's scenes; at one moment the audience is looking at a wall, and the next, once Murphy has 'fallen' into it, they realise they're looking at the ground. Then, as Bill draws stars and lines on the wall with chalk, it shifts again, and becomes the blackboard on which Bill is illustrating his discussion about what's going on in his life.

Things in Emmet's world, as well, are continually changing; at one stage he lies a chair down on the floor and 'sits' on it, with the top of his head facing the audience, and makes a phone call, literalising the fact that he is 'on the other side of the world' from the audience. As Emmet increasingly loses his grasp on everyday reality, that lack of equilibrium is indicated by him appearing 'standing' on the side wall and then spiralling around in mid-air until he lands on the other wall — all accomplished by having Townsend hold Murphy's stiff body by the legs and waist and spin him around.

The production's complex treatment of time fed into its playful use of theatrical space — and into its overall foregrounding of its own theatricality. The production primarily happened in that vague, difficult-to-nail-down time zone that Irish theatre increasingly seems to inhabit: Monologue Time. Though there were some scenes between characters, the actors primarily spoke as their characters directly to the audience, in the present tense, as if the things they were describing were actually happening to them at the time (Crowley even instructed the actors to meet the audience's eyes whenever possible).[49] Here was another theatrical element that reminded the audience that what was happening wasn't really 'real', or that rather invited the audience into the experience by asking it to buy into the artifice.

Place and time in *True Lines*, then, were fluid and pliable, which leaves us with, as we canvass the play for its treatment of the traditional 'anchors' of theatre, plot and character. Here the former was completely in service of the latter; the plot of the production, as much as it existed, was the characters' parallel searches for a unified sense of self. Character was the play's central organising principle, and about the only element of dramatic representation that the creators of the production seemed to take as an unquestioned 'given'. It was never challenged that the people appearing on stage were plausible, real-life human beings; even when, as described above, the characters talked directly to the audience, they did so 'in character'.

*

This curious conservatism in the way the production depicted character is significant, for it says a great deal about the larger cultural context in which the production was created and in turn reflected. In her brilliant study of contemporary theatre, *The Death of Character,* Elinor Fuchs argues that the place of character in theatre is representative of the way in which a particular society views the relationship between humankind and the world: '"Character" is a word that stands in for the entire human chain of representation and reception that theatre links together.'[50] Part of Fuchs' project is to analyse the 'particular problem [of] the human figure' in contemporary avant-garde theatre practice.[51]

According to Fuchs, the shattering of ontological certainty that characterised the twentieth century, particularly the second half of that century — the absolute destruction made possible by the advent of nuclear energy; the rise of deconstructivist theory with its challenge to the notion of the point of origin of any idea or text; the 'swoon' and 'free play' of a post-modernism, with its aesthetic of pastiche and its valorisation of emptiness — caused many theatre artists to challenge the notion that it's appropriate, or even possible, to represent a unified human presence on stage. Fuchs traces the origins of her 'death of character' theory back from Ibsen through Stein, Brecht, and Beckett, and focuses on the 'aversion ... to the idea of autonomous character' of such contemporary artists as Robert Wilson, Lee Breuer, Meredith Monk, and Elizabeth LeCompte.[52]

But character is far from dead in *True Lines*; on the contrary, seen through Fuchs' lens the piece seems an attempt to keep character alive and unified in a world that seems determined to shatter it. As Fintan O'Toole has suggested, if *True Lines* had a thesis statement, it would be Emmet's plea: 'I just want to be continuous.'[53] What *True Lines* communicates is the exhilaration, but also the anxiety and confusion, of people experiencing a certain kind of freedom for the first time. As O'Toole put it, 'it is the best expression yet in our culture of the world of the new generation of Irish emigrants of the 1980s, a world without a centre, a world in which cultures and people are like colliding atoms continually crashing into and bouncing off each other'.[54]

Crowley conceived *True Lines* as an 'homage' to the Quebeçois theatre director Robert Lepage, whose work Crowley says he had 'on a pedestal' at the time he made the show. There is much in *True Lines* that was indeed clearly inspired by Lepage's work: the devising process by which Crowley and the actors made the show emulates the object-based collaborative creation which Lepage practises; and the transformational quality of the staging is similar to the visual storytelling for which Lepage is well known (Crowley acknowledges that the person-as-plane image in *True Lines* was directly lifted from Lepage's opus *The Dragon's Trilogy*).

But more importantly for this argument, a defining element of Lepage's work, which *True Lines* also mirrors, is its prioritising of character as its central organising principle; Lepage's productions, too, refuse to relinquish the notion of unified character, and are often constructed around stories of people on searches — for their families, for artistic inspiration, for their selves.

It is telling that Crowley, who was and is well-informed about international theatre practice, gravitated towards the work of Lepage rather than that of the post-modern avatars Fuchs discusses — Wilson, Breuer, LeCompte. For what Lepage's and Crowley's cultures have in common, of course, is that they are both former colonies (or, in the unique case of Quebec, still partly colonised), and I'd argue that this tendency to hang onto character — even as the international theatrical tide may be turning against it — is a particular characteristic of post-colonial theatre practice. Throwing ontological certainty to the wind is the privilege of cultures where the right to determine one's own identity has not been recently challenged. For cultures still in the process of defining themselves, unified character is clearly much too dear to let go of.

The persistence of character in *True Lines,* then, seems to signpost a certain point on the path of Ireland's cultural decolonisation. The play's perspective and its influences were newly international, but it refused to unmoor itself from representation completely. Another place, then, that we might say that *True Lines* took place is at the crossroads of post-modernism and post-colonialism. By having negotiated that crossroads, or at least found its way to it, *True Lines* seemed to signal a possible way forward for Irish theatre. As Rushdie has argued, 'Description is … a political act … re-describing a world can be the first step towards changing it'.[55] But how much has Irish theatre practice changed since?

*

True Lines was a genuine hit whose initial popularity led to subsequent runs and international bookings. It received excellent reviews both in Ireland and abroad. The number of Irish people I have met who cite the production as a highlight of their theatre-going experiences is remarkable; several young theatre professionals I know say seeing the show is the reason they went into theatre at all.

True Lines itself was a one-off; this group of actors and director did not work together again. Crowley went on to devise another show with different actors, *Double Helix,* which was co-produced by Bickerstaffe and the Abbey and presented in the

Peacock in 1996, but it was not as creatively successful nor as well received.[56] But *True Lines* itself stands as a highlight in what we can see now as an explosion of theatrical activity in Ireland in the early and mid-1990s. Between 1990 and 1995 Bickerstaffe was among some nearly two dozen or more independent theatre companies that were set up throughout Ireland and Northern Ireland, largely by young directors and actors straight out of university or professional theatre training.

These companies joined the 'first wave' of Irish independent theatre organisations — chief among them Druid in Galway, Red Kettle in Waterford, and Rough Magic in Dublin — in producing work of an amount and quality that offered a contrast and challenge to the Abbey and Gate Theatres, which had until that time almost totally dominated the Irish theatre landscape. Several of these companies, including the theatre groups Barabbas, Blue Raincoat, Calypso, Corn Exchange and Pan Pan, and the dance company CoisCéim, were set up to investigate new possibilities in the relationship between text and other forms of theatrical expression. There was a sense in the early nineties of new territory being forged and borders being breached, of a new generation of young theatre professionals re-shaping the theatrical landscape.

Six years later, and the heat has gone off the independent scene considerably. There hasn't been an independent company set up in at least five years that has managed to establish a secure artistic and administrative footing. Many of the 'second wave' companies seem somewhat adrift, producing one or two shows a year but not seeming to forward any specific artistic agenda or message.

There have been isolated instances of genuinely innovative theatre. We've seen several Irish classic texts re-envisioned through a physically and visually-based theatre practice: Conall Morrison's exuberant adaptation of Patrick Kavanagh's *Tarry Flynn* for the Abbey (1997 and 1998), Barabbas' bumptious four-actor version of Lennox Robinson's *The Whiteheaded Boy*, directed by Gerard Stembridge (1997), and Niall Henry's spare, psychologised staging of Synge's *The Playboy of the Western World* in the Peacock (2001). There have been a few excellent pieces of new Irish writing that have been rendered truly remarkable by the uniquely theatrical vision of their original productions, chief among them Donal O'Kelly's captivating performance of his own solo play *Catalpa* as directed by Bairbre Ní Chaoimh (1995) and Pat Kiernan's hyper-kinetic staging of Enda Walsh's *Disco Pigs* (1996).

Some companies have experimented with collaborative creation — Gúna Nua, Quare Hawks, and most promisingly, Calipo, whose works (including *Love is the Drug* (1998) and *Xaviers* (1999)) integrate devised material with sophisticated multi-media technology.

And several of the most memorable theatre experiences in Ireland in recent years were the result not so much of exceptional material as the novel ways in which that material was expressed: John Breen's irrepressibly energetic ensemble rugby play, *Alone It Stands* (1999); Bickerstaffe's hip-hop lambasting of 'Celtic Tiger values', *Rap Éire* (2000); and Tinderbox's hauntingly atmospheric staging of seven short plays about Northern Ireland in a deserted courthouse, *Convictions* (2000).

However exciting, though, these are still the exceptions. A momentum was lost, and a production like *True Lines* stands as one of a few isolated instances of genuinely original theatre rather than part of a continuum of forward-moving theatre practice. The bulk of theatre work being presented in Ireland continues to hew to the traditions of plot-and-character-driven storytelling, and to preoccupy itself with issues of history and national identity.

What happened to the energy and productivity of the early and mid-Nineties? It may be too early to know. But a significant contributing factor is certainly, and ironically, the economic boom which — the powers that be tell us — is the sign of the full-bloom arrival of Ireland on the international scene. Succinctly put, the 'Celtic Tiger' could well be the worst possible thing to have happened to Ireland at this particular point in its artistic life.

The economic upswing of the mid and late-1990s has changed the country immeasurably, doubtless in many positive ways; but one of its less salutary effects has been to price the 'starving artist' lifestyle out of the market. It's no longer possible, as it was for so many Irish artists and arts professionals over the years, to live on the dole and the odd gig and get by very well, thank you, as they pursued the early stages of their careers. Rents have skyrocketed for office and performance spaces as well as accommodation, as have the costs of materials and personnel; putting a show on for a few bob in a room behind a pub (which was, essentially, how *True Lines* came about) is getting harder and harder to do. Even the arts organisations that can pay their artists can't compete with the salaries offered by other industries; many young people who might have considered a career in the arts ten years ago are now entering other sectors simply because the money is so much better.

Doubtless there are new economic and structural challenges facing people who might want to make theatre in Ireland these days, and some might glibly argue that theatre becomes less necessary in boom time — who needs plays when there's so much money to spend? But this very boom, this time of rapid progress, is stirring up societal change; it is offering up contradictions, crises, and challenges that demand the kind of engaged investigation that theatre can provide. The emerging race problem; the ongoing drugs problem; the ever-growing divide between the haves and the have-nots; the equally accelerating urban/rural divide; the wrongs committed by societal leaders, be them religious or governmental, which are being unearthed in the culture of tribunals; the excitement, but also the confusion, of the increasing internationalism of Irish culture: all seem the urgent subject of drama.

What would happen today, say, if you put five Irish twenty-somethings in a room and asked them to make a play about being young and Irish and living abroad? Or, even better, if you put five twenty-something international emigrants to Ireland in a room and had them make a piece about being young and international and living in Ireland?

It would be wonderful to find out.

BEN BARNES

Extracts from Ben Barnes' Abbey Theatre Diary 2000

12th May 2000

Riga visible through the cloudless sky. The aircraft has banked to the left and the blue waters of the Baltic sparkle below. My two-day visit to 'the window on the West' in the Gulf of Finland was full of memorable moments and interesting encounters. St Petersburg is clearly a city in transition. While sturdy German cars flash by from time to time the lasting impression is one of rusted, clapped out Ladas from the Communist era, spewing leaded fumes. The occasional shopping unit at the Gostiny Dvor, grandly described as a department store, carries quality clothing and jewellery with well-known western labels, but by and large the array of goods and window displays is depressingly kitsch and shoddy. The public transport is efficient but the metro vestibules are vast, drab and fetid and every bit as depressing as the Bahnof Friedrichstrasse crossing point into the former East Berlin which was my first encounter, many years ago, with the characterless, utilitarian public architecture of the soviet-styled state. The roads are shocking, the drinks are invariably served tepid, the exploitation of foreigners with enhanced admission charges is shameless, the cyrillic hieroglyphics are impenetrable, the service is slow and the bureaucracy is numbing. My hotel, the Hotel Europa, provides the service, comforts and standards of the cities of the west but this is very much the exception to the rule. And it comes at a steep price. Yet in spite of all this, perhaps even because of it, St Petersburg is memorable to visit. On the evening

I arrived I walked the length of the Nevsky Prospect and
marvelled at the elegant sweep of the buildings along the canals
and avenues and was breathtaken anew by the grandeur of the
Palace Square and the imposing façade of the Winter Palace. It
was floodlit and snow blanketed a decade ago when I walked up
here during the visit of my production of *The Field* to what was
then Leningrad.

On Wednesday I met Brian and Ann Friel (who were over for
the premiere of *Molly Sweeney* at the Maly Theatre) in the lobby
of the hotel and we walked with our interpreter the fifteen
minutes to the theatre. The purpose of my visit was to discuss
production exchange arrangements with the famous Russian
theatre and when I learnt that a production of the Friel play was
imminent I arranged my dates to suit.

We are greeted at the Maly by the Literary Manager, Mikhail
Stronin and subsequently by the Artistic Director, Lev Dodin
who, much to Brian's dismay, ushers us into a room full of
journalists for a half-hour press conference. The irony of Brian,
whose antipathy for journalists is legendary, facing a phalanx of
foreign hacks, was lost on our Russian hosts and with polite
diffidence he managed to sidestep most of what was asked of him.
It was left to me, here on business of my own, to expound on
Brian as the Irish Chekhov and how his own work and his
translations of the Russian masters had opened a window on the
east for us! Afterwards we had lunch at the Dostoyevsky Bar
which Brian insisted on buying as a belated celebratory gesture
towards my recent acquisition of the abbot's cowl. The
conversation was lively and invariably centred around the
personalities and comings and goings in the Irish arts scene: the
cut in Rough Magic funding; the problems at The Gate; the new
chairman of the Arts Council; the debacle of *The Plough and the
Stars* at The Gaiety; the forthcoming Tomas Mac Anna tribute at
the Abbey; the pecking order in the American regional theatre;
the success of Tom Murphy's new play, *The House* ('our O'Neill,'
Tom Kilroy wrote to me, 'only better than O'Neill). I never cease
to be amazed how Brian who, for the most part, lives in the wilds

of Donegal, is so au fait with the cut and thrust of Irish theatre. Inevitably we touched on the breaking Dunlop revelations and Brian echoed my concern that the rampant acquisitiveness everywhere in evidence in Irish society at present and the virtual collapse of organised religion has blunted our sense of civic responsibility and that it is a cause for concern, and indeed alarm, when, in a dangerous vacuum the self-appointed torch-bearers of truth are the journalists of *The Irish Times* and the *Sunday Independent*. As Flann O' Brien might say: what deity must be inserted between us and all harm? God.

After lunch we went to see the last flat of Fyodor Dostoyevsky at Kuznechny Lane. We tried, unsuccessfully, to remember the names of the brothers Karamazov and asked our guide for the proper pronunciation of the anti-hero of *Crime and Punishment*. Brian remarked on seeing the stove in the living room that we always manage to get this detail wrong in productions of Russian work on our stages. It was moving to watch the great Irish writer stroll through the rooms of the Russian master and this interlude in the day's activities was rounded off in the museum shop where he bought babushka dolls for Elishka and Milena ('your wee girls'). In the time between then and the performance I went to a Russian orthodox religious service which seemed to be a form of benediction and I lit candles for my babies as I do in all the churches I have visited since they were born from Notre Dame in Montreal to the little church in the bend of the road between Saltmills and Fethard-on-Sea which I cycled to a few Sundays ago from our house. The performance of *Molly Sweeney* was compelling for the local audience but impenetrable for Brian, Ann and I. Proper names and place names gave us some indication as to where we were in the text but I noted that the aforementioned Fethard-on-Sea, which features twice in the English script of the play, was omitted. It struck me forcibly that if we are to bring a Maly Theatre production to Dublin this would not be it. The Maly is famed for its ensemble, its verve and exuberance and none of these qualities can be released in a play, however good, of successive monologues.

The language barrier, always an obstacle, here seemed insurmountable.

Afterwards the entire acting ensemble of the Maly, numbering sixty or more actors, their families and friends came to a splendid feast in honour of the play and its author. Numerous toasts were given and a sung tribute to the play was made to the air of the Irish rover! This was legendary Russian hospitality and Dodin presided magnificently over the entire affair looking and sounding for all the world like a latter day Suvorin or Stanislavsky. The following day I met him at his palatial offices in the Maly and discussed how we might advance the relationship between our two theatres. I made him a present of a bottle of Irish whiskey but, at eleven in the morning, declined to crack it open with him. Mikhail Stronin interpreted for us as we ranged over the possibilities open to the Maly and the Abbey. It has become clear over the last few days that state support for the theatre in post-Soviet Russia is dwindling and that the Maly survives by virtue of the hard currency fees it can make on foreign tours. In order to keep its head above water it is forced into more foreign visits than it might otherwise do and while the creative exchange we envisage might be in both directions the burden of financing the collaboration will largely fall to us. We did not dwell much on the logistics of any future arrangements as I had aired these matters with Mikhail the day before. We could, therefore, give ourselves over to a discussion of matters artistic. Picking up on my comments from the press conference the day before I explained how much more accessible Irish translations of Russian works are to us and our audiences and how, in recent years, these had taken over from standard and contemporary British versions of the Russian classics. The Irish sensibility is, for instance, attuned to the francophone tendencies in the educated classes in nineteenth-century Russia. It approximates our own historic preoccupation with anglo-saxon culture and fashions and in both cases this proceeds from an essential inferiority complex or lack of self-belief. In Ireland the causes may have been different but the effects were the same. This character abounds in Turgenev and Chekhov and resonates less truly in the British renditions of their plays where the syntax misses the undertow of unease which apprehends at the deepest level that its prosperity is built at the expense of others and the sands of its good fortune are forever shifting.

I took my leave of Lev and Mikhail as blowy snow swept the wide avenues of St Petersburg (the temperature had tipped 75f the day I arrived) and was delivered efficiently by the Maly driver to the airport and hence to the flight which is now about to land in Schipol. I will have time before my connection to get some gifts for my golden girls so I can say without a trace of dissembling, the immortal words: 'from Russia, with love.'

8th August 2000

An intensive few days back in Abbey Street on my return from holidays in the Czech Republic. All of Dublin theatre, it seems, is due to descend on the Abbey this coming Sunday night for a special tribute performance of *A Life* to honour the contribution of Tomas Mac Anna to the Irish theatre in general and the Abbey Theatre in particular. I pop in to the show on Saturday to see if it needs any tweaking. My assistant David Parnell had warned me that Tom (Murphy) and Fiona (Glascott) had gotten very slow in their scenes and although his notes to them while I was away had effected an improvement I still felt that the playing veered occasionally towards the suet pudding of bad O'Neill rather than the soufflé concoction of a Hugh Leonard play. This I call playing outside the genre of the piece and having worked hard to establish a working rhythm between the two period frames of the play I had some re-alignment to do in order to make the time pieces chime in unison again.

The Sunday night was nerve racking. Five former artistic directors, senior actors, producers, writers, directors, journalists, the general public and the friends and family of Tomas flocked to the Abbey. I decided we would bookend the performance with a welcome and short tribute from me, a more substantial tribute from Joe Dowling and the presentation of a bronze sculpture of the Abbey logo designed and executed by John Behan. I was waiting in the wings to come on stage and knew the evening would be a success when I saw on the stage-directors monitor the audience rise to its feet as Tomas entered and watched him give his presidential wave to wild cheers. The night would be buoyed on a tidal wave of goodwill towards this great man of the Irish stage. It was a memorable Abbey night and I was very pleased to have my own mentor, Joe Dowling back on the Abbey stage at the heart of it all. Many, including myself, have been damaged down the years by the political machinations within this theatre and none more so than Joe Dowling who survived to fight another day and has splendidly resurrected his career in the United States. I survived to lead the theatre into the new century and Tomas, well Tomas through his unflappability, his good humour, his larger than life personality and his sheer longevity survived it all and now leans on the lectern before his public and tells them how it was. We have heard it all before but many in the audience have not and anyway it is his night, the man who links us all through from the old Abbey, the Queens and back to Abbey Street and we indulge him, iar stuiritheoir, Amharclann na Mainistreach.

16th August 2000

We were on the high seas again on Wednesday but on a much bigger boat; Stena line to Holyhead and on to Manchester to stay overnight with Julia's parents in Wilmslow before the long drive up to Edinburgh. Julia, Johannka and the children would stay with the Esler's at Kemback and I would commute up and down to Edinburgh as necessary via Leuchars. Johannka is Julia's sixteen-year-old cousin from Prague who is having a summer holiday with us on a break from the conservatoire where she is training to be a violinist. She has already played solo with the Czech Philharmonic so I expect she has a bright future ahead of her. Her visit overlapped with Mimi's (our Czech au pair) sister and friend so that our house at Saltmills was heaving with young Czech women over the August holiday. If you add in my three, who qualify as half-Czechs you would have the best part of a football team.

On Friday I was in Edinburgh for the dress rehearsal of *Barbaric Comedies*. The company are very tired having had a long technical week. You would expect them to be relatively fresh vocally but the opposite is the case as Calixto (Bieito) has insisted on full throttle delivery right through the lighting and flying rehearsals. This sounds like indulgence to me but I keep this to myself for the time being. The production is extraordinary: epic, swashbuckling, satanic, disturbing and beautifully composed in the staging and lighting. Mark Lambert's performance is brave and mesmeric and old stalwarts like Des Cave, Joan O' Hara and Eamon Morrissey are spell bindingly achieving through technique and acting intelligence an intensity of performance which matches the huge energy of their younger colleagues: the six wild sons of Don Juan Manuel de Montenegro and the army of unfortunate young women who are, for the most part, roundly abused physically, and emotionally through four hours of tough drama. My problems with the piece centre around an occasional lack of narrative clarity and the relentless pace and lack of vocal variety and tone throughout. There is, it seems to me, much black humour in the story, particularly between Montenegro and Don Gallant but this is not given time or space to breathe. I suspect Mark and Eamon, who are very seasoned performers, will find this level as the show progresses. The other problem with the production is that it is sectioned between two uneven halves. The first half incorporates 'Silver Face' and 'Blazon Eagle' and lasts two hours and twenty minutes. The second half comprises the third part of the trilogy 'The Wolves Romance' and lasts an hour and twenty minutes. Clearly the play, which comprises three distinct stories, should have two intervals but inexplicably Brian McMaster and James Waters agree with Calixto that the long first half is fine and that one interval will suffice. It is their patch so I defer to them but I file away the resolve to push for a second interval when the production comes home.

Through the previews we have quite a few walk outs but I

ascribe these as much to the endurance test of the two hours twenty minutes without pause as to the scenes of rape, pillage, savagery and masturbation which I expect will be pilloried by those who like their theatre to be affirmative and uplifting and are upset when the darker side of human nature runs amok without the moral corrective that brings sanity and order to the world. Theatre must, however, provoke and shock as well as entertain and palliate if it is to have any meaning in people's lives. When we show the rape of the Sabine women in a room full of civilised people we bring home to them the dark deeds of Srebenica perpetrated in the name of ethnic cleansing in our own time and on our own doorstep. A theatre which cannot have this function quickly becomes a dead theatre. The subscription terrorism of the theatre in America, for instance, has, in my opinion, rendered it, for the most part, moribund.

All that having been said I am unprepared for the storm of protest and criticism that breaks over our production in the days following its opening. I am grateful for the support of the Dublin contingent who came over for the opening: Ali Curran, the Regan sisters, Fergus Linehan from the DTF and Richard Cook who all thrill to the risks been taken by the Abbey with this production and are excited at the prospect of its Dublin unveiling. The British media is fiercely hostile and the story finds its way off the arts pages and into the news columns and the leading articles. Much of the odium is heaped on Brian McMaster and the Edinburgh Festival and while some of this seems heartfelt it is hard not to come to the conclusion that this is payback time as the British media round on Brian McMaster who, it has to be said, has given a hostage to fortune by claiming that the future of the festival may depend on the success of this production. Edinburgh has invested heavily in bringing this Catalan production team and the Abbey together and for artistic and financial reasons need the production to deliver the audiences to the Kings. The payback relates to a perception that Brian has criticised the standards of theatre criticism in the UK, has chosen European over British directors and has generally criticised the

British theatre for a lack of adventure and imagination. If this is allied to the fact that he has favoured Ireland's national theatre as the recipient of this generous co-production arrangement it is not hard to see that the perceived failure of *Barbaric Comedies* would be used as a bata fada mor to beat him with. We get caught in the crossfire. I say 'perceived failure' because the Irish, Spanish and German press are very positive and all the way back to Manchester I try to drive this point home in interview after interview. I had instructed our press office back home that I wanted to respond to all requests for interview and comment about this controversy and not hide behind calming press releases and theatre spokespersons. I believe that if you take the praise you have to be prepared to take the blame. The cell-phone hardly stopped ringing all the way down the M6 between Carlisle and Manchester. I took calls from the *Glasgow Herald*, the *Scotsman*, *The Irish Times*, *The Observer*, the *Irish Independent* and RTÉ Radio News. I tried to get the debate moving beyond the few scenes of sexual violence that had become the focus of the criticism but that was the story and I felt that I was fighting a losing battle. All day I argued with the Irish media not to pre-judge the production on the basis of the British media response. Invariably I had to get out of the car to take these calls because it would have been dangerous to take them while driving and the children, in their exuberance, were giving no quarter to the unfolding drama. Pacing the hard shoulder on the M6 with the rain falling and the traffic roaring by I was about to sign off on my conversation with Victoria White of *The Irish Times* when, out of nowhere, it occurred to me to say, 'you know, in the end of the day the great thing about Irish audiences is that they will make up their own minds'. This made the trailer item on the front page of *The Irish Times* next morning and was subsequently picked up by all the Sunday newspapers. This in turn led to a sense that the Abbey was weathering the storm and that I had played a smart game with the media on this one. Implicit in the statement was an acknowledgement of stormy waters but an appeal to the maturity of Irish audiences and a faith in their discernment. It was the perfect riposte. (I met an ex-PR man, Tom Hardiman, in Galway a few weeks later and he had been at a dinner where *Barbaric Comedies* was being discussed and no less a spin doctor than PJ Mara had remarked on the effectiveness of the sound-bite. One, he said, he would have been proud to have dreamt up!) However, from the daily flood of abusive letters and petitions we are receiving at the Abbey I suspect we are not yet out of the woods with Ramon Maria Valle Inclan. In the meantime, I needed to get back to business as usual.

13th December 2000

On Sunday, I made the one hour flight from Prague, and the funereal malevolence of its architecture, and landed in, what one fancies as, the customary pestilential fog of Budapest. The driver from the Viksinhaz deposited me at the Gellert on the Buda side of the Danube and I had a couple of hours to rest before my meeting with Laszlo Marton. The Gellert is a pre-World War One hotel built around the curative waters which have been bubbling up from a fault line along the Danube since Roman times. The art nouveau baths and pools under the hotel are one of the great glories of Eastern Europe and have played host to the well-heeled of middle Europe in the world *entre deux guerres*. The Gellert must once have been as glamorous as its Mediterranean counterpart, Reid's of Funchal and if its spendour is now dimmed and shabby it still carries the promise of that old world elegance and civility which is everywhere in evidence in the architecture and the citizenry of this magical city on the Danube.

As we drove to the theatre Laszlo told me the story of his production of *Dances in Time*. It is the tale of fifty years of Hungarian history told through the dances of the successive eras and culminating with a return to the right-wing racial tensions and abuses in the post-communist dispensation. Laszlo said that he made the play by telling the cast stories of his own remarkable family life and then asking them to improvise around these stories. In 1956 his mother was offered safe passage out of

Hungary in the time of revolution. The night before they were due to be collected by a lorry that would transport them to the border his mother asked him to choose which of his books he wanted to take with him. The young boy looked along the shelves, hesitated, and finally said he wanted to take them all. When he turned around his mother was in tears and next morning when the lorry pulled up and tooted its horn she leant out the upstairs window to inform the driver that she had changed her mind. 'Why?' a gruff voice asked from down below. 'Because my little son does not want to go.' This scene was dramatised in the production when the small boy loses control of his gas balloon as the crowd jostles towards the departing truck. It floats to the glass ceiling of the lonely hearts salon in which the action takes place and as the lorry revs and the horn is hooted impatiently a human pyramid is formed to retrieve the little boy's balloon. By the time he is in possession of it again, however, his mother has changed her mind. The theatre is packed to capacity for this odyssey through Hungarian history told entirely through the medium of mime and dance and it is very moving to watch an audience so clearly enthralled as the story of their lives unfolds before them.

After the show we had dinner in a nearby restaurant and we spoke at length about Ibsen and Chekhov. It is my hope that Laszlo will direct *The Wild Duck* at the Abbey in 2002 or 2003. He is currently rehearsing *A Doll's House* and we agree that the setting of this play always manages to miss the point. The Helmers are not wealthy people and Torvald only begins his new job in January and his first pay cheque will not be until March. The other salient point about their household is that it has three small children and should therefore be teeming with toys and the bric-a-brac of childhood. These scenographic determinations help to bring these people close to us and makes their dilemma not an academic discussion of feminist politics but a very real personal tragedy from which such abstractions can be extrapolated. Laszlo showed me that he was a director after my own heart when he gleefully told me that he informed his shocked Nora on day one of rehearsals that she lies no fewer than seventy-three times in the course of the play.

At dinner the following evening we discussed the precarious state of Hungarian theatre as the legislators rushed to embrace the glitter of the west and failed to appreciate the gold of their own culture and traditions. I was amazed when Laszlo informed me that he had a meeting with the mayoralty of Budapest at which they said they had an offer from a Hollywood producer to buy the Viksinhaz and augment its staff so that Broadway-style musicals could be staged as part of the repertoire. The officials were nonplussed that Laszlo could not see the advantages to his theatre from such a progressive idea not to mention the substantially enhanced salary that he, as director of the theatre, could command in such an arrangement! I quoted Friel's line from *Translations*: "'Barbarus hic ego sum quia non intelligor ulli" — I am a barbarian in this place because I am not understood by anyone.'

I am on my way home now. Ground speed 416 mph; altitude 39,000f; time to destination 1 hr 23 min; west of Prague; south of Leipzig; north of Bayreuth and on a flight path to London. *Tartuffe* previews this week and Mark Lambert's splendid production of *The Hunt for Red Willie* continues in the Peacock. I expect my new policy positions will be ratified by the board next week and then we move into the implementation phase of Managing Change. The final touches for the programme for 2001 await my attention; we prepare *Medea* for London and I brace myself for the mother of all battles to reform our marketing and PR department. All that lies ahead but all I can think of now is that I will be home tonight. I will creep into bed so as not to wake anyone and in the morning I will see my little girls bearing gifts from the east. My father used to do that at this time every year when he returned from the Smithfield Show in London laden with trinkets and special sweets and the soft brown sugar from England unavailable at that time in our country.

CAROLINE WILLIAMS, KATY HAYES, SIÂN QUILL & CLARE DOWLING

People in Glasshouse: An Anecdotal History of an Independent Theatre Company

Glasshouse Productions was an independent, Dublin-based theatre company, which produced ten shows between 1990 and 1996, including new plays by Clare Dowling, Emma Donoghue and Trudy Hayes, and in addition hosted discussions and debates on the role of women in contemporary Irish theatre. What follows is an anecdotal history of that work from the four company members.

Ostensibly our roles in the company were actors — Siân Quill and Clare Dowling (Clare was later company writer), director Katy Hayes, and producer Caroline Williams. We wrestled the company management between us to various degrees at various times and the artistic direction was for the most part a collective activity, this in itself provided drama of course, as anyone who has ever been involved in collective decision making will concur. The four perspectives as presented in this piece should offer an insight into the workings of the company, our body of work and the passion that drove us to create it.

Siân Quill — Actor
I go on stage asking 'why am I putting myself through this torture?' and exit thinking 'there is no other place I want to be'. The desire to act is that simple.

Katy Hayes — Director

As a director I wanted to work on material that was relevant to my own life experience and there wasn't much of that in contemporary Irish theatre. *Philadelphia here I come!* may well be a great modern Irish play, but I had no special interest in young men emigrating to America in the Sixties. *The Gigli Concert* is a modern Irish classic, but I had no particular insights into a middle-aged man who wants to sing like Gigli. *Observe the Sons of Ulster Marching Towards the Somme* is a marvellous work but very far from my experience, real or imaginary — I had never even read a war comic! As a young director I wanted to work on material that spoke directly to me, to which I could bring something unique, and there wasn't much of it about.

Clare Dowling — Company Writer

In the late Eighties and early Nineties, modern urban Dublin finally booted boggy bits of land off the Irish stage, page and screen. Suddenly people were writing about dole queues and housing estates and southside dinner parties. The characters in these new fictional urban communities seemed very immediate and young and empathetic. Humour was rampant, sentiment gleefully absent. The language would strip paint. There was a vitality and an edge that appealed enormously to me, and when I began writing my first play for Glasshouse in 1992, modern urban Dublin was where I set it, completely undeterred by the fact that I was actually from the country.

Caroline Williams — Producer

In the early days we produced the shows on enthusiasm and fresh air. We were optimists and opportunists, though as the years passed the exuberance was eroded by the lack of adequate funding and even more by the lack of control as to when and where we could present our work. In later years the company did receive some financial support from The Arts Council and Dublin Corporation, though I've always believed the greatest support we received over the years was the classic hidden subsidy — the actors, set designers, lighting designers, costume designers, graphic designers, stage managers, technical operators, runners and others who worked with us for less than their due. Creative teams who made things look great on no money, and who could work miracles with a couple of hundred quid. Though we gained an enormous amount of experience with each production and doubtless dispelled some less than useful naïvety and arrogance each time, each show was a new beginning, from scratch. This constant change and uncertainty seemed tolerable, suited us even, in our early twenties — but we simply couldn't handle it as the years went on.

'Dodgy hubris and other aesthetic principles'

Katy: During our 1995 production of *Vampirella* and *The Company of Wolves*, *The Sunday Times* ascribed to Glasshouse the charge of 'dodgy hubris'.

What the f**k does that mean?

It sort of means that you have too much pride.

Look it up in Chambers.

'Overweening self-confidence, insolence, arrogance such as inviting disaster or ruin.'

That sounds great.

It's Greek. It means that you anger the Gods by wanting to be like them.

And we did.

Glasshouse was a project founded in 1990 to present and promote the work of women in the theatre. Inspirational predecessors would include Charabanc in Northern Ireland and Trouble and Strife in the UK. Ireland has never had an easy relationship with the feminist movement, and Irish theatre even less. The notion of a politically focussed group was alien. The inclusive agenda of a company like Passion Machine had found a niche, both critically and popularly, but the scene was more inimical to feminism. We had never had the upsurge in political drama that had emerged in the UK in the Seventies and Eighties, the neo-Brechtian yawp that produced voices like Howard Barker, Caryl Churchill and Sarah Daniels, and companies like Trouble and Strife and Joint Stock. This is an aesthetic environment, which provides a natural home for feminism. Irish theatre was firmly rooted in realism, and Irish theatre produced 'intimate plays of Irish life' and did it rather well. So we spotted a gap in the canvas, as it were. Between the four of us there was a spectrum of politics and agendas, varying in colour and intensity, but we all felt that women weren't getting a fair shake of the bag. The lack of women playwrights meant that women's stories didn't get told. Female actors weren't being given an opportunity to shine in meaty roles. And the scarcity of women producers and directors meant the decision-making process was overwhelmingly male dominated. We were determined to stop moaning about it and try some intervention.

Siân: In Annaghmakerrig, around that lavish dinner table where artists from all walks of life gather, a discussion arose about the origins of our company name. 'People in Glasshouses ... very good,' remarked one writer. 'It's the whole cynical nature of the theatre business, isn't it? Throwing stones ... he without sin and all that?' Stones? Maybe. Sin? Perhaps. However, in reality, the name 'Glasshouse' just seemed like a good idea one night in 1990, after a few too many pints. But we had a purpose; that much we believed devoutly. In the same year that Ireland welcomed its first female President, we, as a company, aimed to give Irish women a voice in theatre. Historically, it was male voices that were heard at all levels of the theatre system — from writers to management. To change that, one had to fight the system. That fight was informed by feminism. Glasshouse would make no apology for that.

'When I was young I tried to harden myself, in my mind ...'
Ficky Stingers by Eve Lewis, Andrews Lane, November 1990

Siân: There is a certain irony in the way one works as a receptionist by day and waitress by night in order to pay off the bank loan that provided the acting school fees. But bank loans are meant to be delayed. And Clare and I became determined to create roles for ourselves that no director seemed to realise we deserved. We became two actors in search of a play. And, after much deliberating, we found *Ficky Stingers* by Eve Lewis, a one-act drama about one London girl's experience of rape. This poignantly written four-hander is a frighteningly honest portrayal of the foulest crime against women. We booked a two-week lunchtime slot at Andrew's Lane before acknowledging to ourselves that we had no money, director or, indeed, a producer. Enter Katy and Caroline, and in our new office, a smoking table in Bewley's of Westmoreland Street, we plotted and schemed to explode ourselves on the Dublin theatre scene. Not a tenner between us, we begged friends and acquaintances to donate to the arts. We took to the streets, traipsing Dublin looking for £25 ads for the programme. Unpaid rehearsals began in our old drama school.

Katy: To start off we did two English plays *Ficky Stingers* by Eve Lewis and *Low Level Panic* by Clare McIntyre. These were strong plays, very women centred in theme and focus. And presented major challenges to our youth and inexperience: how do you show a rape on stage that captures the horror, but is theatrically convincing? How do you present a naked woman in a bath in a play about pornography, and avoid titillation?

'I want every man in the room to want me ... '
    Low Level Panic by Clare McIntyre, Andrews Lane, June 1991

Siân: I learnt my lines for *Low Level Panic*, our second show, while I waited for punters to leave the restaurant I worked in. Smelling of garlic bread and waitress perspiration, I sat at table 2A memorising Jo's masturbation monologue while the pasta-eaters drained their vino and began a game of strip poker (I jest not). Same venue, same show time, same rehearsal space, Clare McIntyre's play, set in a bathroom, had a cast of three women. I played the fun-loving gal, the dreamer, the one who talks and laughs too much (I knew my hideous laugh would come in handy), the one who dreams of romance, or a shag, or both while luxuriating in the bath. (That bath? — Amazing the things you find in a skip.) My first immersion in the bath was on preview day in front of a healthy-sized audience. I'm in the water/milk Cleopatra solution in my modest body stocking as the play opens. Minutes in, as I splish-splash, the body stocking rolls down and positions itself under one boob. Dialogue continues and I must exit the bath — in a supposed graceful and modest fashion. Ahhhhh! Body stocking exposes one boob to the audience while the other remains hidden behind a clump of wet, shrivelled elastic. Needless to say, from then on it was 'to hell with modesty'. Dublin audiences were well able for a bit of bath nudity, even if it was lunchtime.

Caroline: The production elicited quite a mixed critical response, described by one female reviewer in the *Evening Press* as 'cathartic ... and doubly painful because we witness it every day of our lives,' and she wrote of 'the total involvement of the audience in the lives of these women'. However, the same play, seen on the same day, got an extraordinarily negative review in *The Irish Times*, by a male reviewer, who believed 'so loaded a work is clearly a kind of propaganda ...' and ended with the line 'Brothers, I think that this is one for the Sisters.' Apart from the fact that he'd actively discouraged fifty per cent of our potential audience, this review was a clear indicator to the company that there was a belief out there that plays by women were for women, and that a play which explored women's sexuality, pornography, eating disorders and more was marginal because it was not about men. Such resistance to our work didn't discourage us, on the contrary we found it proof positive that presenting plays by women about women was an important and radical act.

'I drink to forget the future ...'

Out of my Head by Trudy Hayes, City Arts Centre,

November 1991

Katy: The first new play: *Out of My Head* by Trudy Hayes (1991) was a mind-blowing experience. The previous two works were tried and tested, both had had successful runs in the UK and elsewhere, but now we were virgins in virgin territory (to keep the Greek thing going!). We trouped off to Annaghmekerrig, cast, producer, director and writer, and set about developing and test-driving the material. We were inexperienced, but what we lacked in experience we made up for in hard work and, of course, dodgy hubris. The play was a shocking and tragic account of a young Irishwoman's helplessness in the face of alcoholism. We all felt we were onto something new and exciting and challenging. *Out of My Head* was short-listed for the Stewart Parker Award. The bug of new plays had bitten hard and would shape the future of the company.

Siân: It was an actor's dream to travel to Annaghmakerrig with our troupe and spend one week in a room exploring and experimenting with this modern, honest text. I was Lisa, the alcoholic, whose meanderings from lover to lover mirrored her numerous affairs with the vodka bottle. A tragic Nineties heroine whom I revelled in playing, especially because the workshop process allowed for so much creative input. When our excitable noisy group arrived at the big house to commandeer our space, a guest was heard to say: 'Oh, the actors have arrived.' Bernard Loughlin, while passing though the kitchen one morning and seeing three of us actors sipping coffee from saucer-less cups remarked, 'You can take the actor out of the gutter but you can never take the gutter out of the actor.' Sure isn't it that raw gutterdom that has us acting in the first place? We revel in it just as we revel in the limitless boundaries of the craft and, for me, that experience with *Out Of My Head* was just that — limitless.

We returned to Dublin to rehearse in the Actors' Workshop and perform in the City Arts Centre. How proud we were of this piece of innovative theatre, which reflected our own twenty-something lives and appealed to our young audiences. I remember playing to our first school group and, at a part in the play where I am drunk and stripping (I have done shows where I've kept my clothes on, I swear), the shy male character begs me to stop. 'Stop Lisa,' he begs as I'm inelegantly ripping off my underwear. 'Jaysus,' cried one school-going lad in the audience. 'I wouldn't tell her to stop.' Audience participation — don't you just love it? It is with hindsight that I realise the heavy drinking and dysfunctional relationships I helped create for my character in *Out Of My Head* were closer to the personal than is comfortable. But I'm grateful for my lack of awareness then because I believe acting is not therapy. Some therapeutic aspect might emerge as a by-product but *sin é*. It's a job — albeit an insecure and badly paid one — and you get on with it.

'Here's to the coffee shop and here's especially to Mr Counihan who bled the last of the loan money out of us yesterday, may he never get shagged again!'
    Burns Both Ends by Clare Dowling, Project Arts Centre,
                                                    August 1992

Clare: The play's first manifestation was as a rehearsed reading in the City Arts Centre in 1991 and was a very different thing to the finished product. Thematically it was too diverse, but a distinct style was to emerge at this point: that of fast, short, inter-cutting scenes shaped largely by structured movement, and with several characters being played by each actor. The style was partially informed by our lack of resources — with little money for sets, costumes or numerous actors, we had to rise to the challenge of financial constraint.

    What was finally produced in the Project Arts Centre a year later was *Burns Both Ends*, a comedy-drama concerning two young women on the lower end of the socio-economic ladder, Martina and Trish, who escape dead-end jobs in a chippers to become coffee shop entrepreneurs. The play deals with the effect success and ambition has on their friendship, relationships and their familial obligations — in Martina's case (played by Siân Quill) as a young mother. The play was described in the press, variously, as 'an hilarious comedy', 'a mess', 'politically astute' and 'deeply flawed'.

Katy: *Burns Both Ends* was a move into comedy. Though the company's aims and objectives were serious (we were described as 'earnest and hardworking' by *The Irish Times*), there was a strong feel for humour about the place, and frankly, we were all having quite a laugh. This was a fast-paced screwball play about women and private enterprise written in a Dublin idiom. Witty in both its language and physicality, it marked the launch of another new playwright, this time a comic talent.

Clare: The political issues of the play seemed to cause most contention, either because they were perceived as being under-developed, or at odds with the comedy of the rest of the show. We had worked exhaustively on these areas in rehearsal, cutting a lot of the original material, including a scene depicting workplace violence against the character of Trish, because we were always wary of our work being labelled 'worthy' or 'sincere' — which it was anyway. It seemed at times that Glasshouse could stage a play about ten rugby players on a stag night in a strip club and it would be dismissed by some elements as 'worthy' and 'sincere'. Overall, there was a great lack of intelligent critical comment on the type of work that the company was doing, and this says more about the standard of theatre reviewing and analysis in this country than any overly 'sincere' work we were producing. Even when we gave in gracefully to their clumsy labels, and began to wave the red flag with projects such as *There Are No Irish Women Playwrights!*, we could barely elicit a irritated peep out of them. I am still inclined to blame some of this response on the prevalent computer spell-check of the day, which would automatically change 'Glasshouse' into 'Gallstones'.

'But what about …?'
> *There Are No Irish Women Playwrights!* devised by Caroline
> Williams, Project Arts Centre, March 1993

Katy: Side by side with the drama, an archive project was developed to identify new writers and celebrate old. *There Are No Irish Women Playwrights! 1* and *2* were presented as part of focussing festivals on the surrounding issues of women in theatre generally. These presentations of the best scenes from women's writing functioned a bit like a classic hits selection and the audience were constantly surprised at the wealth of material.

Caroline: Researching and presenting these compilations was hugely interesting and rewarding work. We got an extraordinarily good reaction and we came in close contact with people in the academic sector working in this field. *There are no Irish Women Playwrights! 1* was eight extracts from contemporary work and included writers such as Marina Carr, Deirdre Hines, Geraldine Aron and Anne Devlin. Yet again the critics were divided, confirming our suspicion that certain thematic concerns were considered 'unpalatable' to some, such as this *Sunday Tribune* commentator:

> The themes, with the exception of Clare Dowling's charming escapade about two young women trying to start their own business, are wife-battering, alcoholism, babies and war. Surely the human condition as experienced by Irish women playwrights encompasses other sensibilities …?

Yes of course it does, is the easy answer here, women playwrights can write about whatever they wish — however none of the four themes this critic cited seemed 'inappropriate' for the stage to us. Primarily a play is chosen for production on its artistic merit, but why shouldn't these themes be to the fore? There *Are No Irish Women Playwrights! 2* was a selection of work from 1920 to 1970, from Kate O'Brien to Edna O'Brien, and included many other writers better known for writing in other mediums — my particular favourite from the selection was *Tolka Row* by Maura Laverty, for its wonderful scene where Fonsie tells Peggie of his previous girlfriend and her 'coarse appetite'!

Clare: Almost ten years ago, we asked why more women were not writing for the stage. Today, the same question is perceived as passé and embarrassing — surely they're not still banging on about that? But the facts are that women are still not writing for the Irish stage in any equitable number. And given that most of the audience on any given night in any theatre in Dublin will be women, this is a debate that should continue.

Perhaps women just do not want to express themselves in theatre. Perhaps they feel that the stories they want to tell are better suited to other media — books maybe, or film or television. I have written for all three and, given the parameters, some of them are certainly easier than writing for the stage. Maybe women feel they want their work to reach a greater audience than that found in theatre, and good luck to them. But they will not reach a more enthusiastic audience, or a hungrier one.

'I know me own thigh ...'
                    Leapfrogging by Clare Dowling, Project Arts Centre,
                                                            March 1993

Clare: *Leapfrogging*, my second play, left urban realism behind and went into the realm of satire. A one-act play, it explored gender identity both past and present, through a combination of fairytales, movie genres and biblical stories. Jack and Jill, Adam and Eve, and Private Eye Phil struggle along the journey that started with the bite of the apple, through patriarchal society, the feminist revolution, the age of the new man and woman, through to the present day. It was essentially a light-hearted comedy with an edge, and again with much emphasis on the possibilities of form.

I performed in both of these plays — as Trish in *Burns Both Ends* and as Mary Lou in *Leapfrogging*. If I were to do it again, I would have approached *Burns Both Ends* purely in the capacity of a writer, particularly as the play went through so many changes during the rehearsal period. I saw myself primarily as an actress then, and was in the privileged position to be able to write roles for myself — who could resist? But I had learned my lesson by *Leapfrogging* and took only a cameo role.

'I want to peel you like a grape …'
I Know My Own Heart by Emma Donoghue,
Project Arts Centre, April 1993

Katy: *I Know My Own Heart* was a humorous and linguistically elegant account of an early nineteenth-century Englishwoman's life as a lesbian. None of us could remember ever seeing a play about lesbian experience on an Irish stage. The raw passion behind the dainty presentation felt very original and fresh.

Clare: Emma Donoghue's first play *I Know My Own Heart* detailed the life and loves of Anne Lister, a closet lesbian who romped her way through regency England. This certainly managed to get a reaction.

The lack of funding was particularly apparent with this play, given that it was a costume drama, and our efforts were described by one commentator as 'frocks borrowed from someone's dressing-up box', and they were absolutely right. It was no longer a question of rising to the challenge of financial constraint, but rather lying down on the road in front of it.

'No one's laid a hand on me since 1804 …'
I Know My Own Heart by Emma Donoghue,
Andrews Lane, October 1993.

Caroline: Following its successful first outing as a lunchtime show in Project, Glasshouse presented *I Know My Own Heart* as a full length evening show at Andrews Lane Theatre in October 1993. The production did well both critically and audience-wise (this as one of the phrases favoured by the struggling independents at that time — because you'd meet someone and ask how the play was going? Great! Excellent! Fantastic! Hence the follow up question with the catchphrase — and how's it doing audience-wise?)

Though the play was outside of the venue's usual fare, Pat Moylan was enthusiastic and welcoming. The box-office staff were more frank, explaining that they have regulars, people who ring and ask what's on this week and when told the subtitle — A Lesbian Regency Romance — they pause, then they ask and what's on after that? To subsidise their theatrical activities, Andrews Lane at that time used to host music gigs at the weekend. This posed slight logistic problems for us but we would strike our set, such as it was, in preparation for the late night revellers. We were pre-funding in those days so most of the furniture came from someone's parents house, very loosely in the style of the period, or at least not obviously identifiable as not from the period. After one of these gigs on a Friday night at about 1am in the car park there was a bit of a fracas — a gun was fired, someone was shot. Hence the news story in the *Sunday Independent* under the heading 'Man Shot at Lesbian Play.' We were livid at the time, exploring legal avenues and various retorts. Years later it stands out as amusing among the many idiotic press clippings in the archive — and I doubt it harmed the box office receipts a jot. This was one of the periods, Glasshouse not Regency, which I've look back on and question our work practices. I gave birth to my daughter toward the end of the run and I remember having some class of production meeting in the corridors of the National Maternity Hospital. Though this seems bizarre to me in retrospect, at the time it seemed perfectly normal. We were obsessed and driven. It was a time where the work was inextricably linked with our personal lives. Unhealthily so.

'Can a bird sing only the song it knows or can it learn a new song?'
Vampirella and *The Company of Wolves* by Angela Carter,
Adapted for the stage by Katy Hayes, Project Arts Centre,
January 1995

Katy: Producing *Vampirella* and *The Company of Wolves* was a long-time ambition of the company, and finally its time had come. We knitted together the source material of Angela Carter's two radio plays to create a conjoined fairytale narrative with thematic links. Angela Carter was a guiding voice of aesthetic feminism. Her tragically young death (cancer aged fifty) provided a haunting presence behind this Gothic ghoul-fest. We tried to weave a theatrical brocade as rich and luscious as Carter's prose.

Siân: Carter, our on-stage canary disguised as a nightingale, retired to Caroline's when *Vampirella* and *The Company of Wolves* came to a close. Carter (named after our illustrious author) lived a happy life, basking in the glory of her acting debut in the Project Arts Centre. The novelty of playing *Vampirella* and having a pet bird, ridiculously long false nails, a stunning costume (for the very first time), white painted fangs, and easy access to blood pellets was almost too good to be true. And then there was Angela Carter's language, the sumptuous erotic prose she penned for *Vampirella*, a character whose overwhelming desire to be loved ultimately leads to her own destruction. The show was set in the dangerous, crowded woods and in the cold, loveless castle and our reliable Irish weather kindly reflected the mood of both pieces. Being the old Project, the uncomfortably-seated audience regularly enjoyed the outdoor acoustics of wind and rain. We, the cast, on a particularly bad weather night, dressed ourselves upon the grey plastic dressing room chairs for fear the puddles and basins of rainwater would destroy our much-adored costumes. During the interval, we warmed our cold bodies with cups of tea and copious cigarettes as we overheard male audience members debating the pros and cons of our show, and the football, in the adjoining jacks. And, you know, we wouldn't have had it any other way.

Katy: In 1995, following *Vampirella* … and a rehearsed reading of *Ladies and Gentlemen*, a new play by Emma Donoghue, I felt it was time to move on. A company like Glasshouse has an organic life of its own, and I had a sense of my involvement having run its course. I was about to turn thirty and I felt I had to prioritise earning my supper and Glasshouse was a very rewarding but very time consuming project. Changing the world was all very well. But recently married, changing nappies was in the offing and I needed to find some way of making some dough.

'Why would I have a girl's name when I'm as hot blooded a male as ever twirled a cane?'

Ladies and Gentlemen by Emma Donoghue,
Project Arts Centre, April 1996

Caroline: *Ladies and Gentlemen* was undoubtedly a high point for the company and Emma who, having written for many other mediums, has stated that the development and production of both her plays were personal career highlights. Original music for the production was composed by Carole Nelson of Zrazy, and David Byrne stepped in as director following Katy's departure from the company. A wonderful set was created by Irene O'Brien and considering the frugal years that had preceded, spending our grant allocation on this production was pure pleasure.

The play is essentially a love story based upon a real life male impersonator and Vaudeville star Annie Hindle who eloped with her dresser, Annie Ryan, and whose obituary appeared in *The New York Sun* in 1891. The play is also very much about the love of theatre itself, the excitement, the camaraderie and occasionally the drudgery of it all. A very apt and joyful note for the company to end on. It took a couple of months for us to realise, however, that that was the conclusion we had collectively arrived at!

Clare: When I set into writing my third play for Glasshouse, we were tired. I had written three more plays in the interim — *The Marlboro Man* for the Project, *Small City* for the Peacock and *Blood* for the Gaiety School of Acting — and I was personally tired. With a large body of almost entirely new work already behind us, and with all of us moving in other directions by the necessity to make a living, we decided not to develop the show. The company was wound up shortly afterwards.

Siân: As an actor I'm proud of the diversity of roles I've played within my own company. Proud too of the power to create theatre that excited both ourselves and our audiences. Proud that we gave a voice to forgotten and emerging Irish women writers. It was Voltaire who, when asked why no woman had ever written a tolerable tragedy, replied: 'The composition of a tragedy requires testicles.' Balls to that.

Ladies and Gentlemen by Emma Donoghue is published by New Island Books, Dublin 1998.

I Know My Own Heart by Emma Donoghue is published in *Seen and Heard: Six New Plays by Irish Women*, Edited by Cathy Leeney, Carysfort Press, 2001.

OWEN DUDLEY EDWARDS

Irish Theatre in Scottish Festival

An invitation from Dermot Bolger is, culturally and Hibernically, akin to a royal command. This after all is the man who made a series of novelists stop writing novels alone in order to write one all together. It seems an Arthurian feat, a Round Table, a universal Grail-Quest. At our mundane least, it gives him an air of Lord Melbourne asserting collective responsibility of the cabinet, or, as satirised by *1066 And All That*, the doctrine that it does not matter what the members of the cabinet say so long as they all speak at once. (Naturally graduate students with theses to write will not be content with that; they will insist on theoretising about every strand and its putative origin in *Finbar's Hotel*, that admirable establishment whose architects outweigh its amenities.)

I may be whistling an overture as I pass my graveyard. His e-mails via my wife (it is an elementary precaution to have none myself) speak of men in black leather jackets paying calls if the copy does not arrive. He thus transports me — so far, mentally — back some twelve years to the first Scottish production of his own *The Lament for Arthur Cleary*: twelve years gone, but its ending is before me still; Cleary dead apparently in Ireland but seen for the last time facing unknown frontier-guards on the verge of what new world? I focus on Bolger not simply to prefer his raising my curtain to his terminating my existence: his two plays of Edinburgh Festival performance refract in various significance on Scottish culture. *Cleary* is, in many senses, a frontier play, and in 1990 at Edinburgh's Traverse, then in its middle period (the elegant primitive), *The Lament for Arthur Cleary* told its enraptured audience and award-spouting critics that comfort and its cuddly variants were expelled from the Irish stage: no longer could we rely on simple linguistic anarchy, or ruthless skin-stripping anti-hypocrisy, or repetitive drownings or assassinations, or timeless mythologies trapping endless generations, and all the shattering reassurances we knew from Wilde, Shaw, Synge, O'Casey and Yeats. Bolger was to these as Irving Welsh is to Burns, Scott, Stevenson, Conan Doyle and Barrie. None of the analogous ten were all that comfortable for their contemporaries — try Scott on the clearances in *Guy Mannering* or on female punishment of treachery in *Rob Roy* — but Bolger, like Welsh, proclaims a new world, inducing as shudder no ghost-story frisson, only a little dangerous knowledge: the future we guess 'an' fear,' as Burns said to the mouse. Bolger's frontier awoke us from the security in which we had so much enjoyed being troubled by the theatre of Irish despair or disillusion. Even before *Cleary*, Scotland thought of Irish plays as the theatrical exemplar. As classics they could harrow and haunt (but not at the cost of hope). Where does Bolger leave us? Where does he leave *me*, with those damned frontier-guards of his? Beyond Beckett's reassurance, that's for sure.

Scotland was Ireland's frontier, when the original Scots left Ireland to colonise both sides of the North Channel in Dalriada, or in the footsteps of Columba, or whatever way to culminate in conquering (aka marrying) the Picts. A thousand years later, Ireland became a Scottish frontier, giving us today's Northern Ireland and its virtues and horrors. The two countries looked at one another with varying forms of uncertainty, but in theatre terms Ireland has always shown Scotland a symbol of cultural freedom. It lacked English censorship as bestowed by Lord Chamberlain; it lacked Scots censorship as imposed by the Church of Scotland. Ireland told itself it was a cultural desert because it banned *1984*: Scotland told itself Ireland was a cultural oasis because the Irish could attend Shaw's *The Shewing-Up of Blanco Posnet*, and an Irishman could write it. Yeats, bitterly aware of corrosive belittlement in Irish calumny and emulation (as we have learned from Conor Cruise O'Brien's *Ancestral Voices* and

Roy Foster's *Yeats* and from so much garnered and sent forth by
A. Norman [Derry] Jeffares, the master-Hibernologist of Scotland
now in his eyrie on the Fifeshire coast) — Yeats, as I say, made
Conall (Cearnach) say of Cuchulain in *The Green Helmet* (1910):

> For he will never come home, he has all that he
>   could need
> In that high windy Scotland — good luck in all that
>   he does.
> Here neighbour wars on neighbour, and why there
>   is no man knows,
> And if a man is lucky all wish his luck away,
> And take his good name from him between a day
>   and a day.

(It was indeed apposite that the Irish Festival Players, formed
from Dublin and Belfast student actors in the late 1950s, should
have taken this among their Yeats Cuchulain cycle to Edinburgh's
then infant Fringe, performing with resonant acclaim in 1959
even if one night the glasses painted pewter shattered in an
opening toast festooning the audience in flying but fortunately
innocuous fragments.) But Scotland (product of populist religious
zeal and as grimly aware of its reach-me-down London cultural
fads as in Ireland) has its own phrase for what Conall diagnosed:
'I ken't his faither.' In England it might mean you knew the old
Earl; in Scotland, no less than Ireland, it means he started as low
as yourself. Yeats might not offer that reading ('An ancestor was
rector there' &c) but it has all to do with Bolger's frontier. When
The Lament for Arthur Cleary reached Scottish audiences, they
knew whence it came as part of themselves.

What Scotland did not know from personal reading, is the
frontier *Cleary* formed with the original Gaelic poem lamenting
the killing of Art Ó Laoghaire (or, if you insist, Arthur Leary),
which some like to think is the work of his widow, Daniel
O'Connell's aunt, while others whip themselves into ecstasies in
hopes it is not. Whatever the truth, those seem her sentiments, and

in particular the strange, broken half-lines with which it opens — its chant well-backgrounding the Traverse audience gingerly taking its seats — caught the bereavement and bewilderment, the fascination with the cosmopolitanism, the non-Irish career, of her love-object, speaking for Leary's partner as for Cleary's. The poem's doom-laden trot, the hoof-beats of the empty-saddled horse first telling Eibhlín Dhubh Ní Chonaill of her man's tragedy, was not a thing for slavish textual imitation, but the Gaelic sound — even 'dos na daoine nach bhfuil Gaedhilge acu' (as the Abbey used to derisively subtitle its English synopses of Gaelic productions) — gave the beat Bolger required. And if Scots are unaccustomed to understanding Gaelic (though if familiar with their own, they will also be adept at Ulster's — but not Ní Chonaill's Munster), they are used to hearing it in Gaelic programmes on the media: they know of the Gaelic frontier as a fact of life, in time as well as tongue. Bolger's success was to show a horrible cyclical quality in Irish doom, as fully as Yeats' *Purgatory*, but with none of the escape Yeats' form and style might give. (Then, of course, *The Lament for Arthur Cleary* had a masterly Edinburgh production, whereas the *Purgatory* I saw on the Edinburgh stage at the student Bedlam theatre (once the last domicile of the great Scots poet Robert Fergusson when actually an insane asylum) was one where a certain Irish actor hired the then youthful poet Hayden Murphy (subsequently a major Scots theatre critic, notably of Hiberniana) as factotum, dogsbody, front-of-house, programme-seller and boy-in-*Purgatory* — in which last role the protagonist murdered Hayden with the utmost brutality every night possibly for rejection of his offstage erotic agenda. It was, in all senses, frightful.) Bolger's Gaelic-doom-become-modern-doom, returned emigré Musterman entrapped in an Ireland he deemed familiar but found more alien than the foreign lands he had known, were perfectly compatible with a comparably ugly parallel among lost eighteenth-century Highland Jacobites and twentieth-century innocents convinced of their sophistication by a touch from the EC. Alan Breck can be doomed in modern dress no less than Art Ó Laoghaire.

Scotland welcomed *Cleary* with hunger as well as habituation. The Scots are as historically-conscious a people as the Irish, but in a curiously different way. Scots have obliterated large parts of their past at significant moments. Losing medieval history is obvious enough (English philosophers do a much more drastic job for their field), but in modern terms one group might eliminate the Highlands, another the Enlightenment, and so on. Irish nationalist revisionists might like to play that game, but not even they can detonate O'Connell and Parnell out of Irish history, though no doubt in a united Ireland Martin McGuinness as Minister for Education would give it a good old college try. A selective involvement in the past robs the artist of resources of the kind Bolger summoned to his aid so well. So Scots watched *Cleary*, saw the genius and the horror of the bridge Bolger built across historical time, and brooded on the means by which the Scottish historical play could reach such immediacy. It is not a question that makes any sense for a triumphalist culture like England: an *English* history of being deprived of civil rights, such as English scholars dislike admitting in full strength under the Normans, made perfect sense for the Scots readers of Scott's *Ivanhoe*. But the English do not think of a Leary/Cleary form of history, and even their superb self-sacrifice, saving the world in the Battle of Britain and the Blitz, is read by posterity as victory, not — as in reality — heroic integrity in the face of apparent absolute defeat.

The results of the triumphalist English view of the past is unpleasantly evident in international soccer hooliganism, a philosophy that fleshes itself into ideology no less than any other 'ism', eg: Haugheyism, Thatcherism, Paisleyism. The Scots version of that is more uncertain. It had an excellent innings, of course, theologically speaking, when Glasgow Celtic and Rangers were in full fighting trim, and there was sufficient historical consciousness there of a highly Irish kind. (Non-Irish participated vigorously: Celtic fans of Wee Free Presbyterian origin, Trotskyites all, would assure me after a Celtic victory 'The Pope's a great man'.) The serious question arose as to whether hostility in

Scotland to Irish Catholicism was a permanent social factor, and the evidence of competent and relatively dispassionate scholars, including Irish Catholic immigrants such as myself, asserts a decline in Scottish anti-Catholicism so sharp as to minimise it save in the minds of its potential profiteers (or, as they would style themselves, its victims). In any case, the coarse cultures of the Glasgow teams were as good as one another in vituperation: Ranger instructions to seek carnal knowledge of His Holiness were answered by Celtic ones to give comparable service to Her Majesty. Scottish theatre produced some very hard-hitting plays against anti-Catholicism in the 1970s — none supporting it — but it is no longer a profound issue. Hence when Irish culture has studied football-obsession, notably in Bolger's *In High Germany*, Scottish audiences have again been fascinated by what is recognisable in theme but new in approach. There is as much difference between *In High Germany* and Glasgow plays of a quarter-century ago such as *The Sash* and *The Bigot*, as there is between the rules for GAA supporters (which would have included 'banning' attendance at 'foreign' games such as those played by Glasgow Celtic) and rules, or at least customs, for supporters of the international fortunes of the Irish soccer team in recent years.

Scots found *In High Germany* particularly fascinating for its reinterpretation of the uses of football as a theatre theme, although Edinburgh has seen other Irish companies offer simpler if undeniably agreeable alternatives. All turn on team spirit, but Bolger cut a wider swathe in the more difficult quest of fan reaction, pursued into problems of identity and exile. Certainly the earlier Scots plays turned on fan response as well, but this was something obvious to the audience before a word was said: Bolger expected his audience to determine an ideology which in parts would be unclear to his protagonist. As social history, let alone theatre, it was deeply impressive. Irish identity has certainly turned on a variety of strange pivots, from the Abbey Theatre to the Boomtown Rats, but for Scottish audiences *In High Germany* brought home for the first time how so new a cult should have reached so vast a following. That its nationalism and its ethnic consciousness should be so peripheral and indeed so uncertain was a further revelation. Ireland to the outsider often seems to be perpetually talking to itself incomprehensibly but repetitively down the centuries — is it caricatured in J.R.R. Tolkien's Gollum, for instance? Bolger's Ireland was declaring its *raison d'être* in soccer-worship, a marginal cult less than thirty years ago, and almost unknown thirty years before that. Yet what Bolger described was an intensity seldom reached among Irish exiles over the centuries, whether Irish revolution or Mother Machree was in question. Scottish soccer cultists might deplore the sectarian origins of their sport, but they could hardly think of the game without awareness of it. Ireland, supposedly the mother of sectarianism in Scottish Soccer, was now self-identified in a sport whose sectarianism was invisible (who, in Bolger's *In High Germany*, would have had the faintest knowledge of long ago differences between the League of Ireland and the Irish League?). Ireland's soccer pantheon, in fact, had among its highest heroes persons of almost entirely English origin whose religious affiliations were unknown. And the play would also highlight lessons for Scottish internationalism, more particularly as the Scots found themselves ill at ease with English Europhobia. The English problem in the European community is one of never being able to think themselves to be part of it: *In High Germany* reflects high, if peculiar, national identity, but it two-tracks a conscious Europeanism.

Bolger's Edinburgh producers were necessarily minimalist. The Traverse in its middle years took much pride in encouraging its audience's imagination at the expense of sets, thus losing sympathy when going to its present luxurious quarters and its occasionally overweening stage furnishing. Dark lighting and small resources meant that *The Lament for Arthur Cleary* worked in surroundings, which even eighteenth-century originals might have found a little sparse, for all of their victimised poverty. *In High Germany* requires virtually nothing, other than a bench and the suggestion of a station. The impact was analogous to that of radio: having only its content on which to be memorable, it drove a clear message home. In any case this kind of theatre is what the Fringe, at its very best, is about. Lavish productions on the Fringe will usually be at the expense of quality, even of tempo or focus. Theatre that depends above all on what it says forces script and actors into implementation of its implications. And most of the Fringe lacks anything as luxurious as even the old or the middle Traverse. The thousand worlds discoverable in the August days of Edinburgh conjure up their magic most of the time in buildings whose architects never for a moment anticipated a future for them as theatre venue. Schools, playgrounds, church halls, church interiors, masonic halls, health clubs, disused bank branches, graveyards, private houses, bankrupt cafés, delicatessens, motor cars, backs of wagons, pubs, foreign-language institutes, monastery ruins on an island, clubs, settlement offices, canal banks, public parks, botanic gardens, hilltops, and a large hole in the ground awaiting a new building, have given of their best. The result is the largest theatrical showcase on earth, and one where Ireland is a favoured participant whenever it chooses to unroll its mat and strut its stuff.

1990, the year of *The Lament for Arthur Cleary*, staged Ireland's Himalayas. If *Cleary* was Everest, the O'Kelly–O'Hanrahan version of *Finnegans Wake* was K2, Donal O'Kelly's own *Bat the Father Rabbit the Sun* was Kinchinjunga, Daniel Reardon's *Spenser's Laye* was Makalu, and Ulick O'Connor's *Joyicity* was Ulick O'Connor's *Joyicity*. O'Kelly's achievement was gigantic in itself as theatre heroics. His play was a one-person performance in two roles, revolutionary father and entrepreneur son, unravelling the bourgeoisification and capitalisation of the sons of Irish Freedom, salutary in the extreme for patriots and poltroons of any culture, and when finished he was daily out of the Assembly Rooms on George Street, downhill Hanover Street to cross the main thoroughfare on Princes Street, ascending by its gardens past the Hall of the General Assembly of the Church of Scotland on the Mound to breast the hill on Bank Street only to plunge rightwards down Victoria Street bottoming out on the West Bow then sheltering the Traverse Theatre where with Paul O'Hanrahan of Balloonatics he built the blocks of *The Wake* Sheming and Shauning it, Anna Living it up and HCEarwicking it down beginning at 5.30/17.30 having ended *Bat/Rabbit* at 3.30/15.30. Sir Boyle Roche complained that, not being a bird in the air, he could not be in two places at once; but Donal O'Kelly showed how a bat and rabbit could be, when it was half aWake. In energy, resourcefulness, variety, courage, strength, wit, resilience, charm, integrity, social depth-charging and intellectual pyrotechnics the whole thing was grandparent of his *Catalpa* a few years later which would come nearer to total history than anything since Herodotus.

History was in a more self-indulgent mood in 1990 with Daniel Reardon's *Spenser's Laye* performed by Jeananne Crowley and a convincing cast from Connacht Productions in the Assembly Rooms' Ballroom. There was an element of ironic, almost 'ye olde ribaldrie' in the title stimulating imaginations to view it as a great-grandmother-of-*Tom Jones* bodice-ripper-before-the-bodice which in any case undercarpets much of the Gloriana cult, and by the end of the play the Queen is certainly no longer of the virginal variety. Modern scholarship, indeed, suspects that she may have been ex-virgin long before the 1590s when the Reardon Spenser proves the Bard of Loudest Laye. But however jolly-old-romp, the beguiling spectacle had its merit both as history and as philosophy. The Tudor conquest of Ireland was a very nasty business. Objectively considered, it was two groups of savages assailing one another with variations based on the historicity of their previous intermingling, and while Spenser may claim heights of poetic expression superior to any on the Irish side which have come down to us, his powers were enlisted in justifying exploitation by aesthetics. Like Gerry Adams at a later date, he had a genius for assuring his victims that their sufferings were essentially their own fault, albeit his imaginative and poetic powers soar far above Mr Adams' *Peg's Paper* works. Reardon, Crowley, and their comrades deserve the credit for finding the gentle, loving, even humorous, possibilities in Spenser's conquesting, and genuinely seek to heal harms where almost all other imaginative work on the theme (Spenser's included) is evangelically vengeful. Even if much of *Spenser's Laye* is historically nonsense, it is no bad thing for Irish people to admire a great poet inspired by their country however ruthlessly. Audiences left the court of Jeananne Crowley happier and more peaceable than most visitors to the court of Elizabeth Tudor could afford to be. So ecumenical a message was particularly welcomed in Scotland, uneasily aware of proximity to the endless Irish wars, and of housing their spin-offs, Glasgow Celtic and Rangers.

These productions variously symbolised Irish post-war theatre having come of age, although Edinburgh was aware of many other epiphanies ranging from Kilkenny's *The Murder of Gonzago* in 1986 to Cork's *Disco Pigs* in 1997. Dublin is in many ways the least Irish city in the entire island of Ireland. It is much too Anglocentric, whether rudely or amiably, and more conventional than it likes to admit. Kilkenny's Theatre Unlimited was perfectly prepared to get to work on an English (if partly Welsh) author, Shakespeare, disintegrating the word and the work even more radically than the visualisation of *Finnegans Wake* could accomplish, hunching its way into being in a cascade of newspapers worn with more panache than any since Lewis Carroll's *Through the Looking Glass*, deconstructing the proscenium arch and rebuilding it under Hamlet's nose. Postmodernism had hit the theatre, modestly and in a private suburban house, teasingly enough to be also premodernist. It was intellectually mind-boggling; it also armed itself with an excellent sense of humour. *Disco Pigs* has gone on to greater stardom than any swine since Wodehouse's Empress of Blandings, or maybe since Orwell's *Animal Farm*. To me, an Edinburgh-domiciled son of a Corkwoman, the highest poignancy was the rich accents of ancestral sanctity in which the wild new angsts and exultations were cried in their new language now familiar now fathomless crowing its triumphs and grunting its tragedy. It may have been the most energetic play Ireland had spawned, apart from frenzied bouts in individual productions (for example,

Purgatory). Anyhow, the new Traverse, its faithful if fiercely trendy public, and its larger intake-of-the-Festival, loved *Disco Pigs*. The swine that the caricaturists had embedded with the Irish, the swine that the neo-Victorian Sinn Féin and its heirs had rejected, became the swine that now led all the rest. Edinburgh in Festival would fain have filled its belly with the husks that the Disco Pigs did eat and vomit forth. Modern culture has long been accused by its conservative critics of losing sense and meaning; here was a play in which the counter-culture came home, simultaneously proclaiming its own hopelessness and its own music. It was hard to think of a work more negative and more beautiful, and to me at least it was the Cork accent that made it so.

Belfast and Northern Ireland have sent various offerings to the Edinburgh Fringe Festival, including strong poetry, recitals, and gallant performances of bad plays. But Belfast still seems overawed by Dublin, theatrewise, recolonised by postcolonialism. Appropriately, Belfast has provided the best media coverage of Ireland at the Edinburgh Festival and Fringe, notably when produced by Chris Spurr for BBC Northern Ireland.

It seems fairly crazy that Dublin should have made so little use of Edinburgh, so close in proximity, so warm in welcome, so anxious to attract, with such internationalism to assert. Such Irish material as hits the Fringe is frequently in British or other hands. Parish Wilde and finishing-school Shaw, librarians' Synge and mystics' Yeats, political party O'Casey and American college Beckett, draw rein, draw breath and draw the line at accents: that is to say, their own becomes the play. No doubt in the earlier years of the Fringe it was a case of Morningside becomes *Electra* (the gentilities of Morningside meant that 'sex' was what the coal arrived in, and there were no rates, maice yes, rates no, and the church bells went 'cleng'). And how many productions, in Ireland or Scotland (or God save us, London) play *Death of a Salesman* in the New York Jewish lilt in Arthur Miller's ear as he composed it? In any case Irish immigration to the larger island has ultimately resulted in some fine voice coaching, especially among students. When Conall Morrison at Edinburgh University Theatre Company put on *Faustus Kelly* by Myles na gCopaleen aka Flann O'Brien in the mid-1980s, against a design of kitsch-green wallpaper, he cast a highly competent Home Counties young lady of well-modulated standard English as 'Mr Strange' otherwise Mephistopheles. (Perhaps his logic was that of William Lorimer (1885-1967) whose translation of the New Testament into Scots kept the Devil as the sole speaker of English [neatly hitting off his urban sophistication against the rural poverty of Christ].) The effect was a little as if Goethe/Gounod had taken over from Alfred Hitchcock in directing *Rebecca*, to end by the housekeeper giving notice instead of merely setting the house on fire. But apart from this mild incongruity (which might very well have the applause of the author on one of his less bloody-minded days), what Morrison had done was to make a high artistic success of a stage masterpiece systematically belittled in the land of its father ever since its first production in 1943. Morrison's production foretold great things of him, as had his Edinburgh student theatre debut, Martin Lynch's *The Interrogation of Ambrose Fogarty*, indicative of the Ulster Catholic origins he shared with Myles. Morrison's relentless Hibernicity made him a honey-pot to the fair groupies of southeast England, a phenomenon equally visible among subsequent Edinburgh Irish student latter-day Boucicaults and Becketts, such as Colin Teevan and Roddy McDevitt. The performances their direction exacted and extracted spoke volumes for their lineal descent from ancient Irish missionaries (collateral anyway, lest we be haunted by SS Gall and Columbanus, to say nothing of Columba, Ireland's first gift to Scottish theatre [above all on Loch Ness: his co-star the monster has been resting ever since, while the English have had to make do with less indigenous George and Dragon]). They were a little fearful, in all cases, of allowing the perfect rhythms of the Thames Valley to be sullied by hibernicity, but by the 1990s Irish plays received Irish accents, however hard the training. McDevitt solved his own problem at one Festival in a production of what is probably his finest play,

The Lottery Ticket, by starring several members of his own family (the plot required them to eat one another, a device which in a bowdlerised form seems to have inspired the current TV show 'Big Brother'). The director, Ben Harrison, was English and seemed by the end of the run to feel that Ireland's wrongs had been amply avenged. What Harrison, Teevan and McDevitt would not stand for, was the embarrassing English notion of the stage-Irish accent it is assumed any Englishman can do. Much more senior performers and directors were a great deal less choosy: I recall Sean Keogh in Synge's *Playboy* having evidently graduated to courtship of Pegeen Mike after a hard stint in Birmingham to whose intonation he returned at any moment of stress (which is to say, almost all his speaking moments).

That particular Seanín was I believe in Lindsay Anderson's mid-eighties *Playboy* (prompt apologies to the Keogh in question if I have misplaced his intonation: in any case, whether or not he was Brum, he was very far east of Mayo). Anderson had arrived preceded by publicity from a new venture, I think called United Artists, in which a fine group-shot of three interested parties left Fringe-goers under the illusion Pegeen was to be played by Glenda Jackson, the Widow Quinn by Diana Rigg, and the title-role by Albert Finney. It made some casting sense: Pegeen Mike as a latter-day Connaught virgin queen, the Widow as a suitably homicidal ex-Avenger — and what a formidably chilling Regan Diana Rigg had made in someone's *Lear* (Olivier? Hordern? — either way, Rigg's had been the faultless performance) — and no doubt Christy Mahon's venal innocence shared qualities with *Tom Jones* in whose film Finney had starred to Micheál MacLiammóir's luxuriant narration. Synge along with them, though, and you would have some singular accents: still, if the Widow Quinn *had* to have an English accent, a performance from Diana Rigg might reconcile one to the clipped authority of her pride that she 'destroyed her mehn', as it would surely sound. But it was all cheesecake or, insisted Anderson, some publicity menial's error — lucrative enough in pre-performance takings certainly. The production, said Anderson, would tilt away from

Pegeen: modern productions had made too much of her, and he wished to re-emphasise the Playboy. In other words, he knew his Pegeen was not up to the part, nor was she, certainly to anyone who had seen Siobhán McKenna summon the richness of her passion and temper. But Anderson was glibly ready to fight off ghosts from the Abbey: he assured us the great days of the Abbey were in the past, the Abbey interpretation of the play was by now moribund, anyhow Britain had not seen a professional production for twenty years. That required answering. He was told — this was in press conference in all the gracious nineteenth-century architectural imitation of eighteenth-century enlightenment which characterises the Assembly Rooms, where his *Playboy* was to do its tilting — that he might be safe in challenging Dublin: but here in Edinburgh what he really had to worry about was Galway. And so indeed it proved: his *Playboy* was unlikely to fly on one wing very far, but the great film director had hopelessly misread the standards against which he would be judged in Edinburgh. Galway had sent its Druid Theatre Company in 1980 and 1982, and to anyone who had seen its *Playboy* or indeed its *Shadow of the Glen* in the latter year, Synge had attained an ideal in delicacy and authenticity almost impossible for others to reach. Bolger might typify new writing for theatre at the end of the decade: Garry Hynes' company and her Chinese-precise direction opened up the new world in recreating the classics at the decade's beginning. The small space of the Edinburgh student Bedlam was conquered and possessed by Galway with a permeation far beyond the Tudors in Ireland even as reinvented for one of Druid's original plays. A cast trained to a hair, a timing, a sense of mutual relations, a finesse in blocking, a mastery of individuality and ensemble, were all of a professionalism the Royal National Theatre (London) would be proud to own and wise to adopt. And Druid had used its week-long visits with maximum publicity effectiveness, leaping far beyond pre-production exposure norms with announcements of Bailey's Irish Cream reception and greetings to deliver publicly to the Lord Provost of Edinburgh (himself) from the Lord Mayor of Galway (herself), thus entertaining civic reporter coverage, the whole orchestrated with a captivating gentleness by Jerome Hynes whose soft embassy melted some of the most hard-bitten Festival critics into attendance. That was in 1980, of course; when Druid was proclaimed as bringing Synge to Fringe '82, every carpet was red for them. No Finneys, Riggs or Jacksons were needed to woo audiences to their *Playboy*: the word 'Druid' was enough. Nor were Druid, for all their most effectively-deployed modesty, noticeably apprehensive about facing mighty Edinburgh: they were far more anxious, when the time came, about showing their *Playboy* on the Aran Islands. But in Aran also apprehensions were groundless.

Yeats had less difficulty in finding authentic voices in Edinburgh, partly because the content of song and dance in so many of the plays may help stifle the pain induced by cod-Gaelic adulterated by Yeatspeak. That is, if song and dance are well done, and the Fringe has been fortunate in many a decent attempt from darkest Oxbridge or labyrinthine London. But, Druid-style, fine entries from Ireland up the ante, as the poker-players put it. Jim Sheridan brought over his Project Arts Centre's Yeats plays in the late 1970s: the Fringe might have few survivors to recall the student triumphs of twenty years before, but Sheridan's work followed its grasp of the higher promonteries. They might not equal the harpist who entranced Festival audiences in 1959 (all the more with a judicious *Scotsman* photograph swung by the diplomacy of the Irish Festival Players' all-purpose factotum Basil Peterson, late of the Irish Air Corps). But their diminutive dancer could enchant any Celtic hero with her (probably Indian) magic, their percussion was both military and haunting, and their cast of heroes were strong and disciplined, finely juxtaposing their tragedy of *On Baile's Strand* with the mockery of the thieves who begin and end it. Their venue was the Richard Demarco Gallery, and their impresario the voluble, valuable, valedictory visionary Richard Demarco himself, happily ready to extend Celticism to his own Italian inheritance: in fact, he would house major exhibitions linking Ireland and Scotland in fine art, most notably through that pivot of Irish–Scottish mutual admiration, Christopher Murray Grieve, aka Hugh MacDiarmid, to whose memory Demarco devoted a major conference. He intersected MacDiarmid with Yeats (whose likenesses made for another inescapable Demarco exhibition): the intersection was appropriate, even though none of the audience or even the inspired impressario may have known that Yeats and Grieve had intersected their pee-streams on a Dublin road in the early hours of the morning in 1929.

Project Arts and Druid took matters into their own hands, although Demarco's crusading enthusiasms for Celticism certainly sped the call for Project. Yet when Dr Michael Cuthbert, of Heriot-Watt University, took over the Edinburgh College of Art in Lauriston Place in 1985 for an Edinburgh-Dublin Festival-within-the-Festival he did well with Edinburgh use of Irish material, but Dublin was much weaker in its presence, and its Scottish consciousness small. Spaces were much better than Demarco could offer Sheridan in the late 1970s (but Sheridan had used the long narrow approach of Demarco's gallery to make miraculous changes of dimension so that length where needful became breadth, and we could be transported from imaginary seashore to claustrophobic ovens).

The 1985 bouquet had too much of the ad hoc about it — or as a Cockney Scottish Nationalist of the time used to pronounce it, 'haddock' — and the haddock had some antiquity to some of its odours. There was a Shaw pot-pourri on theatre, somewhat self-destructively entitled *Excuse All My Twaddle* and drawn from his letters to Ellen Terry and Mrs Patrick Campbell in what critics complained was a wooden, static, parlour manner. (The audience were fortunate if it did not reach the tedium with which Rex Harrison droned a linked choice of the Shaw theatre criticisms on the official Festival in the late 1970s: he was of course famous for his performance as Professor Higgins, but Eliza Doolittle would not have stood more than a minute of this.) There were collages of Gogarty, and of O'Casey, and a fine recital of John McCormack's favourite songs (including, hilariously,

'When you wish upon a star', usually associated with the Blue Fairy in the Disney *Pinocchio*). But its highest point turned on a transformation of an over-hardy perennial, the one-person play. In general the Fringe programme could be trusted to yield several too many of these, in which some giant of universal culture is resurrected, sometimes from an obscurity just or unjust, and all too frequently showing clear signs of the looted biography from *I-am-born* to *I-died-and-buried-myself.* The Edinburgh-Dublin hosted *Howard's Revenge,* a new play by Edinburgh's foremost historical playwright of the day, Donald Campbell, who discovered J.B. Howard, the Irish founder of Edinburgh's Lyceum Theatre a century previously, as he tried to rehearse his major speech in the stage adaptation of Scott's *Rob Roy* in the intervals of violent altercations with the invisible lighting technician who expressed *his* displeasure by pitching the theatre into Stygian darkness from time to time. During his dries in rehearsal, and between his abuse of the light, Howard (fully realised in all of his Irishry by Finlay Welsh under the direction of Sandy Neilson) managed to recall enough of his life to give a multi-dimensional portrait of an actor-manager on the English theatrical periphery. He even alternated a real Irish accent with a cod stage one for reminiscences of his performance in Boucicault. The result was that we witnessed a play about the theatre which at the same time was a wholly believable hour of the life of a man whose biographical revelations made every sense in the context of what he was doing, instead of bio-picking neither credibly nor theatrically. It is the difference between a recitation — or an audition — and a play. It was all the more appropriate for Edinburgh-Dublin since Ireland had forgotten it ever gave birth to Howard and Scotland gave scarcely a thought to what it owed him.

The honours lay with Scottish theatre in 1985. Ireland is so frequently an uneasy subject for Scots that Campbell's success with Howard failed to generate the inducement for emulation that might have been hoped. Campbell was in any case a playwright who had cut his teeth on subjects somewhat — if not remotely — alien to his ancestral culture: his greatest play is surely *The Jesuit*, on the martyrdom of St John Ogilvie. On the other hand, the Traverse in the 1970s had produced someone's appallingly inept play about the Dublin Easter Rising, *Would You Look at Them Smashing All Those Lovely Windows?* which rivalled the vilest parish pageants of the Golden Jubilee Year, 1966. The early 1970s were not the best time of signals from Ireland anyway, and the Abbey in 1974, while free at last of its Old Man of the Sea, Ernest Blythe, showed little more imagination in bringing the Yeats *Sophocles' King Oedipus*, in a dutifully grim performance in answer to invitation from the official festival. Theatrically, Ireland in the 1970s often seemed to have little new to say, and less new to say about it. The new mood of the 1980s finally achieved its Edinburgh breakthrough on the semi-official level when the Abbey was asked to return, in 1986, not to the Edinburgh International Festival but to the Fringe, specifically by Bill Burdett-Coutts, to perform in the Assembly Rooms annually leased by him. The Abbey was in fact a Scottish watchword (even in its long Blythe years as an Irish cliché): it was the world's first state subsidised theatre. But the Abbey production brought by Burdett-Coutts was very much the new Abbey, a devastatingly revolutionary total-theatre version of Patrick Kavanagh's *The Great Hunger* with mime, dance (or, more exactly, 'lep'), pose, running and everything from vision to stylised contemplation that came to the hand of the highly artistic adapter, Tom MacIntyre. Burdett-Coutts radiated ecstasy with his import, even on the first day of performance when about half the audience left in the highest of dudgeon, having apparently taken the title, *The Great Hunger*, to allude to their ancestral privations leading to their own surviving forebears' settlement in Britain, only to be greeted by this superb avante-garde expressionism conveying the varieties of sexual and artistic frustration suffered in County Monaghan a century later by a poet unknown to them. The plaudits rained down on the Abbey and its courageous host, but in what should have been anxious hours between the box office slaughter of the innocents and the conquest of genuine votaries acquired by the rapture of the critics, Burdett-Coutts showed firmly that the shrewd head running the Assembly Rooms was driven by a genuine artistic heart.

The Assembly Rooms contained a variety of theatre-spaces of varying effectiveness, the finest going to the Irish in 1986. As a venue it was fashionable, especially to a number of English critics who were apparently incapable of finding any other save the Traverse (and wherever Oxford and Cambridge might be displaying themselves). Box office-wise the English critics were in any case less important than the Scots, whose habitual readers knew them, if not their faithers, and could judge their reliability over the non-festival months, and accounted for the bulk of the available audience. The Irish were usually obsessed with their habitual yearning for London approval and a little too ready to consider Edinburgh as Corkbound travellers in slow trains thought of Limerick Junction. But once in the Festival the Irish learnt that a Fringe First from the *Scotsman* was the highest, and also in sales effects the most lucrative, award on offer, save for subhuman exhibitionists named comedians in pursuit of Perrier: and those of them capable of exerting themselves towards salvation, like Owen O'Neill and Ian Macpherson, became playwrights. The Abbey won its Fringe First (Irish productions were eligible even with prior performance at home where Britain could only win if they had no more than six performances before the Festival, a nice case of discrimination albeit, of course, unfair in robbing the Irish of a grievance), and learnt that this had much more to tell its accountants than the news that some London daily's representative had fallen for the second female lead. (The Assembly Rooms actually did rather better when the London *Independent*'s chief Arts reporter became enamoured of one of the venue's staff, and hence gave up all pretence at interest elsewhere, even Oxbridge and the Traverse. I omit any telltale chronological exactitude: sometime in the last twenty years.)

Tom MacIntyre made a triumphant return in 1992, it must be added, with *Fine Day for a Hunt* brought by Punchbag Theatre. (Punchbag itself made other successful returns, as did Rough

Magic, the producers of O'Kelly's *Bat the Father Rabbit the Sun*.) *Fine Day for a Hunt* was staged in the Demarco Galleries, which at that time occupied a great building on Blackfriars Street, new to it since its days of *On Baile's Strand*, and subsequently taken over (and unused) by the Italian Institute. Demarco had begun its theatre work there by staging productions in what appeared to be a coal-cellar whose street door accidentally swung open during one Beckett production, *Company*, thus obliging the producer to interpolate a plaintive request to close it into his text, much as Beckett is inaccurately supposed to have interpolated Joyce's 'Come in' to an intruder when amanuensing *Finnegans Wake*. But by 1992 the coal-hole had been abandoned and a magnificent space accessed on the top floor which brought to life everything imaginable from three lascivious witches (in fiddle, in flute and in fits) for a production of nebular fragments *Towards Macbeth* to culminate in the monastic repossession of Inchcolm Island in the adjoining Firth of Forth, all the way down to an ill-fated staging of Howard Barker's banal poem *Gary the Thief* whose title protagonist not only began proceedings nude and uncomely, but also defecated at the outset, apparently involuntarily rather than in an appropriate anticipation of the two hours tedium that followed. *Fine Day for a Hunt* could ask no finer field, even if neither the externality nor the excrement were required (which, considering the subject, they might have been). MacIntyre has done more to energise theatrical metaphor than any playwright perhaps since Aristophanes, and even the most vigorous blood sports fanatic could hardly recall a more clinking run, as the rising and falling elites were noisily and drastically dissected as thoroughly as their unfortunate vulpine victims.

The Assembly Rooms in 1986 made a second coup by bringing the Dublin Gate one-man Beckett *I'll Go On*, with Barry McGovern, based on *Molloy*, *Malone Dies* and *The Unnameable*, surgically precise in its conveyance of differing intonations of Irish identity, Molloy banal Catholic, Malone expiring Protestant, and the unnameable, of course, unnameable. The *coup de théâtre* at the beginning was gorgeous, with the entire Assembly audience apparently witnessing a horrible case of stage-fright as a voice rang from the wings insisting it couldn't go on, it wouldn't go on, it wouldn't go on, it would go on, it mightn't, it shouldn't, and on it went until finally its owner went on, to thunderous and exceedingly relieved applause. No entrance can have won a more enthusiastic hand in the Festival. It made one realise that Vladimir and Estragon had been exceedingly abrupt and businesslike in getting on the stage before their play even began, though as aficionados know *En Attendant Godot* is in fact a French Resistance thriller. Lighting in the Assemblies was not always a thing of beauty, but *I'll Go On* was as perfect in its lighting as *Howard's Revenge* (by script demand) had been electrically heinous. Malone in particular was enabled to die with mausolear shades of green, cream, white. I still keep on my wall the press-pack photo of his form apparently entombed at the wrong end of eternity: I wasn't at the press conference, but had noticed someone putting a pack in the garbage outside the Assembly Rooms, and, it being a Beckett production, I felt it an appropriate piety to retrieve it.

Beckett had made it on the official Festival before this, in fact Festival director Frank Dunlop had brought over the great Warrilow, in Klurman productions from the United States for a Beckett feast in his very first year, 1984 (a Beckett feast would be a fast if the word in other meanings did not negate the icy precision timing literally every breadth, and very necessary too for the particular play which consists of nothing else). But McGovern by being old Beckett was very new Beckett to Edinburgh, which by now was thinking of Beckett as one of its old reliables, almost the Harry Lauder of Irish playwrights. Beckett himself had not, of course, come to Edinburgh in 1984 (or 1986) so far as anyone knew, but during his feast/fast, two *Daily Express* reporters had been led to squat at Edinburgh Airport in the conviction that they were about to get *the* Festival scoop in his arrival, and there they remained the livelong day in patient expectation … waiting for Beckett.

Having found Edinburgh, Ireland made itself at home.

Dunlop brought the Gate over himself in 1987 with its unmatchable *Juno and the Paycock* where the Dublin tenements arose on the Lyceum stage in all of their ancient horror (the Lyceum had produced an occasional horror of an O'Casey tenement in its own right, in the past, but the horror had been unintentional). Dunlop's successor, Brian McMaster, made friends with Patrick Mason at the Abbey, and the late 1990s saw several productions from him, reflecting his growing Hibernicisation. Mason showed a sensitive awareness of Irish subtleties, more appreciatively than most Irish persons might have shown, but initially he also showed the Achilles heel of Dublin theatre, the arrogant conviction that Belfast is, culturally speaking, its plaything, when Belfast has made it all too clear that it is not. The Abbey's *Well of the Saints* delighted Edinburgh audiences — apart from the Saint himself sounding like the Rev Dr Ian Paisley, which was damned as a joke in indifferent taste and in artistic discombobulation. The richness of the individual performances otherwise, and the beauty of their utterance, offset this, and perhaps the effect might have implied an alienation of Christianity from true Irishness with which Synge might sympathise, but it was still deplored. The modernisation and commercialisation of the miracle hinted by the replacement of traditional water drawing with a tap for the second Act, Edinburgh was ready to forgive if not to forget. The Ulster accent(s) returned to avenge themselves in 1995 when Mason brought Frank McGuinness' *Observe the Sons of Ulster Marching to the Somme*, culturally enshrining the same disillusionment reflected seventy years earlier in England (*Journey's End*) and the USA (*What Price Glory?*) and only capable of theatrical utterance for Northern Ireland now, for the Somme had been as sacrosanct in Belfast as the Easter Rising of the same year in Dublin, and Belfast had lacked an O'Casey to challenge it (though no doubt it could have supplied its equivalent of an Abbey riot in reply). The Mason production was intensely moving, and intellectually profound, marred only by some signs of Mason's undue civility to Dublin assurance that any southerner can do an Ulster accent, as great a fallacy in its way as the English conviction of the ease of Irish vocality. Edinburgh was very much the wrong place for Dublin to stick out a pseudo-Ulster neck: the Scots know where the different shades of the northern accent lie. But, apart from that, Mrs Lincoln, everyone liked the play, other than London critics instructed by their provinciality that they must not.

By this time Mason and McMaster had decided that the Edinburgh official Festival was ready for something a little more modern in theme, having progressed to modern authorship with the great (and by now much Fringe-performed) McGuinness, and Mason proved an interpreter in full harmony with the art of Tom Murphy in staging *The Wake*. Here too were ideal shades of parallel and contrast for an urban-rural Scotland facing the same awkward and undissolved blends in past and present. Appropriately, some of Murphy's premières had been with Druid Theatre, though in its post-Edinburgh days. Mason's hand was now securely Irish. The Hibernicised Englishman had ensured his Scottish welcome, which was more than could be said for the English director of the Gate *Salomé* in 1989, the multiplex playwright Stephen Berkoff, who departed from his Edinburgh Festival production by denouncing his Irish cast and reconvening in London with a new cast headed by himself as Herod. He may, of course, have meant to out-Herod Herod. Ireland had in fact given him a Salomé to die for and a Iokanaan for whom Wilde might have threatened to die, and his lighting man made Iokanaan in his cistern visible (reverentially Dali-esque) while still alive, and well worth the visibility, but blocking and movement recalled Conan Doyle's *The Maracot Deep* in its action on the Atlantic sea-floor, and Berkoff chose to improve on Wilde's borrowings from Ezekiel for the highly Old Testament Iokanaan by interpolating the very different language of Jesus, and the young Syrian and his adoring friend the page of Herodias were apparently played as ancient eunuchs, and it seemed altogether as though London had been given very much the worse part when Berkoff flounced back to it. The Edinburgh International Festival — and Ireland — have been ever so much more fortunate in

Patrick Mason. Perhaps some day he might bring a *Salomé* — in the language in which Wilde wrote it, though not, perhaps, in the language in which Ezekiel wrote it.

Naturally, Ireland will continue to imply work of interest, if not always of excellence. The only time it seriously won a reputation for tedium was in 2000 when *The Barbaric Comedies* came to the Festival. Not having seen the production, I have no views on it. I had been in Northern Ireland, witnessing barbaric comedies of a presumably different kind. But on my return I was startled at the number of normally sane and shrewd acquaintances who complained about boredom at *The Barbaric Comedies*. They were not people easily bored: I do not risk acquaintances who are easily bored (apart from my readers). The word is seldom much present in Edinburgh Festival time, apart from employment by critics from London, who think it barbaric not to be bored in 'the provinces'. But I do not much rely on fellow critics of the theatre, no doubt from childish feelings of professional rivalry. And, it must be said, I am not alone. Most Edinburgh Festival and Fringe criticism is less influential in writing than in speech. Word of mouth sells far more tickets than word on page does. There has indeed been a marked decline in respect for newspaper critics in recent years. The *Scotsman*, under the Arts Editorship of the late Allen Wright, had notoriously high and largely reliable standards. Wright was a great enthusiast for Irish theatre in Scotland, drew many constructive lessons from it for Scotland, and prided himself on being descended maternally from the Allens of the bog of Allen. But the paper never found a satisfactory Arts Editor after his disablement by strokes, in the early 1990s, and its sale to the Barclay brothers resulted ultimately in downgrading of gallant but unfashionable companies, and an embarrassing pursuit of London trends. The Scottish public, purchasers of the bulk of Festival tickets, came to rely more and more on word of mouth, and up to now Ireland could expect good street credibility. *The Barbaric Comedies* somewhat impaired that. It may be unjust, but there it was.

And now there rise before me in the ghosts of so much Irish

greatness in Edinburgh that I flee in the best Ricardian manner wishing them every success in not being smothered or beheaded by some future Richmond. How can I omit Donal O'Kelly's *Catalpa* of 1995 when the Fenian rescue was one-manned even unto its own unsuccessful Hollywood scriptwriter and its own sea-going vessel and not simply the intransigent John Devoy but the very ramificatory process of his endless conspiracy and the deeply sympathetic figure of the innocent American captain ensnared by the sinister liberators? A fine expression of where to take our pursuit of history after Bolger, and a startlingly objective one, O'Kelly giving every participant, even to inanimate equipment, its fair means of self-expression. Or how could I suppress the wholly insuppressable *Mother of All the Behans* resurrected immortally by Rosaleen Linehan first discovered by the audience in the hospital bed of her last days whence she would fly rejuvenated cascading corsets from the back of a screen to remember the glories of the family insofar as her scriptwriting son Brian allowed her to see them, not but what the occasional delay might be caused as when a drunk blundered in the Assembly Rooms stage window from the alley outside to express his regret that the lady did not seem very well and the audience waited with utter civility naturally assuming it to be part of the action and God knows *The Hostage* (which, yes, had also had its Edinburgh moments) sometimes benefited from the unscheduled appearance on stage of her son Brendan its author? And — oh, alright, Bolger, send in the leather jackets to shut me off, the next frontier is mine.

MÁRIA KURDI & CSILLA BERTHA

Hungarian Perspectives on Brian Friel's Theatre after *Dancing at Lughnasa*

1. Friel in Hungary: Context and Productions — Mária Kurdi

Friel appeared in Hungary relatively early: the beginning of the reception of his drama there dates back to the significant year of 1968, which witnessed the translation and successful radio production of *The Loves of Cass McGuire* (1966). The choice of the play was accidental rather than inspired by a conscious process of selection from the writer's first works, yet the discovery of Friel can be seen in the context of intellectual ambitions to bring the latest of quality foreign literature to the attention of the Hungarian public, which had not much access to western cultures other than through printed material, television and theatre, provided those passed as politically correct by the official standards of the era. *Cass* was by all means of the kind, and so was, perhaps more surprisingly, *The Freedom of the City* (1973) whose translation came next, in 1974.

Hungarian drama itself had a flourishing period in the 1970s and 1980s, when censorship was tending to lose of its former rigidity and authors had already learnt how to utilise subtext to the full and make comments about the distorting effects of the socialist system in sophisticated, roundabout ways. The comic mode had its hey-day, given its ability to mask the otherwise quite distressing experience of individual limitations and various forms of social corruption. To offer an example for the homemade theatre that 'entertained' the Hungarian audience while Friel's works were produced one after the other in Ireland and

worldwide, I choose *A szájhős* (*The Braggart*) (1980) by István
Csurka for a brief analysis.

The protagonist of Csurka's play, Lajos Dékány is the freshly
appointed chief columnist of an influential newspaper. The first
scene shows him taking an English lesson, with the task set to
memorise sentences from Oscar Wilde's *The Happy Prince*. Like
the gold-covered prince upon his high column, the socially as
well as financially successful thirty-seven-year-old Dékány
suddenly realises that his world is a sham and he must rebel
against unjust practices and thus grow up at last. First he tries to
turn against his father-in-law by having his corrupt and self-
serving transactions revealed, but the shrewd family patriarch is
too well connected to the political power to be undermined.
Next Dékány intends to expose himself as an incompetent,
morally flawed man whose success was made possible through
compromises and betrayals. This plan also fails because his
decisions remain on the verbal level like a language exercise: he
lacks the courage to face public trial. His identity crisis is
indicated by the purchase of a skeleton made of plaster that he
cuddles and talks to as his twin, his alter-ego, both of them
being spiritually dead in spite of their physical existence. Unlike
the story of *The Happy Prince* and more in the vein of a Wildean
social comedy turned sour, Dékány finally returns to his former
way of doing what his social interests dictate and prevents his
father-in-law, whom someone gave up in the meantime, from
being brought before court. Immersed in the system
irretrievably, he accepts the state of finding himself reduced to a
living skeleton that stays where put.

A major event, coinciding with the country's decisive political
transformation in 1990, was the publication of the volume
containing *Philadelphia, Here I Come!*, *Translations*, and *The
Communication Cord* in Hungarian. After such a prelude, the 1990s
was also the decade when Friel became more widely known in
Hungary. The fast growing fame of *Dancing at Lughnasa* reaching
the country in a relatively short time, the play was performed by the
József Katona Theatre of Budapest in the 1993-94 season with

glowing success: the Hungarians do appreciate dance and music, the wilder the better. Having the sisters very well cast and duly individualised, yet the production failed to reflect on the important dimension Father Jack's stories provide. In 1996 mainly students and academics could enjoy *Translations* performed in English at the University of Debrecen. The timing of the premiere on the eve of the 40th anniversary of the Hungarian revolution of 1956 proved aptly chosen to remind all of the links between the fates of the two small nations pressurised by foreign powers during their history. 1999, the year of Friel's seventieth birthday, saw the presentation of *The Communication Cord* at the theatre of Sopron. In spite of the production's mixed critical reception, the commentators agreed that the setting managed to evoke both the authentic milieu and its imitation.

Philadelphia, Here I Come! had its Hungarian premiere in early 2001 in Kaposvár. The stage interpretation was the work of director András Léner and translator Kornél Hamvai, who ambitiously refreshed the 1990 translation for this particular production. Playing it under the title *Philadelphia, nincs más út!* (*Philadelphia, No Other Way!*), they dismantled the uncertainty in Friel's text, their choice being reinforced by Public, jacket on and suitcase in hand, actually departing at the end. The father figure was similarly 'explained' for the audience: the gestures of love only faintly showing in Friel's old man were blown into the act of tiptoeing into his son's room at night to stroke him and displaying signs of split-mindedness when back in the kitchen. The question arises whether the audience, though in another land and at another time, should not also be allowed to think more for themselves about the plight of the characters as intended by their author. On the other hand, *Philadelphia*'s success in Hungary was well earned by the inventive presentation of the two Gars. The normally clothed Public Gar was paired with a Private Gar always wearing black like a shadow, which interpretation was in place and not overdone, as was the trick of Private first appearing through the wall or standing in the frame of the mirror when Public looked into it. Ultimately, the Kaposvár production made its

audience aware of Gar's essential problem as that of a young man
trying to place himself in an unpredictable world.

2. 'Exiles from Both Places': The Original Plays — Csilla Bertha

> *You're unhappy in the world you inhabit and you're
> more unhappy with the fictional world you create; so
> you drift through life like exiles from both places.*
>
> Brian Friel, *Give Me Your Answer, Do!*

'Who would like to choose Synge's drama as the subject for
his/her MA thesis?' — asked my professor, László Országh. None
of us, all English majors, had ever heard about this playwright
before. Professor Országh then spoke about Synge briefly but so
warmly that I hastened to be the first to volunteer. Thus began
my 'romancing through a romping lifetime' with Irish literature,
before Irish literature in its own right or any Irish studies were
introduced into Hungarian university curricula. I immediately fell
in love with Synge's work, later with Yeats' and some of their
contemporaries, always feeling a deep kinship between Hungarian
and Irish history, literature, sensibilities. But not until I, along
with other Irish scholars from countries behind the iron curtain
were invited for the first time to a conference of the *International
Association for the Study of Irish Literatures* in Graz, Austria in
1984, did my horizon expand to include contemporary Irish
writers for none of their books were then available in Hungary.
Anthony Roche's talk at that conference on Brian Friel's
Translations reconfirmed for Hungarians the sense of familiarity
of Irish literature in general and in particular the relevance of the
issues dramatised in the play. As it happened, a few years later an
especially domineering Romanian customs officer known as the
'pig woman', triumphantly confiscated approximately seventy
books from our backpacks, including several copies of Friel's plays
in Hungarian translation with my introduction, together with
copies of my book in Hungarian on Yeats' drama. When she
turned her back on us for a second, my husband managed to save

some books by quickly shovelling them back into his pack. We were taking those books to friends in Transylvania, not the Dracula-country (although it became that under the reign of Ceausescu) but the old part of historical Hungary that was handed over to Romania in the 1920-21 Treaty of Versailles. Hungarians — approximately three million then, diminishing in number since — thereafter suffered from the cultural genocide of chauvinistic Romanian policy. Romanian became the official language, Hungarian schools were turned into Romanian schools, Hungarian cultural institutions were closed or Romanianised, place-names and often personal names became forcefully Romanianised (for a while even the mention of the original Hungarian place-names in print was punishable), books from Hungary or in Hungarian were confiscated during raids on the homes of resident Hungarians or at the borders as mine were. Friel's *Translations* thus dramatised present reality for Hungarians as late as ten to fifteen years ago. It also appealed to the historical memory of centuries of various forms of colonisation.

Translations had its successful Hungarian premiere at Debrecen University when Patrick Burke from Dublin guest-directed it with student actors in 1996. Even as late as that the haunting feeling of familiarity sometimes proved traumatic. The young woman acting Sarah often broke into tears while rehearsing her role. She was from Transylvania. The deprivation of a people of their language, the forceful changing of old place-names, the erasure of life in ancient settlements were not literature for that actress but living experience as they were for a great part of the audience.

Not surprisingly, together with the parallels in Hungarian historical experience, literary parallels also abound. *The Wedding Feast at Suza* by András Sütő, a Transylvanian-Hungarian play, provides the closest literary parallel with *Translations* — coincidentally, both plays were written in the same year. Both plays depict a tragic loss of collective and individual human values and dramatise a wide scale of social, political, and human attitudes. *The Wedding Feast at Suza*, a historical play about Alexander the Great colonising Persia and attempting to culturally and linguistically assimilate the Persians, actually becomes a metaphorical-parabolical treatment of the plight of the Hungarians in Romania and in those other neighbouring countries where Hungarians must now live as a minority, under similar circumstances. Alexander, forcing Graeco-Macedonian reign, religion, culture, and language on the Persians, plans, for instance, to assure the future annihilation of Persian language and culture and its replacement by the Greek through collecting the babies to be born out of the marriages decreed between Persian girls and Greek soldiers. This new generation, to be separated from their mothers in infancy, will be brought up in Greek culture exclusively.

Sütő, one of the greatest living masters of the Hungarian language, has dedicated much of his art to preserving language, 'our central treasure'. 'The use of language is such a natural human right that it should not even have to be declared as such, yet it becomes necessary to insist on it as long as chauvinism, this seven-headed dragon of our century devours mother tongues, among other things', as he contends. That 'seven-headed dragon' devouring the Hungarian language in the twentieth century, had previously filled itself with the Irish language in the nineteenth. Both Friel's *Translations* and Sütő's *The Wedding Feast at Suza*, while dramatising crucial moments of this process, offer a complex, poetical, and philosophical rather than factual or chronological examination thus opening up the particular cases to include generally recognisable, fundamental human feelings, responses, values, rights, losses.

Friel's plays of course give much more to readers and audiences than just moving political, national-cultural parallels, but that sense of familiarity for Hungarians survives also in encountering his other, less overtly historical-political plays. Moreover, the Hungarian practice of reading behind the lines prompts allegorical readings more easily whether the layers of political allegory are intended to be there or not. Friel's plays continue to speak to Hungarian readers and — alas, less frequently — to theatre-goers, probably with more immediacy than they do to many audiences all over the world. His plays of the Nineties reflect on the changing world not only of Ireland but also of Hungary — this time more closely that of present-day Hungary rather than that of the neighbouring countries where Hungarians live as a minority. Both Ireland and Hungary, at different stages of post-colonialism, have to face the dangers of globalisation, losing national-cultural tradition, heritage, and identity whether due to (concealed) external pressure or self-betrayal. Friel's recurring preoccupation in his latest plays with the artist's role, function, duty, and possibilities under such — and any — circumstances also echoes Hungarian writers' anxiety over their increasing helplessness and powerlessness to heal, having lost the artist's, the poet's original shamanistic powers.

After the huge world success of *Dancing at Lughnasa* many admirers of Friel's work wondered if the success would make him dizzy and drunk and would he seek easier solutions afterwards or would he stop writing since such a popular and critical success can hardly be surpassed. Yet his plays of the Nineties amply testify to his great integrity and self-discipline. He does not recycle the achievements of the exceptionally successful *Lughnasa* but rather goes on searching for new ways of approaching problems and investigating many of his earlier questions. When he revisits the themes and concerns of previous plays, he does not repeat himself but adds new angles to his earlier explorations and deploys new dramatic techniques with great refinement and subtlety.

The Irish drama of the Nineties shows a closer relationship with Synge and Yeats' theatre of the Irish Revival at the turn of the century than with that of the 'second revival' of the preceding thirty years, according to Fintan O'Toole. O'Toole goes on to point out the important difference that the newly emerging unified nexus of time and place is no longer that of Synge's 'single cultural entity' of a shared Ireland[57] but of the individual, of fragments, of 'isolated worlds, closed entities'.[58] Undoubtedly his perceptive observations hold true of contemporary Irish drama in

general but in the case of Brian Friel's plays of the Nineties the
continuity with his earlier work is at least as conspicuous as the
changes. One of the striking features of Friel's drama — at least
from the outside, from, in our case, a Hungarian vantage point —
is just its coherence, integrity, and consistency in linking the
individual plight with that of a whole culture, in dramatising the
most private, psychological aspects of a character in their relation
to tradition or its lack, metaphorically representing the state of the
country or culture and not just fragments of it, reflecting, and
reflecting on, cultural and ontological states.

Christopher Murray's description of the Irish theatre of the
Nineties illuminates Friel's drama in particular: 'Home, history,
identity and intertextuality [...] trends as much as themes [...]
stem from a single polarity, that between tradition and
innovation, always the pulse of Irish theatre.'[59] History, in Friel's
plays of the Nineties, has mostly become absorbed in personal
histories or supplies the background for possible allegorical or
metaphorical readings. Intertextuality, in addition to a dense web
of references to his own earlier work and many other sources,
appears in the translations — adaptations whose number in the
Nineties equals that of the original plays. Home and identity, in a
transformed, sublimated, and increasingly metaphoricised
manner, have become rather a loss, a lack, a search for origin and
source, sometimes combined with a longing for some (indefinite)
faith, the world beyond. The negative presence of a spiritualised
home underlines its ongoing significance and images of
dislocation, dispossession, exile 'supply Irish writers [including
Friel] with a coded language for the articulation of ontological
states.'[60]

Indeed, one of the central issues in Friel's plays is the search
for home as an 'ontological state'. Home in earlier plays, Ballybeg
in *Philadelphia, Here I Come!, Translations, Aristocrats* or *Dancing
at Lughnasa* was related to a physical locale, both concrete and
microcosmic of Ireland. In the plays of the Nineties home as a
spiritual dwelling, made up of personal, psychological and cultural
meanings, can be conjured up from the memories of the past and

tradition and from the realm of the beyond through ritual, song and dance and the magic power of words, hence the foregrounding of ritual in some recent plays, particularly in *Wonderful Tennessee* (1993). In the others Friel's ever evocative language calls 'to the eye [and ear] of the mind' most vividly (ritualistic) dance, poetic images or sweeping orchestra music thus knitting together more seamlessly than before verbal and bodily expression, broadening the scope of his dramatic means. With this he also demonstrates in doing what he talks about: that the spiritual home can and needs to be created or re-created rather than described by the artist. In the Nineties, Friel seems to have been wrestling more than ever (with the possible exception of *Faith Healer*) with the issue of the nature, risk, and responsibility of art's interfering with lives, the special anguish of artistic creation, the possibility of reaching out to the world beyond and bringing the transcendental inside the human being, and the artist's duty and capability of building up a spiritual home for the individual and the nation.

In *Wonderful Tennessee*, Terry, by bringing his family and friends to the pier whence they hope to sail to the hardly visible — and, for the audience, only embodied in words — Oileán Draoíchta, is attempting a sort of homecoming to the scene of a happy childhood memory with his father and, more importantly, to an experience of community with his family and friends. The uprooted, emptied out contemporary city-dwelling characters have exiled themselves from their cultural heritage and in the course of the play are seeking for means to find their way back. Terry's thwarted plan to buy the island clearly shows that there is no literal return to childhood, to the past, to origin, and that you cannot possess what has become a spiritual value. Shaun Richards rightly contends that 'the play does not return to the source in any naïve or absolute sense' but Friel rather 'attempts to salvage something [from tradition] to provide a creative, regenerative point in the contemporary moment of flux.'[61] Richards deploys Homi Bhabha's term: 'incommensurable elements' that form 'the basis of cultural identifications' and refers to Ashis Nandy's 'critical traditionalism'[62] to name what seems to be in the centre of Friel's attitude to origins and changes in culture, the way cultural homogenisation can be resisted.

The search for home in *Wonderful Tennessee* combines with the quest for 'the necessary mystery'.[63] The spiritual, the mysterious, the ancient oneness with powers beyond the human, Yeats' 'Unity of Being', includes culturally defined as well as generally human contents, as does Friel's play suggest through its layering of Greek and Irish myths, customs, rituals, and Christian symbolism. Although Yeats' mythic world has become only a vague desire a century later, the fullness of the mythic, approached through whatever half-heartedly, self-consciously enacted ritual, offers at least a moment's healing, and a half-believed hope for the possibility of repeating the experience once people have found the means. A very limited form of homecoming, true, and rather the beginning of a journey than an arrival but there are stirrings in the search itself.

In *Molly Sweeney* (1994) home turns into even more imaginative and psychological qualities, not even linked to any metaphorical place or mysterious remnants from the past. The entirely inner landscape of Molly's blindness is composed of fragrance of flowers, memories of childhood bliss, the embrace of water while swimming. Yet the vocabulary and imagery connects all this to the notions of home and dislocation, as Molly's description of her fear of 'exile' on the eve of her operation signifies or as she remembers her desire 'to return home to my own world' after only a 'visit', an 'excursion' to 'the land of vision'.[64] The parable of the dislocated badgers confirms the notion that the intrusion into Molly's state of being equals dispossession. Returning to her own world, like for the badgers to their destroyed home, proves impossible. Moreover, by being deprived of an organic growth according to her own inner laws, she cannot take the values of the past with her upon which to build the future. That is why at the end of the play, in her 'borderline country' she corrects herself, on reflection, from saying that she feels 'at home', into 'Well ... at ease there'.[65] Molly's realisation, as she explains in her last soliloquy, that '[r]eal — imagined — fact — fiction — fantasy — reality' have become all indistinguishable, could be taken as a postmodern recognition of the relativity of all truth, but, as always with Friel, the post-colonial and neo-colonial experience colour the postmodern. The resulting confusion might be similar but the causes, at least partly, differ: it is the interfering of external forces, acting out of self-interest under the guise of charity and benevolence — in Molly's case Frank and Rice — that changed all the points of reference. The 'engrams' in her mind, the 'incommensurable elements' of her being were shattered, and she was robbed of the 'dignity of particularity' — to borrow the Hungarian András Sütő's words.

The subtle characterisation of the three characters as individuals in *Molly Sweeney*, still allows an allegorical reading in which meaning applies to a whole culture. F. C. McGrath's relating Molly's borderline country directly to the Northern Irish experience of the on-going 'colliding historical narratives' and 'different discourses' that construct reality[66] sounds somewhat strained but the play does evoke the all-Irish experience of the danger of neo-colonisation (coca-colonisation), and globalisation which takes away deeper identity, although instead of direct pressure that traditional colonisation works with relies more on the willing (or reluctant) participation of the victim. Frank and Dr Rice each, from (recognised or unconscious) self-interest, change Molly's 'otherness' into something that appears similar to the rest of the (sighted) world, and in the process of assimilating her, they annihilate her autonomous personality and manage to 'other' her to herself — a familiar phenomenon of colonisation. In other words, her operation throws her into 'the visual equivalent of the linguistic displacement of *Translations*'.[67]

Molly Sweeney as political allegory is even more pertinent to the experience of the Hungarians, both in present-day Hungary and, to a lesser degree, in those neighbouring countries where they are in minority, who, after the long period of the darkness (of Communism), having their sense of seeing atrophied, became extremely vulnerable to the dangers that come with sight. Seeing the world with the bewilderment of the newly sighted, values blur, identity falters or disappears, and the brief euphoria of seeming liberation from one kind of limitation is soon followed by the frustration of the brave new world (of immediate neo-colonisation) that does not offer reliable truths, does not support self-esteem nor self-realisation. Similarly, reading *Wonderful Tennessee*, together with Richard Pine, as an 'allegor[y] of a society which has lost its memory, its imaginative hinterland,'[68] as the expression of the need 'to be in touch again' with the past, history and tradition, with the mythical experience, once embedded in the way of thinking and worshipping of the people, makes this play also deeply relevant to the Hungarian experience of recent depthlessness, manipulated confusion, and the frequently occurring sophisticated-sounding contempt for historical identity. *Wonderful Tennessee* exemplifies a stage of the fast-going and intensive process of giving up national-cultural identity resulting in postmodern, neo-colonial emptiness that so far has hardly begun to be addressed in Hungarian drama. Earlier phases of this motion, in which the totalitarian pressure forced people to give up, betray or conceal their identities, found their voice in history-plays, tragedies, symbolical or metaphorical moral or philosophical parables — such as *The Wedding Feast at Suza* — or grotesque tragicomedies, for example, Géza Szőcs's *The Böszörménys of Kisberek* (1994), another Transylvanian-Hungarian play. The latter renders in a hilarious, absurdist satire a small community's desperate attempts at self-betrayal — to appear other than what they are — in the hope of being able to preserve themselves. András Sütő's poetic fantasy *Advent in the Hargita Mountains* (1995), creates a world where a loud cry (of protest) can start a murderous avalanche, an instance of betrayal and self-betrayal — the absence of the 'necessary vigilance' — can cause fatal destruction and self-destruction. Or *Balkan Dove* (1999) by the same author explores paradigms of inauthentic existence in a unique combination of farcically grotesque and tragically symbolic images deploying as much (mockery of) ritual, dance, and song as *Wonderful Tennessee*, asserting 'the necessity to lie' in order to survive on both an individual and a community level. But these

Hungarian plays reflect a more externally subdued than only internally betrayed value-system, a home-losing in a transitory position between anti-colonialism and post/neo-colonialism.

Friel, after setting *Wonderful Tennessee* on a pier at the edge of the world and *Molly Sweeney* in the nowhere land of the bare stage, in *Give Me Your Answer, Do!* (1997) brings onstage a house with a garden, a traditional-looking scene of family and visitors. But this image of a more fixed home proves transitory since the Connellys have had to move constantly from house to house to lessen the rent. (The financially more stable couple, Daisy's parents also had to move frequently, for another reason: because of Jack's kleptomania.) The other scene on stage is the bleak hospital room containing only a bed and uncovered mattress. This is Bridget's 'home' where she is exiled from her family by her autism. The appearance of her environment suggests the dismal quality of her life, and only the nurse's account of her screams and going wild indicates that Bridget has not quite resigned herself to her position. In this homeless world, home emerges somewhere between the (temporariness of the) house and the (tragic permanence of the) hospital.

If Seamus Heaney could say about Sarah in *Translations* that she is a descendant of Cathleen Ni Houlihan, 'struck dumb by modernity'[69] and James and Mark Farrelly could call Molly a 'symbol of an Ireland that lost its vision'[70], then Bridget can be seen as another image of old Ireland not only struck dumb and visionless but also exiled, alienated, locked away into her allotted corner, shrunk into herself from the (post)modern world, with whom no communication seems possible any longer, whom no sacrifice will transform: 'No change. There'll be no change. Ever.'[71] Yet — at the risk of stretching the metaphor too far — we may suggest that old Ireland, even in her silence and exile, through the grief her loss causes, is still a painful, necessary inspiration for the writer, a mememto of (past) potentials. After losing Bridget, Tom the artist was 'struck dumb' — unable to write anything valuable, only to cry out his frustration in the obscenities of pornography. His weekly excursions to her hospital room seem the only encounters that make his creative energies begin to flow again. These are the only occasions when he speaks about his new book, first as part of his fantasy, then at the end more as reality. And these are the only occasions when he builds up worlds out of words, lively, colourful, comic and beautiful images. In his stories to his daughter reality and fantasy become blurred, just as in Molly's account of her inside world but Tom, the writer, might approach the state where 'The body is [...] bruised to pleasure soul, [...] beauty born out of its own despair, [...] blear-eyed wisdom out of midnight oil'.[72]

The necessities advocated in these three recent plays show a growing doubt in the possibility of preserving or reviving values and a declining faith in the home-creating power of the artist. In *Wonderful Tennessee*, Frank speaks about the 'necessary mystery'[73] for faith or creative energy, in *Molly Sweeney* the 'necessary vigilance'[74], the moral responsibility of the artist-doctor might have saved Molly from the fatal intrusion into her life. In *Give Me Your Answer, Do!* Tom has to maintain the 'necessary uncertainty'[75] about his own talent, although the treatment of this uncertainty is somewhat puzzling and misleading. Tom's behaviour is psychologically understandable as throughout the greater part of the play he nervously waits for the assessment of his work, but once it is found valuable, he feels 'no more than a little bit flattered'.[76] Daisy's summing up of Tom's dilemma of selling 'for an affirmation, for an answer', or to keep the 'necessary uncertainty' for creation and, indeed, for being able to continue, because 'being alive is the postponement of verdicts'[77], convincing though it may be in general, sounds disingenuous in the immediate situation since it comes *after* the verdict is given, after David announces that he is willing, actually begging to buy the archive for a great price. The play does not discuss explicitly the issue of selling the archive to an *American* university but Tom's unenthusiastic reception of the news of acceptance may owe something to this hidden layer of signification. David's words describing his task call attention to the relation of this case to that of the Irish in general: 'I am expected to provide all the Irish material. It's an order. "Deliver Ireland, David.""[78] Significantly, Tom turns to Bridget after he refuses to sell his work to the American library. Where does this leave the uncertainty? After this refused but offered appraisal Tom speaks for the first time in a realistic-sounding manner to Bridget about his resuming work on a book he began many years before and now is getting 'a little quiver — a whiff — a stirring of a sense that perhaps — maybe'.[79] Does not that suggest that some certainty and encouragement is, after all, necessary for the writer and might give an impetus to start again, but on his own terms, going back to his source of painful inspiration? Or does his courageous decision to refuse the entirely external appraisal of his value as writer (and the practical advantages it would bring), together with the greater uncertainty of his power to bring any ease into Bridget's life, give Tom strength to concentrate on his internal needs to write? Would not that suggest that, after all, the real artist's deep drive to heal, in the face of not only uncertainty but also of almost certain hopelessness, still persists?

The artist is bound to live in a 'borderline country', being both insider and outsider, participant and observer of what he/she puts into his/her art. Daisy describes this liminality in terms of homelessness and exile: 'You [writers are] unhappy in the world you inhabit and you're more unhappy with the fictional world you create; so you drift through life like exiles from both places.'[80] The play's conclusion, however, seems to overturn this balance with Tom fantasising about taking Bridget away from the earth in a 'golden balloon'. Whether as escape into the world of imagination or suicide, this last speech indicates his attempt to abandon forever the world he inhabits.

The golden balloon, unlike earlier occurances of the attribute 'golden', is a product of pure fantasy. In *Philadelphia, Here I Come!* or *Dancing at Lughnasa,* for instance, 'golden' in the concluding images becomes engraved in the minds of Gar and Michael as something precious, something life-enhancing, each, being artists in their own ways, are aware of the necessity to preserve memory. By the late Nineties even sustaining memories are seemingly gone. In *Give Me Your Answer, Do!* Tom, in order to find any stories to entertain his daughter with, must invent them. When the culture has left behind its memories, then the only resource is imagination, building up a new dreamland, no longer based on any remnants of the past. Yet would that offer a home? Certainly the conclusions of *Molly Sweeney* and *Give Me Your Answer, Do!* are the most pessimistic of all Friel's plays. The first shows the total failure of any kind of artist — with the possible exception of Molly, who, in her despair, arrives at deeper understanding that, however, leads to her death — and the heroic but probably futile efforts of Tom in the second. And yet the helpless, powerless artist has no choice but to go on, as the Hungarian poet phrases it:

> [f]allen face-first on the litter of leaves,
> and still going on,
> waking the tall
> but sleeping poplar,
> not letting the pine forests
> stitch together, with green needles,
> all that is already mythless,
> but still conscience[81]

3. 'The old has given way all right': Rewritings and Adaptations — Mária Kurdi

Intertextuality, brought into play by 'the process of composition known as the palimpsest'[82] enjoys an admitted currency in the contemporary Irish theatre. The closest antecedents, again, are to be found in the revival playwrights', especially Lady Gregory and W. B. Yeats' ambition to re-translate classics. Friel's comparably unfailing interest in narratives and images from other periods and cultures has produced new examples in the 1990s: the three original stage works of his conceived after *Lughnasa* are balanced by a group of three adaptations. These remake their source plays in ways one can viably distinguish according to Christopher Innes's categorisation of motives underlying the practice. *The*

London Vertigo (1990), based on Charles Macklin's *The True-born Irishman* (1761) is a version that gives 'new relevance to the material', whereas *A Month in the Country* (1992) and *Uncle Vanya* (1998) belong to the type that recovers the 'original bite' of classics through their reinterpretation for today's audience.[83] Filtering the original concerns through the experiential and artistic lens of another era, Friel's rewritings and adaptations inhabit a borderline space between cultures and styles, where the themes of history and identity become inherently dialogical, while that of home is evoked by domesticating the distant and/or foreign. At the same time the new versions are self-reflexive, foregrounding their own procedures, which represent particular Frielian qualities and techniques.

In the context of the manifold connections between plays that flank each other or have their pairs across the author's larger oeuvre, it comes as little surprise that the woman-centeredness of *Lughnasa* has its echo in the closely following *The London Vertigo* and *A Month in the Country*. They both are invested with linguistic strategies that refresh their predecessors' somewhat dated variations on the issue of identity primarily from the angle of gender, thereby refocusing individual concerns and problems. Reshaping them in a given environment, Friel's approach must have been influenced by the fact that in contemporary Ireland the transformation and/or revaluation of earlier hierarchies and communal forms tends to redraw the map of social structures, with various groups obtaining new roles and significance. After the decades when Irish women's sexuality was controlled and they 'had to contend with discrimination and inequality'[84], the liberating changes that took place during the 1990s called greater attention to the pitfalls of gender relations and oppressive constraints on female subjectivity in their social and historical relevance and as part of the national as well as human experience.

It is from the assured vantage point of remaining on home territory and the widened perspective of post-colonial times that Friel reforms the eighteenth-century, Donegal-born but anglicised Macklin's comedy under the new title *The London Vertigo*. In the introduction he claims that Mrs O'Dogherty/Diggerty, the Macklin heroine's forced abandoning of the proudly adopted, fashionable Anglophile habits and changing back to 'decent Dublin domesticity' rewrites the author's 'own biography as comedy/farce'.[85] Friel develops this potentially self-reflexive aspect at the expense of the moralising spirit of the original, subverting it by making the Irish male characters, the judges of the woman, at least as ridiculous as her through their hypocrisy and self-importance. Qualifying the second time as an even more hilarious farce, *The London Vertigo* yet offers the insight that the concomitant tensions derive from a fragmented society. As in the only other matching farce of Friel, *The Communication Cord* (1981), the failure of communication, while a matter for laughter, is presented through its links with the effects of the troubled national past.

The colonially determined identity conflict represented by Macklin is complicated in Friel's version with the confusion of gender relations, highlighting the connection of the two through their absurdities. Powerless and excluded from controlling the matters of his home country, O'Doherty seeks to exercise authority in his own house, over his wife first of all. Trapped between the desire for personal freedom and the imperative to adjust her behaviour to the required mores like the Mundy sisters in *Lughnasa*, the woman rebels by double-acting: the conventional replies she gives in self-defence are contrasted with her harshly outspoken asides. The concluding scene restages from Macklin the speech of O'Doherty about having his wife's ways 'mended'[86] only to be followed by a reversal of hierarchical relations. Making fun of the inherent fragility of mimicking patriarchal domination the last word is that of the woman: to rebut her husband's self-congratulating declaration of moral victory, Mrs. Diggerty winks at the audience as she utters the aside 'For the time being!'[87]

In *A Month in the Country* the female protagonists, Natalya and Vera occupy different positions in the late nineteenth-century landowning class, yet they are equally affected by the limitations of women's individuality. The problem for both is revealed through the implications of falling in love with an ineligible young man,

Natalya's son's tutor. This crucial aspect of the narrative lends Friel an opportunity to dramatise their respective ways of coping with the new experience in sharper contours than the source text. Natalya's loss of balance underlies her very first words in the Friel version, voicing dependency as well as utter helplessness: (*Softly, with brittle, almost frantic smile*) 'Dear God — good God — dear, good kind God.[88] Her entrapment between unconventional desire and the internalised public expectations evokes the Frielian theme of the deceptiveness of language: Natalya's attempts to articulate her confusion undermine her rather than accomodate her feelings. Applied to herself, the adjective 'ridiculous' in her vocabulary signals her keen awareness of how she is perceived, most poignantly in the anti-climactic overture of the confession scene: 'I am in love with you. Strange how I can say it so calmly, isn't it? ... I am calculating and treacherous and — look at me — yes, so ridiculous.'[89] The other adjectives in the same bathetic self-characterisation are hallmarks of Natalya's psychic distortion and self-division, which violate her communication with others. Borrowing Elmer Andrew's words, her 'veering wildly from one mood to another, abusing her power and position'[90] demonstrates her frustration in satisfying her emotional needs in any acceptable form. Being 'deprived of the very means of protest or self-affirmation' by the 'cultural conditioning' of her world,[91] she is in a kind of impasse that underlies her misdirected anger and extreme anguish at being left by the young man: 'And who is he [Aleksey] to decide I haven't the courage to throw all this up and go with him! ... The bastard!'[92] Anticipating Molly Sweeney's psychic dislocation, she wishes to exile herself from the usual order, soon to be re-established. In horror, she even refuses Vera's kind consoling gestures: 'For God's sake can't you see it's the normal that's deranging me, child?'[93]

Being a woman as well as a fortuneless orphan thrown at the mercy of relatives, the doubly marginalised Vera, however, gains voice through the medium of music in Friel's version: similarly to Claire in *Aristocrats*, she plays the piano offstage in several scenes and like the sisters in *Lughnasa* her individuality is expressed best without the conventions of verbal language. As a kind of protest that transcends Natalya's self-destructive trust of words, her resort to music offers a powerful critique of patriarchy. When she has accepted the socially advantageous proposal of the well-to-do but boorish neighbour, her obviously necessary decision to submit her body in marriage to the much older man she does not love is counter-pointed by the spiritual freedom that her sensitive piano-playing conveys. Opposed to Natalya, she can even appropriate the tool of language to identify herself within the given order while asserting dignity: 'I'm no longer a child, Natalya [...] nor your younger sister that you can kiss and worm secrets out of and then betray shamelessly. *I am a woman, Natalya, and I am going to be treated like a woman.*'[94]

In *Three Sisters* (1981) and *Fathers and Sons* (1987) Friel's important innovation was to enhance and vary the role of the minor characters. The later adaptations re-employ the device to place the respective heroines' situation and struggle for self-definition in a broader context. Katty, the maid is provided with more space in *The London Vertigo* than in the source play to indicate that as the 'servant of two masters' she can manage only by role-playing amid the multiple social and gender divisions of the colonised society.[95] To complete the female trio, Friel also elevates the role of Arkady's mother, Anna, in *A Month in the Country*, by allowing her to articulate her female experience through telling stories. She reveals the unavoidable acceptance of the secret violation of marital faithfulness, involving silence to match cunning for the sake of appearances: 'And all the years we were married, at the beginning of every month [...] he went to Moscow for three nights [...] to visit a lady there that he loved. [...] And throughout all those years he never mentioned her to me and I never mentioned her to him. Because he loved me, too.'[96] Both witnessing and living the necessary conformity to double standards and intricate rules behind the rules for so long, her old-age wisdom favours emotional vulnerability as the privilege of the 'less deceived'.

Establishing itself as self-conscious theatre, Friel's *Uncle Vanya* incorporates elements from the author's earlier adaptations. In regard to the theme of gender, the portrayal of Elena as 'more acerbic and arguably more sexually vulnerable'[97] than in Chekhov, brings the character closer to the version of Natalya in *A Month in the Country*. As Robert Tracy observes in Friel's *Three Sisters* several of the monologues are broken into dialogues, subverting 'one of Chekhov's ways of emphasising his characters' self-centeredness'.[98] This, however, can be argued, since some of the monologues do stretch beyond their original length toward thorough self-confrontation. In Chebutikin's speech about his medical failure the sense of personal split is enacted by the character addressing himself as 'you', another that he has degenerated into, but who is not really himself. The interior crisis rendered in terms of doubling recalls a significant tendency of the Irish theatre, culminating in Friel's separation of Private and Public Gars in *Philadelphia, Here I Come!* The new version of *Uncle Vanya* revitalises the method which, at the same time, renders the original characters' regular lapse into self-dramatisation[99] more concrete, for instance when Vanya mourns over the lost opportunities in his life: 'Why didn't you fall in love with her [Elena] then and ask her to marry you? I don't know why you didn't, Vanya. I don't understand that. She would be your wife now.'[100]

In explaining the attraction Chekhov's figures held for him, Friel made the cautious remark that they are not unlike members of his own generation in Ireland, behaving 'as if their old certainties were as sustaining as ever'.[101] This notion, however, is complicated in his *Uncle Vanya* by having the characters use a lot of self-referencing as well as expressions of self-doubt that parallels the way unusual situations or just unexpected turns may press people to reconsider the validity of their opinions. Sonya, in love with Astrov, the doctor discusses his efforts to save forests in the presence of Elena and Vanya with a new conclusion that mediates her worries about interpreting another person's ambition: 'Just encourage that milder climate with your forests and eventually — eventually — a society will evolve where learning will blossom and people will become hopeful again and men will treat women more gently and with a little more consideration. [...] Now I'm embarrassed. Sorry, Mikhail. I'm sure that's a complete distortion of what you think.'[102] Not accidentally from the viewpoint of her private concerns and from that of the public debates in both Chekhov and Friel's times alike, it is her mention of the potential development in gender relations that trails off into uncertainty.

Friel's treatment of the Chekhovian characters involves defining them more precisely according to Tracy[103] which, maybe, just serves to reproduce in some way their familiarity for the one-time Russian audience, as it obviously cannot be restored for the contemporary one in Ireland. The insightful and astute, yet intellectually homeless Astrov's original tendency to 'undercut[s] his own gloom',[104] for instance, is reinforced by having him refer to the performing aspect of his actions in the Frielian version, encouraging a double view of them. This, in turn, draws attention to the adaptation being a piece of theatre conveyed through the author's complex choices to replay the old story with new accents that enable it 'to bite' again. Presented to Elena whom he wishes to impress, Astrov's long speech about ecological destruction concludes pointing to both the intended effect and the risks of reception: 'The old must make way for the new. The old has given way all right — that's obvious. But where is the new? [...] To hell with tomorrow — you're going to grab today, aren't you? And if that means some physical imbalance, some biological discord in the future — too damned bad! [...] End of tedious lecture.'[105]

The fact that the year of the premiere of *Uncle Vanya*, 1998 was that of the Good Friday Agreement and its significant political implications lends some piquancy to Friel's extending as well as multiplying the Chekhovian instances when Vanya's mother is engrossed in reading pamphlets into manifestations of an explicit obsession with commenting on the controversial writings. And what is last heard from the stage in the Friel version is not Sonya's exclamation about the hope to rest but the scraping of pens, suggesting the redemptive potential of writing as action through its jointly private and public as well as self-reflexive relevance for both characters and author.

The postmodern fervour of rewriting has reached the contemporary Hungarian theatre as well, yet its fruits are not so varied within the work of any particular playwright as is the case with Friel. It is, however, challenging to draw parallels. Chekhov and Turgenev, who document their society at the end of an era with major changes in sight[106] inspired some Hungarian artists to re-use their texts in ways that refer to the political tensions of the post-1989 period. Károly Szakonyi's stage adaptation of Turgenev's *Fathers and Sons* titled *Nihilisták* (*Nihilists*) (1989), reinterprets the conflict between generations to highlight the young Hungarians' burnt-out state of mind due to the pervasiveness of the lies they were fed by their elders. In this respect, the play shares the theme of the contamination of language with Friel's theatre: its prologue, an innovation, engages Bazarov in a fierce attack on the devaluation of meaning through the use of empty slogans. Andor Lukáts's 1992 film version of *Three Sisters*, on the other hand, remains very much a unique period piece. It places the story 'on a Soviet military base in Hungary between 1987 and 1991, just before the withdrawal of the Soviet troops. [...] present[ing] the life of the colony in its complete hopelessness'.[107] Stranded in a foreign land, the three sisters are psychically victimised by both the misrule and collapse of the imperial system that is all the more powerfully criticised by pointing to the damage it did to its own citizens.

Friel's engagement with the flux of his times and country as Shaun Richards puts it[108] continues in the 1990s in full vigour, as does his recognition and assimilation by the theatre world of other cultures. What gives his original as well as adapted works new energy continuously is the ability to create images and artistic structures that combine the personal and the universal in ways that mould the changing material to achieve new complexities. Being conscious of the call to transcend the deceptions of language, his theatre constantly revisions itself to reach out to and communicate meanings for its various audiences.

EMILE JEAN DUMAY

Dramatic Terræ Incognitæ: A French Perspective

In France, and indeed Europe in general, the Irish stage has for years been highly rated for its plays, performances, actresses and actors, for the poetical quality of the works, their often outlandish features and sanguine characters. Synge's *Playboy of the Western World* is a significant example being seen on French stages — among others, up to the present day. Speaking again about the French scene, it is generally admitted that the next hit was Sean O'Casey for similar reasons. Yet his plays are a challenge to stage, owing to the constant breaks of tone and the need for footnotes — if such things were ever feasible in a theatre.

Nevertheless I have an impression that the French and the Germans alike acclaimed him as a political godsend in the Sixties. Sean O'Casey was performed at the celebrated Berliner Ensemble, and most of his plays were directed on French stages at the same period, when political commitment and anti-colonial stances were praised in drama, to such an extent that many directors tried their hands at directing some impossible pieces of his that French audiences were not prepared to assess properly, in particular where the religious background was concerned.

What is the situation today? Bearing in mind that I am prepared to consider only the Irish dramatists *after* Friel, I find that their plays are comparatively few on French stages but that, paradoxically, many have been translated, if not published.

To date three of Sebastian Barry's plays have been translated into French, one of which, *The Steward of Christendom,* has been published, and performed with some success. Marina Carr remains largely unknown although her *The Mai* exists in print.

Dermot Bolger's plays have started a career: one of them was first performed in France in 1998, then published two years later when it was staged again: *The Lament for Arthur Cleary*. It is to be followed by the publication and performance of *The Passion of Jerome* in Paris in early 2002. Several of Tom Murphy's plays have been — brilliantly — translated, in particular *Bailegangaire*, yet only *A Whistle in the Dark* has found its way onto several French stages. Fine translations of Tom Kilroy's plays have been published, none of which, as far as I know, has ever been staged. Frank McGuinness seems to be more familiar to French audiences today as two of his plays are frequently performed in festivals: *Observe the Sons of Ulster Marching Towards the Somme* and *Someone Who'll Watch Over Me*. This is probably due to the opening of his works on to the French or the world scene, i.e. the Great War in France, and the hostages in Beirut. Conversely, McGuinness has largely contributed to bringing some great plays by European dramatists to the Irish stages, adapting and translating Ibsen, Lorca, Brecht and Chekhov.

One might say that contemporary Irish dramatists are *felt* to be present in France, either in print or occasionally on stages, but have not forcibly asserted themselves. Of course *they* cannot be blamed for the situation. Are they comparatively left aside for their lack of political commitment? Honestly, I do not think so. Or do they stray too far from the picturesqueness of stage-Ireland? French directors and audiences ought to be all the more grateful to them for doing so. Their commitment, as we shall see, is more to man than to systems, and they achieve it by embarking on exploratory ventures born of an Irish tradition in literature: the interplay of dreams and reality as well as a nimble manipulation of time. The only correlative in France in the realm of drama, tentatively speaking, could be the works of Bernard-Marie Koltès.

Critics can agree that one major feature in recent Irish drama is the use and distortion of traditional themes. However, another trait makes them distinctive. The effect of novelty in many of these plays probably comes from the realisation that they display a spirit of adventure. Many of the major plays of the last two decades embark on explorations of one kind or other. They investigate unknown lands, undermined grounds and unsafe areas. Their favourite locations are often 'borderlines', unusual places, interfaces or kinds of tectonic plates with the double meaning of break and junction. A way of evidencing a world in motion, by having events on stage take place somewhere between land and water, between sanity and insanity, history and legend, tradition and rebellion, or even inside walls. One advantage of drama as a specific literary medium is that it allows the spectators to live on either side of the mirror by upsetting not only the chronological frame but all the available data. Consequently realism becomes in its own right a way of exploring hazy, unsteady, unexplored areas instead of merely describing, however innovatively, only one side of things. By so doing, realism turns into genuine poetry.

As spectators and critical readers of such plays, we stand, in the company of the dramatists concerned, between the comfort of a familiar world and the appeal of the unknown — with the subsequent indictment of the familiar as static and immovable as against the poetic delight of any *terra incognita* where everything is liable to happen. The various stage techniques considered here allows them to step beyond clashes and propound dramatic openings laden with dialectic energy. The exploratory process, on the one hand, gradually reveals things and provides certainty, reassurement, explanations. On the other hand, it dissolves the unknown and gives room to an undefiled and potent newfoundworld. Exploring amounts to a revelation experienced on the move, to an epiphany.

One character can be seen as superbly emblematic of the whole process: the Frontier-Guard in Dermot Bolger's *The Lament for Arthur Cleary* (1989). Performing far more than his obvious task of checking passports, he embodies a protean creature who symbolises the ceaseless plying of the play between fantasy and reality, past and present days, life and death. Spectators are constantly led to make out for themselves, after a few minutes' bewilderment, what new place, situation, or person suddenly comes to life through him.

Equally emblematic is a line by the main character of Bolger's *The Passion of Jerome* (1998). Harbouring his illicit love in a high rise council flat in Dublin, he pictures the place by saying sarcastically: 'Ballymun is Antarctica, shoals of shuffling penguins and a few mad scientists studying them.' This spirit of exploration, investigation and probing first appears associated with psychological ends, the point being to extend the understanding of characters and their behaviours by introducing a variety of angles, opening up new vistas and inventing incremental details. Exploration is also essentially and indissolubly linked to curiosity. For instance, it is significant that Bolger, commenting upon his play *The Passion of Jerome*, describes it as strange, as if he were, so to speak, discovering it after the very act of writing, as a new land, even a new planet which one hesitates to set foot on for fear of being engulfed.

A sense of originality and experiment that prevails in this type of creative writing does not always make it immediately perceptible. The dramatists considered in this essay tend to extend the field of the feasible and the unfeasible, by setting up improbable dialogues, by making use of the objectivity of the stage as a place for living creatures, or by taking advantage of it to promote, if not dialogues among the dead, then at least dialogues with the dead, which are far more efficient and inventive than hackneyed flashbacks. Instances can be found in Sebastian Barry's *The Steward of Christendom* and *Our Lady of Sligo,* as well as in Dermot Bolger's long plays: *The Lament for Arthur Cleary, April Bright* and *The Passion of Jerome.* To various extents these works propound a fantastic and/or surrealistic approach of the world they tackle. We, spectators, sit astride or stand on either side of a border.

Watching Barry's plays, for instance, we can observe a man or a woman mentally ill and at the same time his or her psychological and medical inner picture; and as for the main characters, we realise that they live unaffectedly both inside and outside of their own selves with equal intensity. Only the theatre can achieve this, for films, ideally meant for a dreamworld, would lay too much emphasis on the unreal. The theatre imposes physical reality during every minute of a play, whatever the situation is, and so, paradoxically, builds up delusion more strongly. This applies particularly to the plays under examination here. Moreover the theatre works as a time machine.

In Barry's *The Steward of Christendom* and *Our Lady of Sligo*, the mental, psychological and physical pains of the two 'patients', exhibited on their beds on stage for all to see, do not necessarily lead to recovery and/or salvation, but at least they give the audience an opportunity to know more about them through the flow of words and, in a way, to reshape the tragic life-story of persons on an intimate level. Such probing amounts to a poetic investigation into the personal history of the characters. On a clinical level *The Steward of Christendom* can best be described as a series of fits, whereas the symptoms in *Our Lady of Sligo* rather suggest a sort of senile condition where actual memories of facts are unintentionally rearranged and reshuffled into bewildering poetic discourse.

In both cases the dotted line of the border is drawn by the continuous flow of words. Few instances can be found of jerky or uncompleted sentences, but on either side of this borderline the speech now proves consistent, now falls (or soars up?) into surrealistic bouts. What is exciting is that a dramatist lays hands on a medical case or a phenomenon and makes use of creative means — whether traditional or new — to both convey the pathological data and perform dramatic, poetic and linguistic variations of them.

Both Dermot Bolger and Sebastian Barry open up the gates of a new world. Barry brings to a clash madness and normality by taking into account a private approach to history. As for Bolger, he pictures the coexistence and/or conflict of crude reality and metaphysics in comparatively uneventful but tragic lives. The themes both have selected are such that one speculates eagerly about how the numerous hallucinations and apparitions are staged.

The 'mad' police superintendent in Barry's *The Steward of*

Christendom who was in charge of public order in Dublin on the eve of Independence appears in a hospital bed in the play; and, dramatically speaking, one can say everything is seen, perceived and uttered, so to speak, in his mind or through his brain. Madness is his shelter from history and his current outlook on his past is seen through a series of hallucinations that grow out of real life scenes. For instance, when his daughter brings him his boots in the mental home, Thomas Dunn suddenly erupts and lives the incident twice: at the time it takes place on the stage in front of us, and synchronically at the moment when he was about to don his uniform for the formal transfer of power in the yard of Dublin Castle in 1921. Comparable moments are to be found on several occasions in the play, when a double time scale is applied to characters who are involved both as ghosts, or even living creatures, from the past, and actual persons in the present.

The central figure of *Our Lady of Sligo* is Mai, an enlightened middle-class woman, who, having become addicted to drink is in a hospital ward, terminally ill with liver cancer. She also seems at times to be mentally unstable. The play rests on the close association of delirium and poetic language related to a very accurate memory of her past, casting a feeling of uncertainty, a continuous flutter and unresolved questions on the character's clear-mindedness. Spectators are constantly on the lookout for the true word or the true memory and trying to detect the slightest slip towards delirium. We come to a global picture and appreciation of the woman. Unlike Thomas Dunn in *The Steward of Christendom*, she is fully aware of her decay, although the momentary loss of her memory of recent events always makes the dialogues chancy. The many monologues do not necessarily evidence madness either. For instance does the long monologue at the end of Act One tell *the* truth about her, or just a version of truth? Some time later Mai still believes her father is alive and utters a fine poetic monologue, whereas at the beginning of Act Two the presence of her dead father is mentioned as a character in his own right who speaks like someone alive. The hallucination becomes something factual, unlike the situation in *The Steward of*

Christendom where events occur in the old man's mind.

Here, necessarily because the dramatist wills it so, the spectator enters the explored area and we take the hallucination into account; indeed we live it. Elsewhere in the play a full scene in the same mood *is imposed* upon us: in Act One Mai pays a visit to a friend, Maria, and the visit is merely an evocation of the sick woman through one long soliloquy; but in Act Two this very visit steals into a verbal exchange between Mai and her husband Jack, without the slightest hint that some time has passed or that a break has occurred. Nay, the visit goes on with the arrival of the dead father — objectively — until the scene is resumed off-handedly with Jack, and the nurse, in the hospital ward. The journey and the visit that Mai has just mentioned at length through a third person narrative are brought back to life in the shape of a dialogue, unless it is the spectator who witnesses from the outside two performances of the same important episode, described first, then experienced. Today and yesterday, inside and outside, are ravelled and leave us bewildered. A double status induces a wealth of uncertainty. The situation here is far less clear-cut than in *The Steward of Christendom*. In addition, historically speaking, we stand in some sort of no man's land since the period of life evoked by Mai is located, psychologically, between the colonial status and independence. She experiences the strange feeling of being at the same time English and Irish. Sebastian Barry's language too stands in a no man's land, astride a border between lyricism and realism. Amid the concrete situations and dialogues the dramatist elbows his way as an explorer who occasionally comes across poetic strains — not quite unlike the O'Casey way. Some passages in *Boss Grady's Boys* indeed foretold the *Sligo* play considered here:

> Out of the secret pains and terrors of his mother my child was born. I remember the moon sitting in the corner of the window when it was over, peaceful and pure, the hospital set up on high ground above the Sligo sea and the sea itself silver from the moon.

And I had grappled with those big demons of pain
that had tried to wrench the vitals from my stomach
and I had glimpsed now and then the heads of the
doctor and the nurse poised between my open legs.

In *Our Lady of Sligo* one is closer to one variety of senile decay
where the storytelling of a life drifts to a monologue laden with
amazing remarks 'round the corner'. Let us state it again; in
Barry's *The Steward of Christendom* and *Our Lady of Sligo*, the
borderline weaves its way through the continuous flow of the
language.

In Bolger's *The Passion of Jerome*, the ghost of the suicide boy
who implores salvation does not enter into a conversation with
the protagonist but his words are reported: 'Play Jesus!' he asks
Jerome, the golden boy with stigmata. Dialogues are not
necessarily based on words. In the same play, for instance, a sort
of dialogue of gestures and deeds occurs: who sets the objects
moving, who hammers the nails into Jerome's palms? In the
council flat in Ballymun, which *is* a terra incognita, an exploration
and investigation take place, that bring forth revelations leading to
a fresh era — Jerome is going to change the course of his life and
start from scratch, 'start again as [my]self' towards a more genuine
future. In *April Bright*, life eventually triumphs over a past death
and current hazards, as it is embodied in a baby held at arm's
length to the light of a wide-open window. An exploration can
never be undone: there necessarily was something before and is
something after.

In Bolger's *The Lament for Arthur Cleary*, Cleary's last words:
'Let go' release a sort of exploratory balloon to fly or soar up to
the future when the exemplary life of the hero will perhaps be told
to his descendants — even though the dramatist propounds quite
another meaning, as he put it in an interview: '... for me it is
when Cleary lets go of his past fully and becomes part of another
world or part of oblivion. Throughout the play he has been
incapable of letting the past go and therefore incapable of
understanding the present fully.'

Dermot Bolger's later plays have far less to do with the workings of the mind than Barry's; you need not lie in wait of subtle shifts of consciousness and language. But they display a brutal clash between rationality, the harsh realistic dialogues and the forcible, haunting presence of the apparitions. In *The Lament for Arthur Cleary* there remains some vagueness about whether the dead are actually dead or the living actually alive: the world may be the nether world just as much as what surrounds us in our everyday life, or the world may be but a dream, and then, who dreams it, and what are dreams?

However, things utterly change with *April Bright* (1995), *The Passion of Jerome* (1998) and *Consenting Adults* (1999). A very peculiar world takes shape where walls play a paramount part — ever present, yet ambiguous walls. Walls exist in Barry's latest plays, hospital walls that symbolise and reinforce a mental and psychological confinement. Things are by no means so simple in Bolger's works: in the three plays just mentioned one never escapes, no one ever comes out for air; and the seeming reality of the dialogues is sharply contrasted by the unexpected encounters with the apparitions and other paranormal phenomena. The part played by walls and haunted houses conveys obsessions dating back to infancy, and, at the same time, symbolises doubts about identities and materialises the barriers that have to be overcome when a person wishes to transcend a failure in the self and try to assert him/herself as different after a surge of painful awareness. The walls in Bolger's plays surround and block errors as much as wanderings; they can mean vague fears *or* very precise hazards. Owing to their solid mass (whether they are naturalistic settings, or merely suggested) they stand for the junction and connivance of space and time, and the twofold figure of past and present. The walls, in the plays concerned, serve the purpose of recording time and of course delineate for us a truly fantastic world. One might say that their role is comparable to the part played by bogs in Seamus Heaney's poetry: they are 'historical records' of a sort, and compel the present minute to bear in mind the bygone days.

The straight line of time becomes then crystallised into one intense dot that shapes the performance compulsively and upsets our traditional vision of the world. They also brilliantly serve the purpose of restoring and redeeming the suburban world, for the dark brick walls of the cul-de-sacs, the bare unhealthy-looking walls of the council flats, call up with even more strength, the same rich memories as are usually elicited from the walls of historical buildings. The suburban walls have access to history, in other words they enable the wretched ones to exist, when they usually were denied existence so far. In *April Bright* the walls, as an expression of space, have time sequences collide, with the consequence of widely separate generations forced upon each other on the same stage at the same performance-time. The walls in *The Passion of Jerome* turn the past into something you can touch. Some characters do actually bump into palpable memories; the walls are records liable to upset lives and are instrumental in a moral quest — a wall looks like a blank page where a character can write afresh a new genuine start in life.

The world of Bolger, when we consider the long plays and *Consenting Adults*, never discloses any mental pathology of the senile decay type. The young expectant mother in *April Bright* understandably suffers from anxiety after several miscarriages; Jerome's wife, Penny, is tormented by emotional instability related to the aftermath of a breakdown following her child's death. In the short play, *Consenting Adults*, the female character somehow heralds the figure of Penny, as she too suffers from a serious breakdown and a deep deterioration in her personality, following the accidental death of a child.

Consequently, in Bolger's plays, despite the recurrent feature of a depression syndrome, one cannot contend that the border lies between sanity and insanity: it is rather to be found somewhere between the 'normal' world and the uncanny — the fantasy being both innovative *and* true to the ghosts and haunted houses of yore. In short, Bolger upgrades the old formula and loads it with new dramatic and moral meanings, as the dramatist makes it clear in an interview referred to earlier in this essay: speaking ironically of his potential Irish theatre audience as 'shiny new Europeans', he plainly states what he means: 'It's interesting to examine what makes them uncomfortable and therefore the notion of the middle classes being one generation removed from the bog and also the possibility of the existence of the God their grannies believed in intruding into their shiny secular world appealed to me.' He adds in *The Passion of Jerome* that audiences necessarily had to 'take sides as to whether what was happening was cocaine induced or a supernatural manifestation'. Sebastian Barry and Dermot Bolger, in their own separate ways, can be said to appear as distinctive explorers of time and their characters' selves, through their tackling of mental confinement, hospital entombment or urban duress — just as if the walls of the hospital wards or the council flats had some machines concealed inside them, normally meant for medical investigation, such as X-rays or scans, and operated here by the dramatists as laboratory boys.

Other Irish dramatists also becoming known in France invite us to join them for another type of exploratory venture — what could be called a topomythical or mythico-topographical voyage. The word can apply to recent works by Marina Carr and Frank McGuinness. Her *By the Bog of Cats*, and his *Mutabilitie* can be defined as open-air explorations, even if the atmosphere of *By the Bog of Cats* is rather deleterious. We hesitantly step into a new world where land and water fully play their antagonistic parts. In Marina Carr's play the water stays still but is laden with mystery and holds out against the land of fields and pastures, the land of landlords, of estate, commerce and commodities, of harsh firmness. On the contrary, although not so differently, the water in *Mutabilitie*, rushing and running throughout, is the cradle of creation for it is essentially the gushing spring and fountain of wild Ireland, the river of her poetic rebirth, as opposed to the immovable stronghold of British power.

The hair-raising melodrama in *By the Bog of Cats* takes place at the borderline between dry land and the bog. The bog has always been part of a peculiar geographical approach, associating poetry, legends and assuming a social role of its own — not unlike the forest in Shakespeare's plays. Of such places it can be said: 'You are now entering the Land of Freedom!' And the absolute opposition between the natural habitats is reinforced by the utter difference and incompatibility of the places of abode: Hester Swane's caravan as against the farm buildings where her man is going to move and set up to live with his new wife.

As a matter of fact the exploration of the bog is carried out methodically along within the dialogue. Our amazement increases as a set of strange creatures are brought on: a black swan, then a sort of witch or freak, the Catwoman who acts as a keeper of the area. Hester is a completely independent woman, following after her mother who, in her own days, already spent her time wandering and singing. Hester's words are a discourse about life and death, past and future tragedies, mysterious forces and magnetic attraction. Conversely the Cassidy family is only concerned with money; the land as a place valued solely for its monetary worth only generates relentless bestiality and greed. What is going on is a wild drama: the violent wildness of freedom and the poetic wildness of great legends as opposed to the relentless greed of ownership. This lust for property will be let loose when the Cassidys openly oblige Hester to leave her hut on the bog and want to take over her young daughter Josie on the pretence that *they* can secure a decent future for her. 'You can't grab the Bog!' Hester exclaims, when Cassidy, the farmer asserts 'There's nothin' besides land!' Out of despair, Hester will eventually kill her own daughter then herself after a kind of dance of death. As a matter of fact the play never ventures on to the bog proper but incessantly reveals or hints at its mystery by means of numerous stories or legends lost in the mists of time that no one will ever bother to check. It seems that Hester's father is himself a legendary figure, and came from one eerie Bergit's Island beyond the water. There is also a lot of talk about an unsolved murder case: Joseph Swane, Hester's brother, put to death on a boat. As for the black swan appearing at the very start of the play, whose fate seems oddly similar to Hester's, it makes its comeback as if by magic at curtain fall: 'Hester — She's cut her heart out — it's lying there on top of her chest like some dark-feathered bird.'

The strangely called Bog of Cats is at first evoked as a place for love when it repeatedly makes its appearance at the beginning of the play in little Josie's song:

> To the Bog of Cats I one day will return,
> In mortal form or in ghostly form,
> And I will find you there and there with you
>   sojourn,
> For ever by the Bog of Cats, my darling one.

Later on we realise that the Bog, like the sea, forcefully allures human beings towards its secret:

> The last time I saw me mother, I was wearin' me Communion dress ... down by the caravan, a beautiful summer's night and the bog like a furnace. I wouldn't go to bed though she kept tellin' me to. I don't know why I wouldn't, I always done what she tould me. I think now — maybe I knew. And she says, I'm goin' walkin' the bog, you're to stay here, Hetty. And I says, No, I'd go along with her, and made to folly her. And she says, No, Hetty, you wait here, I'll be back in a while. And again I made to folly her and again she stopped me. And I watched her walk away from me across the Bog of Cats. And across the Bog of Cats I'll watch her return.

And Hester tells us about her secret province with all kinds of magic and poetry, her realm of possibilities, and by so doing she allows us to dream at the edge:

> I know every barrow and rivulet and bog hole of its nine square mile. I know where the best bog rosemary grows and the sweetest wild bog rue. I could lead yees around the Bog of Cats in me sleep.

Towards the end of the play, Hester, when mentioning the 'house' they want to take over from her, conjures up the paramount power of the bog: 'Let the bog have it back. In a year or so, it'll be covered in gorse and furze, a tree'll grow out through the roof, maybe a big oak tree.'

The implicit comparison with the forest world is once more inevitable. Yet, what strikes one even more is the treatment of water: it is no longer used as the tritely romantic frame for a big mansion like Mai's, neither is it a place for a tragedy like Portia Coughlan's, but it serves as a powerful and poetic substitute for the road. Hester the tinker goes out to explore supernatural places where anything can occur. Nowhere then is a safe place for the explorer to set foot on, whereas the road, traditionally associated with these travelling people, paradoxically belongs to the relentless world of farmlands just good enough to shatter all dreams.

In his play *Mutabilitie* (1997), Frank McGuinness takes us round other strange realms and along unexpected avenues. Here again we are concerned with borderland, between the real world and magic, between historical and poetical truth. In order to achieve his exploratory purpose, the dramatist steadily makes us follow close on Shakespeare's heels, by working out an atmosphere not unlike that of *The Tempest*, and by splitting the dramatic material into vivid, short scenes the way Shakespeare often does. Oddly enough, Shakespeare himself as a half-disguised character is called to life, making his appearance amazingly as a castaway rolled into Ireland up the flood of a magic river. The result is a neo-Shakespearian romance where all probability is given up and dreams take over — although McGuinness embarks into a reappraisal of history and an actual investigation of the English colonial power in Ireland. Once more we are led to an exploratory voyage between dreams and actuality, sailing across uncertain seas to eventually set foot on elusive land, just like those who have survived shipwreck in Prospero's island. As a matter of fact the places for drama are a fortress on the one hand, and the forest, on the other. Spenser, the Elizabethan poet, dwells in a stronghold, an isolated, well-fortified castle, an island of colonial power; Sweeney, the Irish king, half-demented, lives in the woods: his abode is out beyond the walls of the castle, a wild and poetic area — the world of the doomed Irish aristocracy. Then, lo and behold, Annas, the king's daughter, and the servant-poet come forward with the prophecy of salvation: a man of their own creed, a Roman Catholic, will come through the channel of the river to bring his good tidings. William, a poet, will sail or swim up the Avon [i.e. the river, aibhne in Gaelic]; he makes his appearance as early as the first scene, and Annas heralds him in the following terms: 'A man will come amongst us. He will be from a river. The water shall save him. The river shall reveal him. He shall speak out stories…' and the bard resumes the announcement in a chanted litany:

> 'And a man shall come from a river,
> He shall gleam like a spear, like a fish,
> He shall kill and he shall feed us,
> He shall lie and he shall heed us,
> He shall give us the gift of tongues
> … He shall sing the song of all songs
> … Bard meaning poet
> River meaning aibhne.

He is an Englishman. The man who will sing the song to save us is English … he is the William our captive called out to.' William, wet through, is like one of the wretched sailors of *The Tempest*: brought about by the flood, he sets about exploring, but his presence sounds like an apparition on the borderline of three worlds: reality, myth, and the theatre. And it is through the medium of drama that the Irish natives ingenuously discover that peace will sweep over their country. Near the close of the play, the king and queen, according to their wishes, have been slaughtered by their own son — an utterly inconceivable murder. Is the war to be carried on against the English, or isn't it better to collapse in absolute death? Such are the terms of the debate. In truth the characters' motives and the bloodbath remain obscure items in the play. Identically the presence of some characters together on stage at the very same time defies common sense. We are not in the realm of reason, we are *on stage*. This is why, once all these fits of wild madness have been exorcised, we can watch a conclusive scene of charity in heavenly surroundings, when a child, rescued from a conflagration, drinks his milk to the sound of music on the river bank. The various worlds which the play is made of incessantly overlap to make up a sort of fade in/fade out: poetic incantation and history, closely interwoven, resemble the bog where water and land are the components of two distinct worlds but, at the same time, make up a whole landscape, which both entices or allures explorers and puts them off.

Water is in some way one of the major ingredients of exploration; it allows unknown modes of life to develop, as well as it isolates from and leads to undiscovered worlds. But it can equally kill the explorer by drowning him.

Water is obviously synonymous with liberty and poetry in *By the Bog of Cats*, and incidentally with power and murder as well. In McGuinness's *Mutabilitie* it is in various ways a principle of salvation and a principle of life, if not of baptism. The last scene calls to mind the bank of the Belmont River in *The Merchant of Venice*. The pastoral scene, the river, the milk of life, the miraculous child, with the accompaniment of music, fill us up with the feelings experienced when we attend the performance of one of Shakespeare's romances. *Mutabilitie* evidences McGuinness's taste for experiment in dramatic manner and theme: it is his way of exploring. In *Someone Who'll Watch Over Me* he observes the reactions of three individuals he has chosen to place in an isolated box, so to speak: the three hostages in Lebanon are monitored in front of an audience. More recently in *Dolly West's Kitchen* (1999), near the border between the Republic and Ulster, that is between neutrality and war, he chooses to put aside Irish citizens and soldiers of the Allied Forces during World War Two, and watches what occurs in such hot surroundings. The dramatist, as a good storyteller and an efficient 'scientist' starts the process by asking questions that could be worded as follows: 'supposing we set a river flowing' or 'supposing we have Shakespeare land on Ireland, what could we do with him, or what phenomena could be observed?' Creative fantasy, based on visible cultural landmarks, and embodied in remote, mythical or dangerously present historical events, experiments and explores Terræ Incognitæ one mistakenly considered familiar. A striking and explosive mixture.

The plays so far examined in this essay share one characteristic feature: they are plays of extremes. Political radicalism is certainly not to be found in any of them, although various strains, stresses and clashes either ethical or psychological are scanned, brought to light and prompted by stagecraft for drama's sake. One might say that provocation is achieved experimentally and poetically, in other words creatively — with intimations of Marivaux's *La Dispute* in the background.

And for that matter, the best conclusive note to what I have tried to show is Tom Murphy's *The Wake*, because it is an excellent example of provocation, of social and topographical exploration, of rebellious, subversive imagination. Vera O'Toole, an Irish-born New-York call-girl, has returned to her native island to pay tribute to her deceased granny by attending some sort of wake. As a matter of fact the spectators, as well as the other characters of the play, become the witnesses of a merciless onslaught on a stronghold in the heart of the city. The girl is hiding in a hotel that can be seen as a mysterious, wild island, just as much as an impregnable urban fortress, or some pocket of resistance: she has taken refuge there with a notorious former lover and is determined to face up to the decent, righteous members of her family who will stop at nothing to wrench the inherited hotel from her. Vera has crossed the sea to land on an unexpected Terræ Incognitæ — Ireland, the immovable place of die-hard traditions that smokescreen the worst greed and trickery.

The initial stage-directions make it clear that she arrives by night at a nameless spot. Vera is a diffident explorer whose ways are secret and illicit. As she very soon puts it, 'where *can* I go? No place in my *own* home to go to! Had a bottle, didn't have a message …' After a short while she will find a haven, the company of a former lover, Finbar, a boozy dropout. They will together lock themselves inside the hotel she ought to inherit, awaiting to be stormed; and under such circumstances her journey is made to appear as a challenge: as Murphy puts it, 'perhaps she will defy her family again with Finbar: perhaps this is why she came here.' And the family circle are the wild, native cannibals who are so anxious to *eat* the bold explorer: 'We want the hotel. We want to get our sister out of that place. We must.'

This is followed by bedlam and booze when Finbar and Vera exchange words in their fortified camp, after which one witnesses a scene very much like a skirmish — Henry, the 'decent' messenger sent by the tribe, tries to approach the rebels and start a parley:

> *She (Vera) has gone out with mugs/plates and fires them. They smash outside.*

> VERA: Fuck off!

> FINBAR: Fuckin' Jesus —

> HENRY (off): Don't shoot! … Don't shoot! Friend! A friend!

Friend or foe? Henry will eventually be allured by Vera's good looks and the opportunity of a fine booze, after brilliantly taking stock of the situation: 'These marauding family expeditions happen on a national scale. A member of course is sacrificed, but it is done for the greater good of the pack.' And the image of the fortress besieged by wild natives comes up some time later when Henry declares: 'The drums continue for three days, I believe: then they attack.' To which Vera rejoins: 'And I've bolted the door. Because when they arrive they're going to have to break it down to get in here.' Indeed they will stop at nothing, will send a priest, the gardaí, even an ambulance to take off the 'raving lunatic'. However, after a general meeting which in no time turns into a rigmarole and a pandemonium of songs, it appears that Vera has managed to stand fast and never given up her rights. The savage rites end up in a drinking bout and sleep. All things considered, Vera's expedition has proved successful! She has blasted customs and traditions by flying the flag of provocation on the mean land of Éireann. By so doing she has written an unexpected additional chapter to the time-honoured journey back home of the Irish from all over the world.

This is the way that many protagonists of contemporary Irish plays strike me from the perspective of France. They are the worthy sons of Brendan, sailing to people and islands, halfway between reality and fancy, towards untrodden shores where the sea begins and ends. It would be hard to claim that they herald a brighter future for mankind; however, through their minute scrutiny of Ireland, they urge all possible audiences to consider the earth and her inhabitants at large with a fresh eye.

BREANDÁN DELAP

Never Mind the Quality, Feel the Gaelic

There is a tale from ancient Greece of an innkeeper called Procrustes who stretched his guests or cut off their limbs to make them fit the standard-sized bed his inn provided. It is as apt a metaphor for the state of drama through the medium of Irish as one is likely to find. Dramatists and theatre companies, frequently with the best of intention, have operated under the assumption that potential audiences should be cut or stretched or otherwise 'adjusted' to fit their plays rather than adjusting the plays to suit the audiences. One of the underlying problems in recent years has been that everybody wants to write the great Irish play but nobody seems to want to produce accessible and entertaining material that doesn't affect literary pretensions. There are many Beckett wannabes in the Irish language scene, but few Bernard Farrell wannabes. The last twenty years have consequently seen an endless conveyor belt of plays that long to be taken seriously, being produced by companies hopelessly out of sync with the needs of the audience. If Pirandello had been an Irish speaker he probably would have renamed his famous play 'Six Authors in Search of an Audience'.

The weight of this legacy has meant that despite almost eighty years of various levels of state subvention, the Irish language dramatic tradition is still in its infancy. If anything, it seems to have gone into a tailspin. A tradition of sorts did exist in some of the Gaeltachts — Gaoth Dobhair for example had its own theatre and an award-winning company — but interest seems to have waned in these areas in recent years. Equally much of the talent that manifests itself in the healthy university scene seems to fall by the wayside. There is no shortage of new material being written by members of An Cumann Drámaíochta in NUIG, UCC and the University of Ulster but their hothouse flowers tend to wilt in the light of post-college day and few go on to stage plays at a higher level. Equally, many budding talents who received training and bursaries from Amharclann de hÍde seem to have gone missing in action, presumed back in the daytime job. The subordinate status of drama as a literary form is further underlined by how few universities include it as a module in their Irish degree programmes.

Small wonder then that some of the most talented actors and dramatists in Irish have concentrated more on television than on the stage. The phenomenal success of TG4's 'CU BURN' — a quirky comedy series set in a funeral parlour in Donegal — was due in no small measure to the humour and style of acting that was prominent in Aisteoirí Ghaoth Dobhair's productions during the Sixties and the early Seventies. Equally, many of the actors in 'Ros na Rún' — TG4's flagship soap opera — cut their teeth in the pantomimes that An Taibhdhearc toured Connemara with.

It could be argued though that Irish drama left the people rather than the people leaving drama. Plays in Irish are often perceived to be difficult to understand, with a language that doesn't reflect current speech patterns and containing actors who are uncomfortable with Irish. Audiences have got used to hacking their way through complex plots and unfamiliar language and have come to expect only intermittently passable entertainment for their troubles. There has also been a tendency to concentrate on esoteric subjects for select audiences. Amharclann de hÍde, for example, chose *Tine Chnámh*, Liam Ó Muirthile's epic poem cum end-of-world cabaret, to launch their arrival on the professional scene in 1993. Set around the bonfires of St John's Eve, *Tine Chnámh* is undoubtedly one of the finest poems ever written in Irish but its language is so sodden with symbolism that it left a lot of the audience back at the lights. As a statement of intent it sent out the message that theatre was an elitist hobby for the chosen few. This set the tone of future productions.

I am not necessarily arguing for a dumbing down or inferior product or for the return of parish pump drama. Nor am I suggesting that audiences should check their brains in at the cloakroom just because a play is in Irish. But if the boundaries of Irish language theatre are to be expanded it is imperative that a corpus of clearly plotted and accessible modern plays be encouraged and promoted to co-exist with those plays that aim to reach a higher level of literary attainment. They need not necessarily be mutually exclusive concepts.

One of the most obvious problems that have beset Irish language plays over recent years has been bad pronunciation and shaky phonetics. Fluency in Irish is not always seen as high on the list of priorities when it comes to casting a play and as a result it is often hard to grasp what the actors are saying. This in-built deficit has become all too predictable in Irish language drama and has dogged many fine productions. Audiences have been remarkably patient and understanding over the years, stoically accepting shoddy workmanship and inferior goods as the almost inevitable consequence of staging a play in a minority language. The Dublin-based professional company Amharclann De hÍde and Galway's An Taidhbhearc have been among the main offenders in this regard. Much of the humour and subtle nuances of some good scripts have been lost upon the audience due to bad pronunciation or incorrect emphasis. Yet the actors these companies used were often professionals who were highly regarded in their field. At the other end of the scale you have outfits like Aisteoirí Bulfin, Aisteoirí an Spidéil or Aisteoirí Bhréanainn, comprised wholly of amateur actors, who cannot compete with the production values of the professionals but who perform with an insider's sensibility and a clear understanding of the language. This raises the question: who are the professionals and who are the amateurs? If an actor is unable to pronounce words properly can he really be regarded as a professional? In the casting of a play, would the director be better off choosing well-known and professionally trained actors with little Irish or should he plump for native speakers with no formal training? Once again they need not be mutually exclusive concepts. It is high time therefore that The Arts Council applied the same artistic yardstick for the funding of Irish language theatrical companies as they do for their English language counterparts. Foras na Gaeilge, whose remit is to promote the language and is in no way qualified to judge the theatrical merits of plays, has become the main source of funding in recent years. This can only make for bad theatre.

Perhaps the most worrying aspect of Irish language drama over the past number of years though has been the apparent dearth of new material. A large number of recent productions have been adaptations of classic poems or novels. Some like Na Fánaithe's version of *Bullaí Mhártan* (1989) have even infused much ingenuity to the material that had been lacking in the original. Others like the Abbey's imaginative adaptation of Máirtín Ó Cadhain's *Cré na Cille* (1998) and the Project Arts Centre's version of Myles na gCopaleen's *An Béal Bocht* (1994) have justifiably achieved canonical status. But many other adaptations have been noticeable for their lack of dramatic interplay and have felt like watching a recitation of prose. The creative drought is all the more remarkable in view of the fact that Irish language writers frequently express frustration at their lack of recognition. Writing in a minority language can be a lonely business. This is particularly the case with Irish as there is no tradition worth mentioning in the Gaeltacht areas of reading material through Irish. People who emigrated traditionally wrote letters home in English even when Irish was the language of the household. Equally English tabloids (and Scottish in the case of Donegal) will always outsell Irish language publications in the Gaeltacht. Drama, however, can transcend these boundaries as well as reaching outside the ghetto and therefore affords the writer a platform to showcase his work to a wider audience than poets or novelists can ever aspire to. This craving for recognition has yet to be reflected though by a significant volume of newly written Irish plays.

Another trend in recent years has been the translation of well-known plays from the Anglo-Irish canon into Irish. Many like the

Amharclann de hÍde's translations of some of Synge's lesser-
known works (*Pósadh an Tincéara* and *Chun na Farraige Síos*
1996) have been billed as the reclamation of texts that were
already larded with Gaelicisms — a kind of literary 'Bringing it all
Back Home.' The speech patterns in the originals, it is argued,
reflect a certain aphasia that crept into the dialogue of
communities that had recently experienced a changeover of
languages. The people in these areas still thought through Irish
but used English words to express these thoughts. It is clear that
Synge exploited this linguistic interchange, drawing heavily on
Gaelic syntax and locutions to forge his uniquely bilingual
dramatic language. The dialogue in his plays often sounds like a
literal translation and it was felt that it should follow naturally to
translate them back into Irish and re-annexe them into their
original cultural context. This prodigal son approach has been
taken to extremes, however, and will only ensure that Irish
language drama dwells in the perpetual shadow of its Anglo Irish
master.

It's refreshing though when the translation turns out to be
more compelling than the original as was the case with
Connemara-based writer Mícheál Ó Conghaile's translation of
The Beauty Queen of Leenane (*Banríon Álainn an Líonáin*), which
was chosen as the flagship production of the highly successful
Féile 2000 festival that was held in Galway in October 1999. Ó
Conghaile stripped the play of its affectations, displaying a
sensitive ear for the vernacular, which the original production
sadly lacked. Martin McDonagh's conventional linear narrative
was replaced by something more meditative and fluid. This in
turn made the characterisation more convincing. The tone and
texture of the play was also a radical departure from the primary
source. Ó Conghaile's curt, evocative dialogue had the effect of
blunting the skittish humour of the original, making it easier to
sympathise with the characters rather than treating them with the
comic derision favoured by McDonagh.

That said, Mícheál Ó Conghaile is a very fine writer in his
own right and should be encouraged to produce original work

rather than translating major box office hits. The trend towards translation is in some ways a new take on the shambolic policies pursued by the Government's Irish publishing company An Gúm in the 1930s, which saw some of the best writers the state has ever produced translating English classics in the hope that some of the techniques employed might rub off on them. This produced the farcical situation where you had precocious talents like Seosamh Mac Grianna translating *Ivanhoe* and Pádraic Ó Conaire writing for children. Admirable and all as recent productions have been therefore, they cannot mask the inescapable fact that the translation of second rate kitchen-sink dramas is a very thin basis on which to erect a sustainable tradition of Irish language theatre.

If the national theatre has a clear and coherent policy towards the Irish language, they have kept it very well hidden. The Nineties began brightly enough with Alan Titley's linguistically subversive *Tagann Godot* (1990) and Seán Mac Mathúna's *Gadaí Géar na Geamh-Oíche* (1992) a bittersweet tale set during the War of Independence with a particular focus on the frustration felt by Irish soldiers returning from the Western Front. Since then, however, the policy seems to have gone into freefall and appears to operate on an ad hoc basis, depending on the whims of whoever happens to be the artistic director. The long-standing tradition of using the Peacock Theatre to stage a number of Irish plays annually, for example, seems to have been discontinued. The Abbey has produced little of any value in recent years and certainly hasn't encouraged any new talent.

Tom MacIntyre's attempts to blow the dust off classical eighteenth-century poems and remould them into modern fables are a case in point. *Caoineadh Art Uí Laoghaire* (1998) was a poorly cast, turgid affair while with *Cúirt an Mheán Oíche* (1999) MacIntyre managed to transform the greatest comic poem ever written in Ireland into an extended revue sketch. Much of the prickly wit of the original was replaced by long-winded ranting rhetoric that was both pretentious and self-indulgent. No amount of technical audacity could compensate for the dramatic and linguistic shortcomings of these efforts. The Abbey toured with the latter production, and boasted what seemed like the laudable intention of taking art to the people, playing in small halls from Inis Meáin to West Belfast. What they failed to mention, though, was that the script was beyond the understanding of most of those who attended the show and that the standard of Irish was so poor that it was hard to grasp the unintelligible babble issuing from some of the actors mouths. The result was at best patronising and at worst insulting. Not surprisingly audiences voted with their feet. Is it any wonder then that Irish language enthusiasts accuse the Abbey of lip service and condescension?

Despite the absence of a cohesive strategy from the National Theatre, Irish language drama has flourished in the last ten years. The initial impetus came from Dublin, though Galway and Belfast have since taken up the mantle. From the outset Amharclann de hÍde was bold in its scope and ambition. Founded in 1993, with a generous funding of £90,000 per annum provided by Bord na Gaeilge and the Arts Council, the company aimed to produce plays of the highest standards of production using professional actors, writers, directors, musicians and technical staff. It was also intended to stage a season of Irish plays every year and to establish a full-time professional company. Though based in Dublin, Amharclann de hÍde toured extensively bringing their shows to the Gaeltacht regions as well as Belfast, Cork and Galway. Their early productions followed the well-established path of adapting well-known literary works from page to stage. Director Michael Scott took a foreign language approach to the company's first two productions — Liam Ó Muirthile's *Tine Chnámh* and Seán McCarthy's adaptation of Pádraic Ó Conaire's short stories *Mallachtaí Muintire*:

> I am in a sense following the same policy of work I pursued for the Dublin Theatre Festival with shows such as the Swedish 'Pygmalion', the Peking Opera, Franca Rame, Pistol Theatren, where the language of the company did not for a second hinder the appreciation of the show.[109]

The problem with this approach was that most of the audience were fluent Irish speakers while once again many of the actors lacked proficiency in the language. Consequently, there were times when the plays did indeed feel like they had been written in a foreign language. Paradoxically, the language became a barrier rather than a key to a greater understanding of the plays.

In many ways Amharclann de hÍde was ahead of its time attempting to break new ground in a tradition that had so far struggled to find its feet. The company attracted fierce criticism from some quarters from the outset. Doubts were cast on the artistic direction and some felt that its somewhat lavish budget might be better employed elsewhere. Biddy Jenkinson, for example, chose the Oireachtas awards ceremony of 1994 to fire a shot across the bows of Irish language drama. Jenkinson laid claim to the title of 'the most prolific Irish language dramatist' having won no fewer than six Oireachtas awards for newly written plays. Despite the apparent dearth of material available, however, none of her plays had ever seen the light of a Dublin stage. In its haste to create a professional identity for itself some felt that Amharclann de hÍde had been a little too quick to distance itself from the existing talent. This is all the more remarkable considering the subsequent success of Aisling Ghéar's production of Jenkinson's *Mise, Subhó agus Maccó* — perhaps the most stunningly inventive play ever written in Irish.

The company's growing pains were further exacerbated when Cathal Ó Searcaigh fired an exocet in their direction at the opening night of Aisteoirí Aon Dráma's production of his play *Tá an Tóin ag Titim as an tSaol* in Belfast later that year. He queried the wisdom of Amharclann de hÍde spending money on the translation of plays from English to Irish when they could be harnessing the pool of talent already available. (It was commonly believed in Irish language circles that Michael Harding's *Ceacht Houdini* (1994) had originally been written in English.) The policy of investing money and resources in talent that is more likely to come to fruition in another language was nothing short of bizarre. Moreover, the frequently cited excuse of lack of suitable material available ran the risk of becoming a self-fulfilling prophecy.

Since its inception, though, Amharclann de hÍde has had as many highs as lows. Éilis Ní Dhuibhne's *Dún na mBan Trí Thine* (1994) was their first big success. The plot centres on a housewife, whose horizons have been severely constricted by domestic duties, and who finds sanctuary in listening to the voices in her ears. There is an underlay of Irish folklore in the play as well and the fantastic is neatly incorporated in the literal. Ní Dhuibhne has the rare gift of engaging both emotion and intellect and making you care greatly about the outcome. Her next foray into theatre, *Milseog an tSamhraidh* (1997), was billed as a post-feminist take on the famine but felt more like 'The Attack of the Cannibal Lesbians' and was met with critical coolness and box office mediocrity. Other notable hits include the modern reworking of Mairéad Ní Ghráda's *An Triail* (1998). Thirty-five years after it premiered on a Dublin stage, the play speaks as eloquently as it ever did about the plight of unmarried mothers and unplanned pregnancies and has occupied pole position in the Irish language repertoire for many years. Few of Amharclann de hÍde's other shows have managed to dislodge it since.

One of their biggest successes though was Liam Ó Muirthile's *Fear an Tae* (1995) — a kind of 'The Singing Detective' meets 'One Flew Over the Cuckoo's Nest'. Set in a closed ward of a psychiatric hospital between St Stephen's Night and New Year's Eve, the play charts the fortunes of a detox patient as he enters the maelstrom of the institution. His fellow inmates include a schizophrenic, an epileptic and a rip-roaring drunk. Into the emotional cauldron comes the symbolically named tea-man, Matt Sweeney, a man who operates an alternative system of authority to the rest of the hospital staff. Physically deformed, but far from intellectually infirm, he acts as a catalyst in the unfolding psychological origami of the patients. Ó Muirthile's play provided a fascinating insight to the problems that face an alcoholic and explored the fine line between socially acceptable and unacceptable behaviour. His characters weren't paraded as freaks but as volatile chemicals that needed to be handled with care and were brought from the depths of despair to the threshold of hope.

It was unfortunate that the second play produced during the 1995 season was eclipsed by *Fear an Tae*. Antoine Ó Flatharta's *An Solas Dearg* was set in a production studio in Connemara, and revolved around the burgeoning media industry that had developed at a phenomenal rate in the Gaeltachtaí in the lead up to Teilifís na Gaeilge (now TG4). On a broader level, however, it explored the influence that Hollywood has on our daily lives and the very nature and value of heritage and identity as the new millennium unspools. Ó Flatharta is a native Irish speaker from Leitir Mealláin in Connemara and unashamedly writes in his Gaeltacht vernacular even if at times this constitutes a flagrant disregard for an caighdeán or standard Irish. The play was therefore peppered with English phrases, that have sneaked their way into everyday speech, and although the dialogue may have upset the purists it had an authentic feel about it. *An Solas Dearg* was in many ways the most important play produced by Amharclann de hÍde, providing the audience with an excellent evening's entertainment without sending the low-brow metre into the eponymous red zone.

Of all those working in the field of Irish drama, Taidhbhearc na Gaillimhe has had to face up to its inadequacies and the shifting demands of audiences. Founded in Galway in 1928, the theatre has a proud tradition as a stepping-stone for young talent coming through the ranks of the UCG dramsoc. Mícheál Mac Liammóir wrote, directed and played the lead role in An Taibhdhearc's first production — *Diarmuid agus Gráinne* — and amongst the many actors who launched their careers in drama there were Siobhán McKenna, Caitlín Maude, Maolíosa Stafford and Mick Lally. In the past three decades, however, An Taibhdhearc has been perceived to be operating at a very primitive level and living off past glories, a thought borne out by a succession of withering reviews in Irish language publications. The following extract from Alex Hijmans' review of Seán Mac Mathúna's civil war drama *Hulla Hul!* seemed symptomatic of the malaise:

Dún do shúile agus smaoinigh ar dhráma sa Taibhdhearc. An bhfeiceann tú é? An seit: seanteach tuaithe Gaelach (an troscán bogtha thart rud beag ón uair dheireanach a baineadh úsáid as an dearadh seo.) Na cultacha: seanchaite. An chaint: Gaeilge iontach saibhir ag cuid, drochGhaeilge ag cuid eile, agus é deacair a dhéanamh amach in áiteanna. Na haisteoirí: as áit — don chuid is mó. Tar éis na hoíche deiridh, cuirfear an seit agus na cultacha thíos staighre faoin stáitse go dtí go léireofar an chéad dráma eile. Tarlaíonn sé do chorraisteoir fosta…

Close your eyes and think of a play in the Taibhdhearc. Can you picture it? The set: an old country house (with the furniture slightly re-arranged from the last time that this design was used). The costumes: tattered. The dialogue: some actors have very rich Irish but others have poor Irish and are sometimes difficult to understand. The actors: mostly miscast. When the curtain comes down on the closing night, the set and the costumes will be taken downstairs and stored under the stage until the next production. The same applies to some of the actors…[110]

The theatre itself has an air of faded elegance about it and is in dire need of a facelift. The lack of proper air-conditioning means that it can often get stuffy and the actors have to compete with the din of overhead fans during the summer months. Yet there is much reason for optimism. An artistic advisor has been appointed and recent productions would suggest that the theatre has considerably spruced up its act and is in line to reclaim its position as the Irish language's National Theatre.

One play which bucked recent trends was Joe Steve Ó Neachtain's *Níor Mhaith linn do Thrioblóid* which made its audacious stage debut in Taibhdhearc na Gaillimhe in October 2000 and must rank as one of the most accessible and entertaining plays written in Irish in recent years. It played to sell-out audiences and even had a re-run — a rare case of an Irish play being a commercial success. The curious thing is that the play will probably hardly even register a blip on the Irish language drama graph in years to come. High art or literature it ain't, yet it struck a chord with Gaeltacht audiences, something most other Irish language plays failed to do.

Set in present day Connemara the play deals with a specific locale but with universal emotions. The story revolves around the ramblings of an old schoolmaster on the eve of his wife's funeral. He's lonely to the point of desperation, but not very popular with the neighbours. One by one, his children return home for the funeral and all of them clearly have their own skeletons in the cupboard. The plot is intricately constructed with the family's convoy of woes dovetailing nicely with the smutty innuendo of the neighbours. Ó Neachtain spent many years writing the script for Raidió na Gaeltachta's long running soap opera *Baile an Droichid* and clearly has a sensitive ear for dialogue. This was most evident in his capacity to twist the knife and the master's deafness afforded many opportunities for snide asides. And therein lies its strength. They came from all around Connemara to listen to well-known local actors like Peadar Lamb and Diarmuid Mac an Adhastair deliver comic lines in the local idiom. They expected to be entertained and for once they weren't disappointed!

Hot on the heels of *Níor Mhaith linn do Thrioblóid*, came *Pádraic Ó Conaire,* a warts-and-all account of a forgotten genius, a hopeless drunk and an inveterate sponger. Pádraic Ó Conaire cut such a colourful literary figure that the task of separating the man from the legend is an awesome one. Narrowly plinthed on Sister Eibhlín Ní Chionnaith's biography of the author, Diarmuid de Faoite's mesmerising one-man show proved that few things are as theatrically gripping as fact — as long as you don't let it get in the way of a good yarn.

De Faoite delved beneath the iconic status of the author and revealed a man of both creative brilliance and emotional fragility. He took on a vast assortment of roles — from Michael Collins to Mícheál Mac Liammóir — cleverly montaging the author's nationalist and socialist views with samples from his work.

Ó Conaire, whose oeuvre stands comparison with that of Maupassant, is regarded by many as the first professional Gaelic prose writer, yet it is thought that he earned no more than £700 from his work. His writings were also subject to an intellectual lynch mob led by an tAthair Peadar Ó Laoghaire and de Faoite's dramatisation of the correspondence that passed between him and other pillars of the Gaelic Revival was bellyachingly funny. Equally illuminating was the author's lively debate with Liam O'Flaherty, a native Irish speaker from Inis Mór, who chose to ply his trade in English while Ó Conaire continued to plough a lonely furrow in Irish. Comic, tragic and wonderfully compassionate, *Pádraic Ó Conaire* was a dramatic *tour de force*.

Another beacon of hope is An Taibhdhearc's innovative scheme Fuadar Feabhra which was set up in 2001. Inspired by the Druid's Debut scheme, Fuadar Feabhra aims to promote a fresh wave of material in Irish and provided an opportunity for aspiring writers to stage their plays for the first time. The first crop of plays (*Cleite Faoileáin* by Aodhán Ó Ríordáin, *An tUisceadán* by Nuala Nic Con Iomaire, *Banríon an Chéad Dath* by Ruairí Ó Broin and the wonderfully surreal *An Fear a Phléasc* and *Seacht gCéad Uaireadóir* by Mícheál Ó Conghaile) all showed promise and played to healthy audiences. Fortunately, it is planned to expand the scheme and develop it into a bi-annual event. The advantages that can accrue from such an approach are considerable given the current scarcity of material.

Irish language drama of course needs to be judged not in isolation but in the wider context of efforts to promote the language in general. Nowhere has the recent growth of interest in Irish been more apparent than in West Belfast. The past two decades has seen the development of six all-Irish primary schools, one secondary school, a weekly newspaper, a cultural centre, a restaurant and a technological centre in the area. Not surprisingly then, it stands to reason that the Irish language's only full-time drama company should be based there. Since its inception, Aisling Ghéar has been churning out plays at a rate of one every two months, even if in some instances it's been a case of never mind the quality, feel the Gaelic. The word 'professionalism' implies more than gainful employment though, and some of their early productions have tended to lack polish. The wisdom of staging overwrought translations of *Shirley Valentine* (2000) and *The Shadow of a Gunman* (2001) has also been questioned. They have been criticised as well for the lack of money and energy that is set aside for publicising their plays. But Aisling Ghéar are a company with lofty ambitions and an adventurous outlook. They also have the added advantage of having a spanking new theatre at Cultúrlann Mac Adamh-Ó Fiach at their disposal while the simultaneous translations that they provide ensures that they can tap into a wider audience. There is no shortage of courage either which was most evident in Gearóid Ó Cairealláin's excellent translation of Eugene Ionescu's *Amédée* (1999) and in the casting of two ex-IRA prisoners to play the lead roles in Peter Sheridan's *Dialann Ocrais* (2000), a fine and painful piece of work set during the Hunger Strikes of 1981.

But the company's most notable theatrical triumph to date was its mesmerising production of Biddy Jenkinson's *Mise, Subhó agus Maccó* in May 2000 — a postmodern take on contemporary Irish mores. Heavily influenced by ancient Irish literature — and the Aisling in particular — it is a daring and original show that flits effortlessly between the abstract and the actual. The play tackles the runaway train of modern Irish affluence head on, contrasting it to an older more erudite nation of poets and scholars. Mise, her husband Subhó and Maccó (who is on the run from something that is not overly apparent) are mutations of the Celtic Tiger society, living on a construction site beside the City Hall for longer than anyone can remember. They are essentially outsiders peering in, more attune with nature than mankind. A precise and tactile writer, Biddy Jenkinson initiated the audience into previously neglected range of insights, subverting traditional plotlines and turning theatrical convention on its head. Even hardened cynics were moved by the sheer force of imagination displayed.

A burgeoning theatrical tradition depends on a regular supply of actors and for the first time since the foundation of the state actors can aspire to make their living from Irish language drama. John F. Kennedy's definition of economic success as a rising tide that lifts all boats is as true for the Gaeltacht as for other parts of Ireland. There is less emigration from these areas and by consequence, there are far more potential actors, producers, directors and writers available.

The advent of TG4 has also provided many openings for actors with Irish. Unfortunately, many of their programmes have been dogged by the same in-built language deficit apparent on the stage. Some of the same actors, who see Irish as a stepladder to success, have slipped through the net and have managed to make a career out of incoherent patois without making any real effort to brush up on their pronunciation. But the Gaeltacht-based soap opera *Ros na Rún* (which is filmed in An Spidéal) has been a big success and has ensured a significant swelling of the ranks of Irish speaking professional actors. A strong case could be made therefore for the relocation of Amharclann De hÍde from Dublin to Galway in order to capitalise on this burgeoning growth. It is quite possible for an actor, for example, to juggle a regular role in 'Ros na Rún' with the odd foray into theatre. Moreover, the actors have a long lay-off during the summer months and would presumably welcome the chance to supplement their income. Opponents would argue that the language needs to be decentralised from the greater Galway area (Údarás na Gaeltachta, TG4, Raidió na Gaeltachta and *Foinse* are already based there) and that there is a real danger of a brain drain from the other Gaeltachts. Be that as it may, does it not stand to reason that an Irish language theatre company should be based in an area where the language is still the popular means of communication and where there is ample professional talent available? Though there must be careful weighing of the foreseeable costs and gains of relocating Amharclann de hÍde to the Gaeltacht, I believe that the idea merits serious consideration.

Such a relocation could dovetail nicely with the campaign to build a theatre in Connemara. Though first mooted almost thirty years ago, the plan has taken on a renewed momentum in recent years and now appears to be a realistic prospect. The political will seems to be there at present and the most significant hurdle left to be surmounted is the location. The committee campaigning for the theatre appear to be undecided as to the relative claims of Ros Muc, Carna, Indreabhán and An Cheathrú Rua. Connemara's tradition of agitation should ensure that the theatre would be a forum to air social issues, not just entertainment.

The challenges confronting Irish language theatre are immense and reflect those faced by other minority language communities. At the Abbey's lively public debate *Stage Irish* in 1999 Welsh dramatist, Ian Rowlands, expressed his frustration that a new generation of actors and writers were deserting the stage to concentrate exclusively on the more lucrative lure of S4C. But television needn't be seen as a threat but as an opportunity and Irish language theatre's best chance of salvation may be to piggy-back on the soufflé success of TG4. By the same token, Raidió na Gaeltachta could help by developing a series of radio dramas. The station's schedule will be greatly increased in the coming years and such a series would at the very least fill a hole as well as providing a plinth for showcasing new talent.

Be that as it may, there are many positive signs and reasons for optimism and it doesn't seem too fanciful to imagine that in the next twenty years Irish language drama will at last become a cultural force to be reckoned with. Neosfaidh an aimsir.

RONAN MCDONALD

Between Hope and History: The Drama of the Troubles

'All drama is based on conflict.' The adage is so often repeated that it verges on cliché. If true, it may be that a troubled social and political context like Northern Ireland would provide a rich source of dramatic material. Certainly the wealth of drama that the Troubles have produced suggests that social turmoil feeds a robust stage. If drama is founded on conflict, then in another sense conflict is founded on drama. Many of its metaphors and concepts are borrowed from the stage lexicon. We often hear references to the 'theatre of war' or to contesting global interests being played out on 'the world stage'. The conflict in the North has been especially prone to this sort of metaphor, this sort of conceptual seepage. From murals to marching seasons, Northern Irish political and social life teems with gesture, display and performance. A bomb explodes in London and is dubbed a 'spectacular'. Even the peace process leading up to the Good Friday Agreement, with its carefully scripted moves and counter-moves, historic handshakes and carefully gauged concessions and counter-concessions, has been a sort of balancing 'act', a series of pirouettes done in the full glare of the 'media circus'. A society of competing nationalisms will reflexively dwell on the construction of 'identity' and self-conscious identity is rarely far from a performance of one sort or another. Never more so, one might add, than when identity feels under threat, as the yearly marching season and its associated stand-offs amply demonstrates. It may not be insignificant, countering the unhelpful old stereotype about Northern nationalists, like oppressed American blacks, having all the best songs, that the Protestant contribution to drama of the Troubles has been at least as significant as the Catholic one. This is not just a recent phenomenon. There is a notable tradition of dramatists who treat Protestant identity as an overt theme, from St John Ervine to John Boyd to contemporary playwrights like Christina Reid and Gary Mitchell.

The connections between politics and drama have a long history in Ireland. From its origins at the start of the last century, the Abbey was always a self-consciously 'national' and sometimes 'nationalist' theatre, where the stage was regarded explicitly or implicitly as an arena where the soul of the nation would find its communal expression. And if drama found itself flirting with politics, then the relationship was mutual. The 1916 Easter Rising, that totemic moment in Irish republicanism, is often conceived as a sort of street theatre. With its air of self-conscious sacrifice, as opposed to pragmatic militarism, its status as gesture and symbol, it is little wonder that Michael Collins scornfully described it as having 'the air of a Greek tragedy'.

So the politics of the Northern conflict, and even, crucially, its many violent manifestations, often borrow a vocabulary of performance or spectacle. This may be one reason why Northern playwrights have struggled to find suitable means to engage with the civic strife around them. Many of the pressures are the same as those felt by poets and novelists, the need to find an idiom or mode of expression that will address the political situation while still remaining true to artistic creation, to be a public artist, without being a propagandist. The dilemma, in other words is to avoid on the one hand an isolated, apolitical artiness and on the other a coarse agitprop. The dilemma, however, takes on a specific tinge in drama and not just because of the historical intimacy between theatre and politics in Ireland. Excluding film and television, the theatre is the most public of the literary arts. It is communally produced and communally received and the corresponding onus on drama to address public events is often greater than that, say, on the privately experienced lyric poem. If, on the one hand, there are pressures on playwrights to address themselves to the 'situation', there is a corresponding need to develop techniques of refraction. In other words, distancing strategies are often developed in drama that strives to present the Troubles and its various complexities in a fresh light. The central danger of all writing about the Troubles is the danger of cliché. If we see cliché as the tired use of language, a use that calcifies and deadens imagination, then it is the verbal equivalent of tribal entrenchment, a spasmodic reflex towards the familiar and the reassuring, the instinct to go with the grain.

Given drama's public nature, and given the corresponding pressure to address issues of social strife, it is not altogether surprising if it has sometimes been regarded as a platform for social communion and cultural self-definition. In many instances its performative possibilities have been explicitly styled as a contributor to reconciliation and political healing. The Field Day Theatre Company, founded in 1980 by Brian Friel and the actor Stephen Rea (who were quickly joined by a number of other high profile directors), unabashedly sought to find ways of re-imagining and re-enacting entrenched political positions, of discovering a mythic 'fifth province' in Ireland, beyond the hackneyed historical roles and established stereotypes about the Troubles. Field Day sought to probe deeper than conventional, realist forms had allowed and initiated a drama of ideas, which would not baulk from history plays and experimental forms. The movement came to be criticised for being overly nationalist in its emphasis, but the notion that theatre has a public role and could even help political healing is not confined to nationalist perspectives. A Protestant, socialist playwright like Stewart Parker saw theatre as a vehicle for reconciliation, a surrogate peace process in the cultural rather than political realm:

> … if ever a time and place cried out for the solace
> and rigour and passionate rejoinder of great drama,
> it is here and now. There is a whole culture to be
> achieved. The politicians, visionless almost to a

man, are withdrawing into their sectarian stockades.
It falls to the artists to construct a working model of
wholeness by means of which this society can again
begin to hold up its head in the world.[111]

So, to return to the beginning, if drama is sourced in conflict, in Northern Ireland it has also been regarded as working in the cause of unity. There was a feeling in the Eighties that theatre had to take on a more serious role than hitherto. That it ought to shuffle off its tradition of 'this-is-how-it-is' social realism or the formulaic domestic dramas of families torn apart by political violence in the interests of a more daring, more formally innovative theatrical register. Enter a more cerebral drama, a theatre of ideas. A number of dramatists, such as Brian Friel, Tom Kilroy, Stewart Parker and Frank McGuinness, addressed the Troubles in these terms, at once distanced from the object of concern but also seeking to sound some of its deepest structural strata.

Not surprisingly, then, some of the most notable achievements in drama from the North have been formally innovative plays that are self-conscious about language and tradition and that deploy interesting amalgamations of dramatic modes. Departures from naturalism have been commonplace: the divided stage in Brian Friel's *The Freedom of the City* (1973) and in Frank McGuinness's *Observe the Sons of Ulster Marching Towards the Somme* (1986), the treatment of language and style as themes in themselves in Friel's *Translations* (1980) and in Stewart Parker's *Northern Star* (1984), or, more recently, the use of multiple-role acting to blur divisions between imagination and reality in Marie Jones's *A Night in November* (1995) and Owen McCafferty's *Mojo Mickybo* (1997).

Marie Jones is the most prominent figure to have emerged from Charabanc Theatre Company, a movement set up in Belfast in 1983, initially to provide work for five unemployed actors. Operating at the same time as Field Day, Charabanc also addressed issues of social strife and political division but with a very different sort of theatrical practice. Like Field Day, the movement went on tours around Ireland and abroad. Beginning with *Lay Up Your Ends* (1983), a play about the 1911 strike of Belfast women linen mill workers, Charabanc staged a number of plays, utilising improvisation, collaborative writing, and popular, inclusive forms, including street songs and multiple-role acting. The group emphasised theatre as an instrument of social awareness and sought an audience beyond the urban middle class. From the start, Charabanc put women's issues to the fore, tending to treat issues of contemporary social concern through productions rich in humour, language and theatrical vitality.

Another significant strain in Northern Irish theatre, associated (though not exclusively) with Field Day is the history play (or its cousin, the memory play) where questions of identity and tribe, of colonialism and political domination, of violence and betrayal, issues central to the troubles, can be examined in a less blurred and contentious context. In other words the dual and perhaps paradoxical function of the history play is to gain critical distance from the constricting confusions of the actual conflict while at the same time approaching an understanding of that conflict by plumbing its historical origins. A random selection of plays that thematically address the Troubles in the form of a history play include, Brian Friel's *Translations* (1980) and *Making History* (1988), McGuinness's *Observe the Sons of Ulster*, Christina Reid's *Tea in a China Cup* (1983) (which could also be classified as domestic drama and a memory play), Stewart Parker's *Northern Star* (1984), Tom Kilroy's *Double Cross* (1986) and, most recently, Gary Mitchell's *Tearing the Loom* (1997). The list is far from exhaustive.

Of course, not all the plays to have emerged from the Troubles have been history plays or have been formally experimental. There have been plenty of conventional domestic and kitchen-sink dramas, lots of social realism and romantic melodramas that have used the conflict as their backdrop. Domestic drama that seeks to engage with the Troubles has frequently followed the example of Sean O'Casey, where the external political situation is presented as an ominous and intrusive presence, destroying the possibility of happiness that its protagonists attempt to grasp. A play that overtly models itself on O'Casey is Christina Reid's *Joyriders* (1986), which begins with the characters in a make-believe theatre, watching the tragic climax of O'Casey's *The Shadow of a Gunman*. These are working class, disenfranchised petty criminals on a Youth Training Programme, brought to the theatre by their supervisor, Kate. At the end of the play, the death of Maureen, shot by soldiers as she tries to rescue her glue-sniffing brother, Johnnie, after he has stolen a police car, mimics that of O'Casey's Minnie Powell. As well as showing the background of the Troubles — the punishment beatings by the IRA, persecution by the British army — the play also shows the centrality of class and socio-economic issues to the fates of these teenagers. Like O'Casey, the play's core theme is that of tragically wasted potential. The teenagers, it is hinted, would thrive if the situation was not as riven with class and sectarian conflict as it is. Instead the play works its way through to a shockingly violent conclusion. There is little optimism. The idealistic Kate had been involved in the Civil Rights movement in the early Seventies. However, she is now reduced to fighting for the survival of the Youth Training Programme, which she knows merely functions as a sop to the hypocritical pieties of local politicians. Shadows are cast even over the future of Arthur, who during the action is awarded a large compensation as a result of being shot by British troops.

A lack of optimism, a sort of inherent fatalism, has sometimes been ascribed to dramas of social realism. Sometimes this tendency has been seen as restrictive, as Field Day's penchant for experimentalism would suggest. In Northern Irish domestic dramas, the atavistic pressures of 'The Tribe' often take on the hue of destiny; those that seek to escape it through love across the barricades or, indeed, by replacing it with another political agenda, end up defeated. This model can encourage a sort of quiescence, within which the characters have no control over their future. All too often 'politics' becomes an external, intrusive force which ruins 'ordinary' lives. The O'Casey model becomes simply a sentimental endorsement of the family, in which, typically, stalwart, heroic women vainly try to keep house and home together despite the misguided idealism or feckless irresponsibility of their menfolk. For critics of domestic drama, the deeper motivations of politics and identity, and specifically the idea that a domestic space might itself have some relation to wider political structures, are inadequately explored.

However, domestic drama of the Troubles should not be dismissed as uniformly lacking in depth or always historically naïve. To be sure, realism of its nature tends to foreground 'human' above 'political' concerns. However, there are other ways in which political complexity can be imported into the domestic realm, without sacrificing the focused, concentrated exploration of human conflict (not to mention the advantages in audience recognition and identification) that realism can provide. One device that has been used in Troubles drama to bring politics closer to domestic realities is to set paramilitarism within the home, not as an external intrusive force, but as part of the fabric of the family from the outset. Anne Devlin's *Ourselves Alone* (1985), for example, treats the fate of women within a republican family. It demonstrates how women's lives are caught up in the forces of paramilitarism and, while it shows how destructive this is to the day-to-day lives of the women, it also addresses the issue of political involvement at the core of domestic life, rather than constructing politics as a threatening monolith that de-stabilises it from outside. Hence there is a more developed recognition of the ideological basis of the family that also offers a critique of nationalism from a feminist perspective.

More recently, the plays of Gary Mitchell deploy a similar device within a loyalist milieu. Whilst conventional domestic dramas show the home disrupted by outside political forces, Mitchell shows those forces to be already incubating inside the home. In his plays, a Mafia type situation prevails, where home and family are inseparable from the violence that sustains and ultimately destroys them. Hence *In a Little World of Our Own* (1997) shows how a loyalist hard-man, Ray, seeks to protect his mildly retarded younger brother, Richard, with a violence that descends into frenzied rape and murder. In *Trust* (1999), we have a family saturated in paramilitary racketeering. But conflict between the husband and wife, Geordie and Margaret, derives from her urge to protect her family, not by resisting the paramilitary influence but by deploying it in order to protect her son, Jake, from being bullied at school. Far from the pacifist women of O'Casey, Mitchell's women are often as thickly involved in the fray as the men. The 'Mafia' structure adds a layer of complexity in that violence and paramilitarism are the glue that holds the family together before they become the source of its destruction. There are criticisms to be made of Mitchell's work, but one of its strengths is that it avoids sentimental, simplistic oppositions between family and society, domesticity and politics, women and men.

The socio-economic structures underlying family life are most explicitly brought home when Mitchell adds an historical dimension to his domestic drama. *Tearing the Loom* (1998) dramatises the divisions in the Ulster Protestant community during the 1798 rebellion, treating the brutal suppression of the United Irishmen by the fledgling Orange Order. A strikingly violent play, which begins with a garroting and ends with a man bleeding to death while a woman is slowly hanged, it examines the tragic fate of the Moores, a family of weavers. The son David is drawn into the local Orange lodge by stories of butchery visited upon Protestants by priest-led rebels in Wexford. As so often in Mitchell's drama, notions of masculine identity and its precariousness are as central a concern as those of reactive Protestant bigotry and, as in *Trust* and indeed in *In a Little World of Our Own*, Mitchell uses father-son relationships to reinforce this troubled inheritance. There are two father-son relationships in *Tearing the Loom*, one between Robert and David, the other between Samuel Hamill, grand master of the local Orange lodge, and his son, William. William had been involved with Ruth, the daughter of Robert, who has now taken up with local United Irishman, Harry. While the play probes the origins of political violence, it also recognises the connection between the social position of both families and wider economic systems, many of which are exploitative and exclusive. Robert and his mother Anne insist on the irrelevance of politics to the lives of the family. What is important, for them, is only what goes on inside the home:

> ROBERT: Let me tell you what is of true importance, Ruth. Everything within these walls is of the utmost importance to us. Outside of them nothing can compare.
>
> RUTH: These walls can protect us from the wind but not from tyranny.[112]

Robert voices the position of conventional domestic drama, where home and family take precedence over abstract political ideas. But the play undermines his belief by showing how deeply implicated domestic life is with wider socio-economic structures. For instance, Robert is trying to organise a marriage between Ruth and William not just to preserve the integrity of the home, but to ensure the economic advantage of familial connection with the wealthy Hamills. Similarly Robert's urge to preserve patrilineal succession — the play begins with him trying to teach David how to operate the loom — is a desire to preserve wealth and social 'respectability' as much as familial integrity. Simply put, the social position of the Moores cannot be separated from wider social and sectarian injustice. The final image of Robert, tied to the loom as his daughter is tortured, symbolically indicates how the 'loom' represents a force of succession that is as much disabling and hidebound by tradition, as it is a principle of reassuring domestic continuity.

Tearing the Loom stands out from Mitchell's growing corpus. He is more known for his depictions of paramilitary families in Rathcoole estate in Belfast. His departure here is a commemorative gesture for the bicentenary of the 1798 Rebellion. As already seen, however, the history play was recurrent in Northern drama during the Eighties and into the Nineties, partly because of the implicit Field Day credo that throwing light on the past would illuminate current schisms, that ancestral voices, the ghosts of history, would dispel the atavistic antagonisms of the present. So there is a sense in which the 'history play' might be seen as forum for political progress. However, one could argue, that the prevalence of the history play also indicates a hidden fatalism. History plays, especially those based around well-known events and episodes, almost always rely on a heavy investment of dramatic irony. Unlike the characters on stage, the audience typically knows what is going to happen. This is crucial because the characters, effectively, are pre-destined as far as the audience is concerned; in one sense what happens to them is beyond their control. When we watch *Translations* we know that the Famine will shortly decimate the community, even without the reminders of the smell of the blight throughout the play. We watch *Observe the Sons of Ulster* with the ever-present awareness of the massacre of Ulster's 36th Division at the Somme, even without Pyper the Elder's guilt-fuelled reminiscences.

So for all the talk of 'the fifth province' and the imaginative rewiring of cultural structures, the history play is, in an important sense, a narrative that relies on pre-destination. Much more so, perhaps, than the domestic drama that it was designed to usurp. Yet this is not a weakness. Inevitably, a long-standing conflict is going to give rise to feelings of entrapment and hopelessness. If drama can point the imaginative route towards conflict resolution, surely it should also express the communal sensibility. If this includes feelings of despair and fatalism, drama should perhaps reflect this tragic sense, not just replace it with pat comic alternatives. If the stage is taxed with simply providing oblique promises of Utopia, forever deferred in real life, then it is merely an upgraded form of propaganda.

The last play Friel produced with Field Day, *Making History* (1988), is a significant instance of how the history play relies on structures of pre-determination. Set in 1591, this play treats an episode in the life of Hugh O'Neill, the earl of Tyrone. Having already sworn loyalty to Queen Elizabeth and married Mabel, a recent English settler, Hugh is forced to make a choice between English and Irish culture, between the forces of the crown and the old Gaelic clans, with whom they increasingly conflict. O'Neill is acutely aware of the significance of the choice he has to make, aware of himself as 'making history'. But the play is not simply about the enduring effects of these events on the historical stage. In another sense 'making history' refers to the process by which these events are recorded for posterity. While O'Neill ruefully contemplates his role in history, pondering how future generations will remember him, Archbishop Lombard, who is writing the biography of 'the O'Neill', is aware of how contingent and perspectival any record of history inevitably is:

> I don't believe that a period of history — a given space of time — my life — your life — that it contains within it one 'true' interpretation just waiting to be mined. But I do believe that it may contain within it several possible narratives: the life of Hugh O'Neill can be told in many different ways. And those ways are determined by the needs and the demands and the expectations of different people and different eras. What do they want to hear? How do they want it told?[113]

In the final scene of the play, when O'Neill is a bitter and broken exile in Rome, we discover that Lombard's book will be a whitewash, that it will glamorise and mythologise O'Neill, turning him retrospectively into a Gaelic hero. O'Neill simply wants Lombard to tell the truth, to acknowledge his many failings: his own erstwhile Anglophilia, the incompetence of the Gaelic leaders that led to the rout in Kinsale; 'I need the truth, Peter. That's all that's left. The schemer, the leader, the liar, the statesman, the lecher, the patriot, the soured drunken émigré.'[114] What we have here is a conflict of historical perspectives: between O'Neill's notion of history as objective and Lombard's wily spin-doctoring, designed to cater for the desires of the demoralised Irish. On the one hand, the play strikes at the dynamics of nationalist myth-making, preferring the integrity of O'Neill to Lombard's opportunism. Yet at the same time it affirms Lombard's belief that history is made and re-made — a process of which, after all, the play is itself a part.

So there is a dilemma of historical understanding. In one respect, *Making History* seeks to rehabilitate the past. To open up new dimensions of understanding by revealing how artificial historical narrative is, both in terms of the choices that are made and in terms of how the story is structured and told. In other words the play is advancing a principle of historical flexibility, partly in order to re-orientate many of the inflexible positions and inherited roles in the socially divided society from which it was written. But in another sense *Making History* relies on the connivance of an audience, fully aware that Gaelic civilisation will be swept away and that the 'Flight of the Earls' will open the way for the colonisation of Ireland. This is an historical fact, regardless of how an alternative strain in this play seeks to demonstrate how flexible and changeable the story becomes in the telling. The writing of history — historiography — may be contingent, moulded to some extent by the perspective of the historian, but there is another sense that what happened is utterly recalcitrant — it cannot be changed. It is only our interpretations of what has happened that mutate, not the past itself. So if historiography is flexible, history is not. If the future is full of endless possibility, the past is rigidly linear: fate, the will of the gods, is just that linearity anticipated in advance. In a sense, then, the past (and hence history plays) has all the inexorable irremediability of the most pitiless fatalism. In that respect, the 'history play', given its deep reliance on shared dramatic irony, is a secular expression of the sort of fatalism we traditionally associate with Greek drama. Though without the machinations of inscrutable gods, and however open O'Neill's decision is for much of the play, the House of O'Neill is as doomed as the House of Atreus.

Perhaps the prevalence of the history play, together with this sort of secular fatalism, is one reason why there have been several Irish adaptations of the Greek classics in the past twenty years, including Tom Paulin's *The Riot Act* (1984), based on Sophocles' *Antigone* and Seamus Heaney's *The Cure at Troy* (1990), a version of Sophocles' *Philoctetes*. The latter has given us one of the most quoted of lines from the literature of the Troubles, even coming to the attention of Bill Clinton's speechwriters:

> History says, *Don't Hope*
> *On this side of the grave.*
> But then, once in a lifetime
> The longed-for tidal wave
> Of justice can rise up,
> And hope and history rhyme.[115]

Like so many other plays to have emerged from the Trouble, *The Cure at Troy* treats the opposition between the aspirations and actions of people and the countervailing flow of history — regarded, significantly (and perhaps suspiciously) as a force outside of human control, though we can hope for the occasional 'rhyme'. In *The Cure at Troy*, as in Heaney's poetic work, art is seen as a crucial connecting force between 'fate', the will of the gods or that which has been pre-ordained, and 'hope' or human agency. Poetry operates 'always in between/ What you would like to happen and what will –/ Whether you like it or not'.[116] Ten years before the action of the play, the warrior Philoctetes had been abandoned on the island of Lemnos by Odysseus, because of the unbearable stench from his rotting foot, incurred as the result of a snakebite. Now Odysseus has returned to the island with his lieutenant, Neoptolemus because they need the bow that never misses its target, given to Philoctetes by Hercules, in order to win the Trojan War. Treating the need to leave behind grudges and past wrongs in the interests of mutual advancement, *The Cure at Troy* also considers the excruciations of compromise, of turning one's back on long held principle or, to put it in more familiar terms, of 'selling out'. It is also a passionate appeal for trust and civic diplomacy, not the unscrupulous wiliness espoused by Odysseus, but the far more honest and honourable methods that Neoptolemus cannot give up. First staged by Field Day in Derry's Guildhall in 1990, we can perhaps feel the intimations of the end of the conflict, that were soon to be nurtured.

The distancing techniques deployed by many playwrights in treating the Troubles and the tendency to try and look at social realities and political strife in fresh ways means that many of these plays often incorporate allegorical dimensions. In other words the audience is invited to hear echoes of contemporary strife in events on the stage not directly concerned with the conflict. There are, then, allegorical suggestions in *The Cure at Troy:* does Philoctetes ulcerated foot represent the corrupt, stagnant situation in Northern Ireland? Does his original abandonment by Hercules on the island of Lemnos betoken the abandonment of the nationalists by the Irish state? Or of the Unionist by the British? Partly, perhaps, but we have no definitive answer. There is a difference between the suggestiveness, say, of a mythic play like this and the one-on-one correspondences one would expect from full allegory. Many allegorical plays can be criticised for too close an identification with their object of reference, so that a process of simplistic decoding takes the place of dramatic subtlety and richness. Perhaps the most direct allegory for the Troubles is Bill Morrison's 1992 trilogy, *A Love Song for Ulster*. This series of three plays uses the fate of one household and three generations as an easily decipherable allegory for the Irish struggle, from the Anglo-Irish Treaty to the first stirrings of the current peace process. The first play, 'Marriage', tells how Kate has been abandoned in the North by her mother Mary and forced into marriage with John, a stolid Protestant and Orangeman. The echoes of partition are not difficult to hear. At first the marriage is strained as both parties seek to conform to their pre-ordained roles, he dominant but reluctant patriarch, she submissive housewife. As soon as the marriage settles into a semblance of contentment, John is shot dead by Mary's brother, Gabriel, and she is subsequently raped and co-opted by John's more brutal brother, Victor. The three plays go on in this style, offering allegorical equivalents for many of the main events of the following seventy years: the Second World War, the outbreak of the Troubles, the arrival of the British army, the Ulster Workers Strike, the Hunger Strikes and so on. Finally, as all three generations gather round the table, the play concludes with portents of reconciliation and the end of the conflict.

The allegorical references in *A Love Song for Ulster* can occasionally seem didactic and restrictive. Yet the experiment is not without interest. Perhaps the most significant feature is the Beckettian exchanges between Mick and Willie. This working-class pair operate like a sort of chorus, commenting on the action, before they assume the role of characters in the middle of the second play. As the stage directions tell us, they *'begin the play as ghosts, become real, and end as ghosts again'*.[117] Amidst the trivia of much of their conversation is Willie's obsession with the biblical story of Abraham and Isaac. This story chimes with the play's dominant concern with generational succession and parental-child relationships, with violence, abandonment and betrayal. But, above all, it is interpreted by Willie as a mythic treatment of the conflict between human aspiration and divine decree, between agency and fatalism, hope and history:

> WILLIE: I know about history. History always leaves out what people felt about it while it was happening. It always leaves out that most people didn't like it, didn't want it, protested about it and were generally fucked by it.[118]

Willie cannot fathom why Isaac went with his father, why he did not put up a struggle. The pair continue to ponder the question, recognising that the tale, like recorded history, is incomplete, simply serving to reinforce the message of the 'old men' who are telling it. It has a happy ending, where Isaac's life is spared, simply for propaganda purposes: 'To show the rewards of blind obedience. That's why the story is not interested in what

Isaac felt. He's just there to show that even with his own father's knife at his throat he submitted to authority of his earthly father backed up by his heavenly father.'[119] Willie thinks that Isaac should have kicked his father 'in the goolies the minute he started coming at him with the knife and rope'[120] and this in a sense is the moral message of the play. Authority, especially quasi-divine authority that brooks no questioning, needs to be resisted. So, too, should the rigid ordinances of patrilinear succession. During the play, sons are tragically caught up in the violent machinations of fathers and father-figures. A deterministic model, in which identity and inherited roles are bequeathed from father to son in tribal succession, are presented as the enemy of emancipation and individual self-realisation.

The gender exclusivity here is deliberate and highlighted in many Northern dramas, by both men and women. Indeed, gender identity, particularly exaggerated, violent masculinity, are so intimate with notions of tribal identity as to be inseparable. Just as the characters on stage are often 'performing' their national and cultural identity, so too are they performing their masculinity. We see this continually in the work of playwrights like Christina Reid and Anne Devlin who, often examining the Troubles from the perspectives of female characters, expose the vagaries and injustices of gender politics. As already seen, another playwright who recognises the connections between the performance of masculinity and the performance of a Protestant working-class identity is Gary Mitchell. He too is recurrently interested in the formative relationships between fathers or father-figures and sons on the brink of maturity in whom they invest their hopes and pride. Interestingly in his play *In a Little World of Our Own*, the story of Abraham and Isaac is also invoked. The play treats three brothers, local UDA heavy, Ray, his 'simple' brother Richard of whom he is ferociously protective, and Gordon, who is engaged to Deborah and is struggling to live up to his fiancée's strong religious faith. Gordon ponders in Act One that, if he were Abraham and had been asked to kill his own son, he would have refused. Later in the play he is put in a version of this position.

Richard has an unreciprocated crush on Susan, the daughter of another loyalist leader, Monroe. Susan, it seems, has spurned Richard for a Catholic boy, Michael. In a scene that occurs offstage after a dance, Ray gets involved in a stand-off between Richard, Susan and Michael. Having chased Michael away, Ray, in a violent frenzy, ends up severely beating and raping Susan. Ray has been planning to pass this off as a crime of Michael's by violently coercing a false confession. The intermediary between the loyalist families, Walter, knows the likelihood that Richard — widely known as a stalker of Susan and as a 'retard' — will be blamed, no matter what story is offered to the Monroe family. The solution he offers to Gordon, the one that will involve least bloodshed, and still adhere to the brutal codes of paramilitary retribution, is a tokenistic shooting of Richard in the knee:

> What I'm talking about here, Gordon. Is a little nick. Not a bullet in the head or a shattered kneecap … it's not about the wound it's about the act and it's about the will to carry out the act, that's remorse and that's respect. This act will be a tremendous piece of courage and this act, believe me, will be an act a man like Monroe will have to respect.[121]

Hence, as he later remarks, Gordon finds himself in an analogous situation to Isaac. The decree of tribal ordinance, the Mafioso code of honour that Mitchell often invokes, here takes on the role of divine instruction, again bringing home the idea that identity and tribe can be a sort of a restrictive destiny. So the story of Abraham/Isaac is deftly incorporated into a play intimately concerned with notions of patriarchy and symbolic paternity: Gordon, and especially Ray, are surrogate father-figures to the vulnerable, child-like Richard. But with a symbolic stroke at the end of the play, Mitchell ends up inverting the myth. In the last Act, Susan dies in hospital but not before fingering Ray as her rapist and murderer. As Ray lies wounded in the living room, with Monroe's crowd outside waiting to finish him off, he begs

Gordon to kill him. In the mêlée which follows, Richard ends up shooting Ray. Symbolically, this is a son killing his father. The action has moved from the Isaac/Abraham myth to the Oedipus myth. And this importance of overcoming the father is a familiar theme in Irish drama, from *The Playboy of the Western World* onwards. While Abraham and Isaac — the move to kill the son — represents the entrapments of authority, of history, or inherited identity, the symbolic killing of the father represents the opposite: the escape from authority and the fatalism represented by the tribe. So in a sense, for all the bloodshed, *In a Little World of Our Own* ends optimistically, much more so than *Tearing the Loom*, where it is the children who are killed. Perhaps, the symbolic overthrow of authority at the end of the play might be a register of the peace process, a subliminal recognition of political moves away from entrenched positions and atavistic loyalties.

In general, with the change in the political atmosphere of the North, we find a shift from history plays and the experimental dramas that characterised drama of the Troubles in the Eighties. There has been a return to domestic and realistic dramas, by writers like Mitchell, Daragh Carville and Michael Harding. There are a number of reasons for this change. Parker's premature death in 1988 robbed Northern Ireland of one of its most eloquent and penetrating playwrights. Field Day seemed to run out of steam in the early Nineties, signifying the end of one of the richest sources of theatrical and intellectual production in the North. Theatrical movements like Belfast's Dubbeljoint have continued to generate drama about life in the North, and produced Marie Jones's work after Charabanc. But the tradition of a 'theatre of ideas', such as that attempted by Field Day, has ebbed. It is as if political success has sappped energy from theatrical innovation. Yet one could make a case that realism — or at least the staging of a recognisable, contemporary social reality (not always the same thing) — is the dramatic form natural to a functioning society. This does not mean that arresting subject matter and unexpected conjunctions cannot be attempted on the realist stage. Nonetheless, when a polity is fragmented, when cause and effect seem mysteriousy disconnected and social life continually in crisis, drama buckles into new and unfamiliar forms. Similarly, there is something a bit odd and fetishistic about continually calling up the spirits of your ancestors through the medium of history plays. Perhaps this sort of intellectual, self-conscious drama occurs when politics intrudes into culture, when culture cannot function normally. There is always a political dimension to cultural production but during times of crisis, the two become indistinguishable; drama becomes a mode of political imagination, rather than an organ of cultural expression. Often, as argued in this essay, social conflict can be the engine for urgent, innovative drama. Yet, it can also be restrictive. To borrow a formulation of G.B. Shaw's, you are never more aware of your leg than when it is broken. When it is functioning normally you can forget about it. The same goes for identity and politics. The history play and cerebral drama is the natural theatre of politics. But this exploration of communal memory can be at the price of seeing the lives of recognisable people dramatised on stage, the people who live next door rather than in the seventeenth century. For this sort of theatre, a certain amnesia is necessary, just as we forget about how our leg functions, when we want to start walking. The hope for Northern Irish theatre of the new century must be that political success will free theatre to reflect the culture of Northern Ireland, rather than reflect upon its politics.

MIC MORONEY

The Twisted Mirror:
Landscapes, Mindscapes, Politics and Language
on the Irish Stage

The extraordinary upsurge in new Irish theatre over the past decade and a half has seen some major additions to, as well as reinventions of the repertoire. Most of the work is very specifically Irish, and yet a great deal of it has proven to be bizarrely exportable. But what is it that makes the bestiary of the Irish stage so keenly recognisable at home, and yet simultaneously so appealing to international audiences? And what chimaeric image of Ireland is created in the process?

A decade ago, the theatrical world began swooning to Brian Friel's bittersweet *Dancing at Lughnasa*, with its dreamy nostalgia for a Donegal that seemed to have evaporated. There was great innocence and deceptive simplicity to the piece, along with a Dennis Potter-style use of music and memory. The parting narration touched delicately on the suffering that later befell the characters, but apart from that, and an excitable flurry of dancing on tables, little disturbed the amber world of gentle Donegal accents and soft emotional cadences.

Since then, the voltage of Irish stage performance has risen considerably. We've had the gung-ho unleashing of Riverdance from Perth to Broadway, with its shock-troops of thundering Irish dancers — the 'Flying Squads' as they are known in the business — hammering away to the jagged, propulsive counts of Bill Whelan's re-codification of the old dance music. Generally, these last years have seen the Irish star rising ever higher thanks to the peace process in Northern Ireland and, under the waning influence of the Clinton presidency in the US, the 'greening of the White House' — with the Irish lads 'scrubbing the muck off the shamrock', as a character mutters in Paul Mercier's play, *Ourselves Alone.*

But I'd love to have been a fly inside the skull of an American diplomat, or a senior CIA operative, watching the Irish theatrical offerings at the Island: Arts from Ireland festival at the Kennedy Centre in Washington in May 2000, as the latest deranged beasts of the Irish imagination reared up in front of them.

There was the demented, imagistic energy of Donal O'Kelly's performance of *Catalpa*, which colourfully revitalised Irish race-memories of the Antipodean penal colonies. Rough Magic dusted down Stewart Parker's sublime *Pentecost*, charting the utter societal breakdown of the dark days, literally, of the hellish Loyalist Workers Strike in 1974. Then there was the willfully crazed, routine incest of Marina Carr's *On Raftery Hill*, with that appalling and unforgettable scene in which Raftery, played by Tom Hickey, climbs up on top of his daughter, and deflowers her in the best Irish family tradition. Oh, this was pig-in-the-cabin stage-Ireland alright, hurling red-hot potatoes out at you.

Certainly, Carr crashed through the barriers of yet another taboo — and certainly, to my eye, there seemed nearly as much unease in the playing as in the gutted audience reaction at the time of its premiere. But with her heightened Tullamore tinker's argot and coarse, lyric vinegar, Carr exemplifies a whole wave of contemporary Hiberno-English dramatists who conjure fantastic landscapes out of the vernacular, almost to a Syngian/O'Casey template. Yet despite the archaic idioms, theirs is an utterly contemporary world as they lure you down the back lanes and bothairins of the Irish psyche, often illustrating the worst excesses of humanity, which scream out at us from newspaper court reports.

On Raftery's Hill had all Carr's hallmarks and caucus-race characters of hardened strange women, addled old birds and sacrificial lambs — as laid out in a magnetic series of plays over the 1990s such as *The Mai, Portia Coughlan* and *By the Bog of Cats*. Perhaps because I saw *On Raftery's Hill* in Galway under the same flaying whip-arm of director Garry Hynes, I later very much associated it, perhaps mistakenly, with McDonagh's Leenane Trilogy. It seemed to stalk around on similar melodramatic, provocative, even satirical stilts. The engine of both productions was one of menace and frightening intensity, while the language constantly strove to best bury the barb in the soul of the adversary and twist it. This taste for cruelty is becoming increasingly prevalent in the new, younger-minded drama.

It still baffles some people how Martin McDonagh's merciless Leenane Trilogy tore around the world like wildfire. From Leenane to the howling antics of *The Lieutenant of Inishmore*, McDonagh's work is as much deliverance-style pisstake as powerful pastiche, with its acid blarney and junk-culture Connemara. Like Shane McGowan's best work, it's a blistering re-imagining of the Irish experience from a first-generation London-Irishman. McDonagh's Connemara is a vicious, swaggering cartoon creation with all the aesthetics of a Tom and Jerry cartoon, yet which is utterly, weirdly recognisable — thanks to his undeniable handle on the old idioms and mindset and landscape.

Yet just look at how Irish performers are scoring abroad, particularly in the UK — deep, dank parodies of their own culture. Look at our standing army of comedians who have emerged triumphant over the last decade, from the Tommy Tiernans and Deirdre O'Kanes to TV writers Arthur Mathews and Graham Linehan who so superbly timed the utter daftness of Fathers Ted, Jack, Dougal and Mrs Doyle on Craggy Island. Untroubled, wild self-parody and hyper-charged melodrama seems hardwired into a lot of new Irish writing and performance — or maybe what is expected of it.

At this point in Irish history — at a time of unprecedented wealth in certain private pockets — it may seem sad and reductionist to assert a colonial dimension to this often buffoonish translation of ourselves, negotiating a comical, exotic identity within a dominant Anglo-American culture. But it's certainly had a long history, analagous to the emergence of black perfomers in the US from comical minstrelsy and grotesquely gesticulating dumb-show tap routines.

In this light, it's interesting to ponder the theme of the latest Irish success — Marie Jones's fondly amusing *Stones in His Pockets*, which catapulted recently from a successful run on London's West End to Broadway and a clutch of Tony nominations. It's a play about a pair of comical, gormless no-hopers, finding themselves and each other whilst hanging around as extras in an American film shot in Ireland. It's a curious reappraisal of the little people of Irish history and the way their stories are invisibly subsumed into the actual making of it.

The chief weapon for Irish dramatists, of course, is the strangely universal appeal and the creative use of the old Hiberno-English dialects, with their beautifully involuted syntactical shapes that emerge partly from the translations of nineteenth-century Gaelic revivalists, and partly from the rich idioms which still survive up and down the country, and indeed island. Sometimes, the Irish protrudes like bones through the hungry hide of the unsuspecting Bearla. In his recent *Dictionary of Anglo-Irish*, Diarmuid Ó Muirthile lists a vast amount of Irish words and phrases that he asserts still inhabit the English language as spoken here.

It is interesting too that there is such evergreen life — in Ireland, at any rate — in the thatch-lifting intellectual play, *Translations*, by the man from Greencastle, County Donegal, Mr Brian Friel. Written in 1980 to launch Field Day, *Translations* remains an astonishing feat to so formally engage, through drama, with issues of language and colonisation and the engulfment of one culture by another, as the mappers trawled the countryside, renaming and respelling the landscape, in what was ultimately a repressive military operation.

Riffing elegantly on the doublethink of Northern Ireland where, say, the city of Derry/Londonderry has two names depending on the slant of your identity, Friel illustrated the bizarre ironies of native hedge schoolteachers knowing Latin and

Greek classics but no English — alongside reminders of how, say, the Great Liberator Daniel O'Connell declared that the old language was a barrier to modern progress.

Indeed, one of the strangest things I ever saw was an Amharclann na hÍde production which translated Synge's harshly tragic *Riders to the Sea* back, so to speak, into Irish and brought it to Inis Mean. Whatever the piece lost or gained in the retranslation, it was bizarre to see the urbane company playing in full costume to an audience that included old women in the audience with authentic multi-coloured shawls and pampootees — fetching up an image of Irish theatre in a constant vortex of translation and re-representation.

Interestingly, as I write, Paul Mercier has returned to the original Irish text of *Diarmuide agus Grainne*, and discovered that many meanings were over-elaborated in Standish Hayes O'Grady's baroque Hiberno-English translation, which so influenced Yeats and Lady Gregory in their search for an Irish literary theatre, as Bearla.

Then there is the strange business of new 'adapations' of classics by Irish playwrights: arguably manufacturing Hiberno-Ibsens, Hiberno-Chekhovs or Hiberno-Turgenevs. Rather than working from the original, say, Russian, playwrights are more often than not working from existing English translations, meaning that the Hiberno-versions are another important little step away from the integrity and mindset of the original.

Despite the Gaeltacht in his home county, John B. Keane has long extolled the Elizabethan virtues of Kerry English — its richness of phrase and euphemism, and indeed its delight in language for its own sake. Linguistically, scholars characterise Elizabethan English — in the texts that remain, of course — as the most uninhibited in the history of the English language — indeed it gave us the astonishing wealth and grain of Shakespeare.

Ó Muirthile quotes another academic, the late John Braidwood of Queen's University, Belfast: 'Today probably only the Irishman, especially the Southern Irishman[*], and some

---

[*] With one eye on Ulster Scots, and the other on the treacly dialects of the North in general, I would query this qualification.

Welshmen, work in the Elizabethan linguistic, mastering the language, whereas the rest of us, with pusillanimous notions of correctness and good taste hammered into us at school, let the language master us.'

Most academics date Hiberno-English back to the Elizabethan age and the early seventeenth century. Ireland's comparitive remoteness, insularity and largely oral culture all conspired to conserve the more baroque features of Elizabethan English. The word 'crack', for example, now erroneously gaelicised as 'craic', in fact appears in the work of poet Edmund Spenser (who, as Sheriff of Cork, recommended that the unruly Irish be put to the sword) as 'crake': to boast loudly and raucously.

Ó Muirthile and others credit Hyde, Yeats, Synge, Lady Gregory et al for intuitively recognising that, by 1900, the Irish had forged a new language from the one they had been forced to learn: a kind of musical creole from which the new dramatists could create and heighten a new and fictive literature for the spoken art of the Irish stage.

Synge: 'In a good play, every speech should be as fully flavoured as a nut or apple.' It is a testimony to the robustness of the Hiberno dialects, from Dublinese to those in the lonesome wesht, that despite the neutralised, middle-class Anglo-tones of RTÉ broadcasters, there are still rich motherlodes of knotty, scuzzy accents and idioms for playwrights to plunder and embellish, with remarkable musical fidelity — creating worlds a whole lot more pungent and punchy than the smell of nuts and apples.

In the hands of good writers, with lyric power welling up inside them, the liberating rhythms of the Irish vernacular tend to open the door into a primitivism, an ill-mannered eruption into the psyche as though of some unconscious force, of something oral and uncivilised; a wild, untamed elastication of reality.

Again, one could assert a colonial and class-based dimension, gradating across from mannered, urbanised Dublin, with its own gross internal inequities and register-shifts of accent and idiom; to Tom Murphy's great epic vernacular symphonies of disaffection in small-town Tuam — upending Shavian drawing rooms and Big House dramatic tropes with chaotic forces often unleashed in the crucible of alcohol. Briefly, the social pecking order seems to shimmer and collapse in the heat of the night's drinking, only to re-congeal once the genie goes back into the bottle in the hangover dawn.

It is interesting that in 1961, when Tom Murphy's *A Whistle in the Dark*, written in that violent, growling lyrical vernacular, took on the raging sense of social and racial inferiority of the 'fighting Carneys' in Coventry, London critics howled down the 'anthropoid apes' of Murphy's creation — earning him little affection from the then Abbey director Ernest Blyth. How the cycles of taste have turned.

In his last two plays *The Wake* and *The House*, both at the Abbey, Murphy has stuck to his abiding vision of small-town Irish life, tinctured by the murderous hunger for property. Meanwhile *The House*, set in the late 1950s, nastily echoes the land-lust of John B. Keane's Bull McCabe in *The Field*. In both plays, Murphy paints a haggard but convincing vista of families bound by little more than mutual contempt and shared ownership.

Murphy always points up the unassailable caste-systems within these narrow-minded communities. For example, in *The House*, you have the vulnerable, pallid creatures at the top of the pyramid, the delicately traumatised old Anglo-Norman family of Mrs de Burca and her three daughters. Then you have the cute, local propertied class of the shleeveen publican-auctioneer, and the well-mannered solicitor who has escaped the slums of Barracks Street. Below that again, you have the raucous, 'native' codes of the pub, where the monstrous male energies collide — disgruntled locals clashing with the uneducated, criminalised, wide-boys who annually return, cash-laden, from the building sites and criminal underworlds of urban England and the US.

This latter zone is wild with expletives, but with its own codes and hesitant language of inarticulate need, as Murphy probes into an understratum of Irish society, with all its personal dereliction, learned self-loathing, atavistic male aggression, and cruelty. He constantly pinions the virtually colonial disdain the upper classes have for the untamed poor, clinging to hopeless underclass estates like the one in *The Wake*, which everyone sneeringly refers to as 'the Punjab'.

This echoes such prejudices as often surface among the new Dublin playwrights, who frequently refer to characters from outside the Pale as 'culchies' or 'bogmen' — neatly fitting the colonial snobbery of terms like 'bog-trotters' (or 'bog-wogs', as recently surfaced as an example of British military parlance in Northern Ireland). The rural/regional term for Dubliners arose as a pejorative for those turn-of-the-twentieth-century urban loyalists who aspired to waving little Union Jacks, or 'jackeens', that were handed out to children for Queen Victoria's visit.

If one goes back into the theatrical record, an uneasy image of the ignorant, sometimes ape-like, rural Paddy prevails. Christopher Fitz-Simon in his book *The Irish Theatre* (1983), dates the first consciously created stage-Irishman to the 1594 play, *The Battle of Alcazar* by the Archbishop of Cashel, George Peel. Peel's characterisation of the Norman-Irishman, Maurice Gibbon Fitzgibbon, reveals a rather early, simian piece of onomasticism, while Shakespeare introduced his own ill-educated, rustic Irish bumpkin, Macmorris, as a minor character in *Henry V* (1598).

Naturally, native Irish characters popped up in the work of Irish playwrights like Farquhar, Thomas Sheridan, Richard Brinsley Sheridan, Macklin and O'Keeffe — highly popular, comic parts, often tricky but charming rogues, with names like O'Blunder or, more ominously, O'Trigger. English playwrights boiled these stereotypes down with gusto into the comical, bibulous, colourful eejit of a stage-Irishman. Fitz-Simon identifies two types of Irish stage-archetypes stretching back at least to the seventeenth century: the parasite-slave, a lazy, crafty rogue — or the drunken fighter-braggart, which conforms to the *miles gloriosus* of classical comedy.

In the nineteenth century, as Darwinian ideas began to percolate, Irish actor-playwrights arrived like Tyrone Power (1797-1841) and Dionysius Boucicault (1822-90), thanks to an emerging Irish middle class and the opening up of the new, receptive American theatres. Power left behind masterpieces like *O'Flannigan and the Fairies* — a clear forerunner to *Darby O'Gill and the Little People*, or indeed that recent Leprechaun movie for which actor Colm Meany was so roundly denounced by Irish-America. But Boucicault was the consummate actor, impresario and playwright, and his plays still enjoy the odd, soft-headed revival — often for the benefit of summer visitors to the Abbey.

Born in 1822 in Gardiner Street in Dublin, Boucicault, by the age of twenty-six, had had thirty works performed in the West End. In 1878, he wowed New York with his 'Irish trilogy' of *Arrah-na-Pogue*, *The Shaughraun* and *The Colleen Bawn* with its roguishly resourceful, charmer-hero, Myles na Coppaleen who saves the day, and indeed the girl.

Even in England, these plays were spectacularly popular. It's extraordinary that *The Shaughran*, set during the Fenian uprising a few years previously, even saw benefit performances in England for Fenian prisoners in British jails. Queen Victoria attended *The Colleen Bawn* three times — the last play she ever saw, as Prince Albert collapsed and died shortly after one performance, and Victoria rarely attended any public events thereafter. Set around the Lakes of Killarney of Boucicault's fervid imagination, the Colleen is pure begorrah stage-Irishry, and even Conall Morrison's ironically winking production at the Abbey recently failed to polish the chestnut up to any convincing gleam.

It's interesting that although Boucicault's high-flown melodrama was seen as anathema to the ideals of the Gaelic revival and the early Abbey theatre, these aristocratic types created a romantic, primitivist stage-Ireland, which itself often became risible, arguably until Garry Hynes put vicious manners on Synge's *Playboy* again. For decades after independence, the recycled sets at the Abbey provided a kind of static reality studio for generations of writers who wrote, and still write, for the staggering range of exaggerated accents you hear simultaneously on the Abbey stage, whatever the idiom of the original text.

But now that a certain freedom of expression and a newfound

respect for regional identity is opening up in Irish theatre — as much in the big houses as in the independent sector — writers are returning anew to the rhythms and music and scepticism implicit in the old vernaculars, and creating new literary forms.

It's an irresistible allure for a writer to learn, inhabit and wind around inside these idioms, even if younger writers do not always seem aware that they are entering into a deep history of theatrical stereotypes. Sometimes, they boldly re-appropriate the weaponry of belittlement. More often, the dialects are just used to generate the sheer colour of withering insult, or simply to wield the blunt bladders of humour. Certainly, the old talk makes for an enormously flexible instrument for engineering surreality and absurdism.

Interestingly, there are a number of remote, poetic rural voices active along the border: Vincent Woods; Michael Harding's thrashing anguish in the presbytery; even some of Dermot Healy's occasionally loonish, soul-raking stage poetry; and Tom MacIntyre's wild celebratory use of a kind of phalloidal dementia to enliven the landscape, or to eviscerate resonant history as he did in his acerbic-heroic *Good Evening, Mister Collins*.

Clones man Pat McCabe's mad tale of border butchers, *Loco County Lonesome* has hit the road again, while his own stage-adaptation of his novel, *The Butcher Boy*, remains a lambent memory. More recently, Declan Gorman's Drogheda-based young Upstate company have been making inroads with Gorman's topical, sometimes morally didactic, satirical meditations on life in the peace-process Borderlands.

In this context, Conall Morrison's vital, imagistic adaptation of Patrick Kavanagh's novel of testosterone-driven, nature-spiritualised, re-remembered youth, *Tarry Flynn*, was an auspicious coup on the West End. Whilst researching it, Morrison investigated old recordings in the Ulster Folk and Transport Museum of Cavan people speaking in the 1930s, in accents and dialects so rich and hermetic, they were probably unintelligible in neighbouring counties.

Many of the regional voices on the Irish stage today speak

from the experience of the small town. No matter how anachronistically 'culchie' John B. Keane must have sounded to the Dublin theatre managers who so studiously ignored him in the 1960s and 1970s — don't forget all those great Dublin jokes like the one about the Kerry woodworm found dead in a brick — Keane's work was acidly engaged with Listowel society and its hinterland people who would wander into town of a fair day. Nowadays of course, partly thanks to Ben Barnes and the old Groundwork company, Keane is one of the biggest bankers of the main Dublin stages, stacking arses onto Gaiety seats with comedies like *The Chastitute* — or in the Abbey, 'serious' plays like *Big Maggie*, which Garry Hynes recently roasted of all maudlin sentiment.

Billy Roche wrote clearly in a Wexford mindset for his inter-referential Wexford trilogy, even if the casts in various productions didn't always adhere to the exact, earthy diamond of the local accent. Gina Moxley's nowhere-crossroads Cork was also rather an urban re-imagining of childhood in her hilariously 'autogeographical' *Danti-Dan*, which reached back into the cusp of cruel, uneducated, pubertal sexuality; with a remorselessly bold girl-child trying out amorous manoevres on a young simpleton. Set on a country bridge beside an old Button-A-Button-B phone box, to the strains of young Larry Gogan on the wireless, it had a tawdry-golden modernity, which had all the lost romanticism of a John Hinde postcard.

Cork also has its Enda Walsh, interestingly enough a Dublinman who — sensitised to the fragrant, nasal, melodious, gutty, old-underclass Cork patois — has crafted his own ornate, relentless wordscapes, like the extraordinary, druggy babytalk dreamworld of *Disco Pigs*, which having toured the continents, has now being committed to film by Kirsten Sheridan. More recently, Walsh delivered himself of the dank, dark claustrophobia of *Bedbound* with its secret-compartment underbelly of urban Cork, with a father and daughter walled up in a piss-stained cubicle in the house; she like a pallid and demented sea-bottom creature, thanks to the paranoid predations of her disturbed, widowed, warring father.

More recently, actor Eugene O'Brien emerged with *Eden*: two bleak, cross-cutting monologues (directed fittingly enough by Conor McPherson), set in an Irish midlands small-town, and written in a machismo, adrenalised dialect you could cut with a slurry-shovel. It was an arresting, if not entirely successful piece, about a blighted marriage with two kids: the young father drinking himself useless, whilst nursing infatuations with local lassies. The barroom flog of the lad's humour, played bombastically by Don Wycherley, was more convincing in the writing that the frailer, awkward, victim-like attempt of the wife (despite Catherine Walsh's keen performance) to negotiate her own pleasure, eventually with a stranger down by the canal.

Although from rural Wicklow originally, Loughlin Deegan lived in Limerick for some time before he wrote his hugely diverting debut play, *The Stomping Ground*. With a keen, deliberate ear for young-minded vernacular, as well as absorbing fragrant Limerickisms ('I'm as sick as a small hospital'), Deegan's major theme is the edgy manner in which young men communicate. More recently, for Red Kettle, he produced *The Queen and Peacock* about gay Irishmen marooned in once-liberating exile in London — ultimately inspired by John Crowley's influential devised show, *True Lines*.

Meanwhile, stage-Dublin is its own sprawling territory. The old outer suburbs crop up regularly in such hardy perennials of the southside as Hugh Leonard's *Da* and *A Life*, or indeed the darkening comedies of Bernard Farrell, and his humoristically confused South Dublin/Middle Ireland of the imagination; full of basically decent characters helplessly muddling around for solutions to situations far bigger than themselves.

Farrell so closely reflects and ribs his audiences, that it is interesting that his plays have never travelled abroad — unlike say, novelist Maeve Binchy whose work has been targeted for adaptation by the likes of the Fishamble company — chatty, fussed-up skits of the antiseptic pretensions of the middle classes, their womenfolk forever in neurotic/cosmetic/dietary distress. There was more darkness and realism and uncomfortable emotion somehow in Joseph O'Connor's young-minded but strangely accurate *Red Roses and Petrol*, set in an overgrown suburb in which family formalities threatened to all but collapse.

But the incursion of the more gnarled Dublin vernacular onto the stage has a curious and sporadic history. Like its Cockney counterpart, the old Dub working class accent is historically associated with the broad slap of the pantomime dame, or the stereotypical pair of ould ones, with their malapropisms and false teeth-shifting double entendres — typically, common-as-muck creatures trying to put on airs.

In Belfast, you have the cosily alarming May McFettridge buttering up the Grand Opera House audiences, while in Dublin, the mantle of Danny Cummins and Maureen Potter at the Gaiety seems to have passed over to Brendan O'Carroll and his comedies of Mrs Brown, the sewer-mouthed, chain-smoking, power-widow. The humour is bludgeoning in its physical directness. Dismissing the eloquence of her daughter's gallant Special Branch suitor, Mrs Brown is likely to croak, 'sher that's only man's talk for "show us your knickers"'. A lot of the mirth has to do with urine samples or 'swallowed' rectal thermometers, in fact anything to do with the puncturing of the anal sphincter. But by God, O'Carroll works his, or maybe her, audiences spectacularly.

Under the circumstances, it's little wonder that our northside Taoiseach Bertie Ahern took voice-coaching at the Gaiety School to iron out his 'dis, dat, dese and dose' — as though in an attempt to cleanse himself of this underclass idiom, an uncouth dialect of insult and complaint — despite its ornate, melodious codes and rich oral-literary slang.

On the Dublin stage, it was probably O'Casey who first dignified the archetypical comedy of Captain Boyle and Joxer Daly with the momentous, long-suffering decency of Juno and her fellow-tenement people, in O'Casey's cinematic transliteration of the Dublin slums. Set against the brutal conflagrations of the independence struggle, his three big plays have an enduring appeal, thanks partly to his extraordinary ear for the Dublin vernacular — indeed, like a balladeer, he inserted a number of fresh catchphrases into the common tongue.

It is intriguing that his later, socialist, anti-war stage-poem, *The Silver Tassie*, originally rejected by Yeats at the Abbey, has now been immortalised in Britten-style operatic form by Mark-Anthony Turnage — a fine production of which was recently brought home to Dublin by Opera Ireland, directed by Patrick Mason. The *Tassie* experience soured O'Casey to Ireland and its priest- and police-dominated society, and he continued to excoriate it, perhaps best in his satiric-absurdist *Cock-a-Doodle Dandy*, which I once saw performed by a bunch of prisoners in Mountjoy, who particularly relished firing off blanks to jolt awake the captive audience of perfumed visitors. The play shares some of its fantastic literary/vernacular tinge with the work of James Stephens and indeed Flann O'Brien whose various porter-metabolising characters have become synonymous with the great Dublin comic actor, Eamon Morrissey.

But in terms of big Dublin realism, and the greater socio-political canvas, no one has quite equalled O'Casey's achievement. The great gouger and republican Brendan Behan tossed off a couple of scurrilously heartfelt plays in the 1950s, like the death-penalty prison drama *The Quare Fella* at the Pike in 1954, and *The Hostage*, first produced as *An Giall* by Gael Linn in 1958, a bawdy Guests of the Nation-style yarn about a British soldier held in an Irish brothel. Both still get the odd raucous revival, and of course, Niall Toibin has swaggered about for years in the narrator part in the stage-adaptation of *Borstal Boy*. Peter Sheridan finally committed his own adaptation to film in 1999.

Other landmarks in Dublinese theatre include the late James McKenna's *The Scatterin'* in 1960, a bleak and poetic lament which Paul Mercier revived in the Gaiety in the 1980s. McKenna's Dublin was a reduced, humdrum world on the outskirts of the rock and roll era. The 'big men are dead', one character bemoaned, while the bums are 'crawling around in the sun like corpses on sick leave'. The only future was 'to jail or to England' for its crews of young underclass teddy boys, and the central character nearly manages the latter — only to get nabbed on the emigration boat for stabbing a Kerry guard.

Heno Magee's *Hatchet*, from the early 1970s, is another important portrait of inner city life — a spare but colourfully written piece about in-your-face, violent, tenement Dublin, and a gambling, hard-drinking family of no-hopers and jailbirds in no-go Summerhill. The gargle-sozzled wit is set against the vicious violence between unemployed menfolk, and the law is nowhere to be seen.

The late Seventies were the heydays of the Sheridan brothers, Peter and Jim, in Dublin theatre, and the inequalities evident in the rougher side of Dublin provided the major theme of their left-leaning work. From 1976 to 1980, they galvanised a company in the Project Arts Centre and churned out play after play, which are now iconic memories in the heads of those that saw them.

Typical of the work was *The Liberty Suit*, written by Peter in collaboration with Mannix Flynn: a prison yarn about a guy from Sean McDermott Street who ends up in Artane. Memorably staged in a big Olympia production in 1976, it saw Flynn playing himself to great acclaim as the jailbird-turned-actor. Another piece was Jim's *Mobile Homes*, inspired by their own circumstances, when both Sheridans and their families were living in caravans on rented lots, thanks to the accommodation crisis of the time. Plus ça change.

Another piece written by Jim, *The Last Post*, was a history of Ireland as refracted through the monocle of Brigadier-General Kitson-Clarke, British Army Commander-in-chief in Northern Ireland who oversaw the introduction of internment in 1971. This was done as a Communist Party production, and went to Cuba in 1981.

Although the staging was stylised, the performance style under the Sheridans was always social-realist and agit prop. Maybe their biggest hit was Jim Plunkett's Great Lock-Out epic, *The Risen People* (adapted from Strumpet City), which they revived four times in the Project in those years — and far less successfully in the Gaiety in the early 1990s, after more than a decade not working together. Jim broke into film with *My Left Foot* in 1987, based on their stage-adaptation of Christy Brown's *Down All the Days* at the Oscar in 1981 — and the film is now on the school curriculum.

Peter went on to work in Dublin Community Theatre, forming the City Workshop that played a history trilogy of ould Dublin: *The Kips the Digs, The Village*, about the Monto; *Pledges and Promises*, about the collapse of the docks in the 50s; and *A Hape of Junk* — all using inexperienced local actors. This led on to the founding of CAFE with Annie Kilmartin, the Grapevine City Workshop and the Northside Community Action Project. One well-known piece of Peter's was *Shades of the Jellywoman* with Jean Costello (who plays Rita in the TV soap Fair City), one of the women from the City Workshop, based on her own life in the inner city.

But more often since, when it comes to good nutty ould Dublinese on the stage, there is more of the macho, pigeon-walking, hardchaw strut to the new drama. Expletives came into their own in a big way with the dawn in the 1980s of the quintessential Dublin company, Passion Machine, and the early theatrical vision of Paul Mercier in *Studs* and *Spacers*, or Roddy Doyle's mad-headed *Brown Bread* (about a bunch of lads kidnapping a bishop) which went from the SFX to the Olympia, before Roddy went mega with *The Commitments*.

These expletives, erupting from the underclass accents, were a gesture of ebullient defiance against bourgeois social mores, and asserted their own mock-macho modes of appropriate behaviour. The plays gave vent to a new breed of comical head-the-balls who confidently leapt up onto the rostrum; punctuated their lines with aggro-karate routines; shifted their crotch for emphasis; and mimed the odd loaf into somebody's nose-bridge just for added menace — all drenched with percussive swear-words. In the 1990s, actor Anto Nola was still reliving these John Godber-influenced salad days with his plays *Too Much Too Young*, head-hopping to ska music; or *Fully Recovered*, a more questioning piece about life in a upholstry factory.

In one sense, this was re-appropriating the hard-man

caricature — or the idiocy of Brendan Grace's *Bottler* — and blowing it back like a whirling gobber over the class barricades. Certainly, there is often a very thin line between stereotype, satire and the genuine article, and the emphasis of the playing was crucial.

This upbeat, knockabout sensibility spilled onto the big screen when Roddy Doyle's comedies like *The Commitments* arrived (Ballymun residents were none too pleased, seeing the neighbourhood depicted as full of horses, shattered concrete and burnt-out cars). But there was something daftly genuine in those early works before the darker dramas that later surfaced. I often rerun lines in my head, such as in *The Snapper*, when actor Colm Meany interrupted an argument with Ruth McCabe about their pregnant daughter, to suddenly round on the terrier with displaced frustration — 'Jaysus, how much shite can come out of one dog?'

Despite its similar meaty vernacular, there was a far more feeling, morally searching strain in a couple of plays written by actor Brendan Gleeson back then: *The Bird Table*, about a misfit in the civil service; and *Breaking Up*, about the ending of a young relationship that had produced a baby. These betrayed a melancholic, more realistic mood, which somehow fed into some of Mercier's later plays.

Generally, the early Passion Machine idiom exploited the inbuilt anti-authoritarianism and scepticism of the Dub-idiom, and made a virtue of dingy realism and the gift of laddish slagging, which even middle-class audiences seemed to love — even if they wouldn't necessarily tolerate such 'colourful language' in their own living rooms or work-spaces.

In the theatre, the Dub-macho frequency is still being finessed in new work like Ken Harmon's recent *Wideboy Gospel*, tightly directed by Jimmy Fay. Set against the riots in 1995 after the England-Ireland soccer friendly when English yobs flung the terraces at Irish police, it painted a rough world of criminalised and paramilitarised West Dublin estates. Ronan Leahy played a low-level mad-bastard loser, negotiating his fellow psychos through a staccato script which was pure Dub baroque — a great encrusted, compacted thump of contemporary slang. But this was manga material, really, with the lad's humour preventing much real pathos or penetration. It was choreographed like one long martial-arts manoeuvre: karate turns and air-punches, the percussive nose-hiss with every head-slap — just nastily amusing entertainment, looking for somewhere to go.

But while Dublin has been enjoying a certain gangland-glamour on the silver screen, from the regrettable *Courier* in the 1980s to *The General* and the Veronica Guerin movie *Though the Sky Falls*, a more curious twist on the hard-man Dub-noir genre has emerged in Mark O'Rowe's idiosyncratic pieces, particularly *Made in China*, as directed by Gerry Stembridge. This production abounded in shades of the brutally homophobic, gay subculture of the Kray twins, and of course, more martial arts stuff strutting around to Mametesque hard-core Dub staccato.

O'Rowe displayed unfettered relish in the violent, genito-urinary passages of the piece, and the language packed enough masculine punch to open large exit wounds out the backs of the heads of, say, a Maeve Binchy audience. There were Tarrantino and rap-mythology flavours to the three-handed stand-off between two hard-men and the gormless young apprentice, but it will be hard to forget the queasy magnetism of the anally mutilated, manically destructive psycho — a role that fit Andrew Connolly like an SM leathermask. Sometimes, O'Rowe's intoxication with the florid vernacularity led him to write, rather distractingly, for low laughs. But this was exhilaratingly irresponsible theatre, and it'll be interesting to watch O'Rowe mature and expand on his instincts.

In the last few years, Paul Mercier has entered the most hubristic stage of his career, scratching at the limits of theatre with his manic Dublin trilogy: from *Buddleia*, the tale of a house from first tenants to demolition (the Passion Machine lads truly gloried in that scene), through to *Native City*, an alternative history of twentieth-century Dublin no less, from end-colonial times to 1990s racist assaults — all told, decade by decade, through the uses of an inner-city, now deconsecrated church.

Mercier's work since has been equally ambitious, and although always resonant, not always technically successful. *Ourselves Alone* is a kind of auto-generational play told through seven monologues from characters united by personal history — attending UCD in the 1970s/1980s, labouring in a German gherkin-factory, and later meeting life's rough justice in various ways. There is a lot of truth and feeling in this piece, although in the early form in which I saw it, you had to struggle to comprehend it.

More recently, Mercier wrote *Down the Line* for the Peacock — interestingly, the first time his work has been directed by someone else (Lynne Parker). Set in an 'ordinary' suburban home throughout the 1980s, as the kids gradually leave the nest through matrimony or alienation, this was soap-flavoured realism, with no serious message really, other a certain kind of melancholia watching everything, including family life, moving on towards the autumn years.

One important Dublin play to emerge in recent years, and which travelled to the UK with its excellent cast — was Jimmy Murphy's *Brothers of the Brush*, a visionary piece of lad's realism in the black economy of the building trade — a raging piece of work dramaturged by David Byrne at the Peacock which exposed the realities of the cash-in-hand lifestyle, once the day comes along when a lad becomes a father.

Jimmy's next two plays at the Peacock were less focused, more maudlin affairs, bemoaning homelessness in *A Picture of Paradise*, or in *The Muesli Belt*, the disappearance of a way of life associated with an ould Dublin pub about to be pulled down by the pig-ignorant Celtic Tiger. But Murphy remains an interesting voice, and although I haven't seen his *Kings of the Kilburn High Road*, it seems to have struck a chord.

Perhaps the most successful Dublin playwright to emerge over the past decade has been Conor McPherson, who has defied many stereotypes with his casual, understated monologues. I first came across *The Light of Jesus* — later re-christened and simplified as *The Good Thief* by Garreth Keogh — an Irish road-movie monologue about the moral dilemmas of an ordinary decent crook on the run with a kidnapped woman. When McPHERSON first staged it, under his own direction, he made an intriguing use of slide-projection, with a voice-over regularly intoning left-field quotations on morality from Plato, Hume et al.

Despite a mixed attempt at dramatic dialogue in *The Weir*, monologues, and the dramatic ironies of unreconstructed, pathetic masculinity, remain McPherson's territory. *This Lime Tree Bower* was a hilariously uncomfortable piece narrated by a series of straight-faced, laconic Dublin blokes who, with jaw-dropping insouciance, drawled out matter-of-fact admissions of cruelty, abominable selfishness, or the functional relief of simply having a wank.

The dense medium of alcohol, first visited in *Rum & Vodka* — an early monologue about the reality tunnel of a grotesquely pissed night in Dublin town — has now become the central characteristic of McPherson's creations. *Port Authority* again delved into the stomach-curdling realities of what young drinkers and alcoholic thirty-somethings do to themselves — never mind the philosophical geyser in the old people's home, keeping aflame life's little pleasures, alongside the secret embers of a romance, which might once have happened.

Again in *Dublin Carol*, the grim certainties of alcohol addiction are the issue here, as much as the central character's job as an undertaker, which scarcely impinges on his Christmas Eve boozing in the office. It's a bleak, Pintry scenario, the man's grotesque habit having estranged him from his family, and now from his wife's impending death. It's a more convincing part than many of McPherson's older characters. Generally, McPherson's work is utterly male-centred, with a grimly philosophical tinge — quietly excoriating his characters by exposing their hard-wired, anti-social desires, and offering little antidote other than black humour.

In recent years, there has been remarkably little direct social or political engagement in Southern drama, apart from notable exceptions such as Donal O'Kelly's *Asylum, Asylum*, or Joe

O'Byrne's *It Come Up Sun* for Passion Machine — both on refugee issues. It's interesting that this reticence occurs only a few miles down the road from Northern Ireland, and perhaps reflects less a post-colonial social confidence than an embarassed legacy of censorship, reinforced by a strong critical allergy to agit prop and advocacy in the theatre.

Even Jim Nolan's strange, meta-theatrical, historical drama of his Waterford parish at the Abbey, *Blackwater Angel*, sidestepped the rich resonances of tunnelling backwards in time to the tale of a former Cromwellian soldier who had benefited grandly from the Munster Plantation. Nolan's concerns were less with the colonial inequities or societal backdrop, and more on the soldier-character (played with star-power by John Lynch), and his agonising over his mystical gift of healing. The only real engagement with the historical period came, oddly enough, with the closure of the theatres under the puritanical Republic, through the device of a very Shakespearian underground English theatre troupe, and its young foundling in whose singing the former soldier hears the voice of God.

History is embroidered deeply into the fine fabric of Sebastian Barry's hyper-poetic plays, but he rarely allows big-world politics to cloud the theatrical after-life which he brings to his oft-non-conformist Protestant ancestors. Certainly, his work charts the decline of the Protestant identity in the south of Ireland through a haunted gallery of florid, childish play-language and the imagined voices of the little left-over figures of history, such as the utopic, clean-living sect doomed to die out on the inhospitable island in *Prayers of Sherkin*.

In this production, as in most of his earlier plays, he was served extremely well by director Caroline Fitzgerald, and later by Max Stafford-Clarke, with Barry's greatest success, *The Stewart of Christendom*, featuring one of the late Donal McCann's truly great roles. Once the Chief Superintendent of what he called Christendom, Dublin Castle, the old man babbles, incontinently but heart-breakingly, from his dotage in the County home in Wicklow. Here as elsewhere, Barry takes a more variegated than bipolar view of Irish history, although his sympathies might be best expressed by the remark of one wittering aunt-character about the bould Michael Collins, 'with a tally of carnage, intrigue and disloyalty that would shame a tinker'.

Perhaps unsurprisingly, the easing of the Troubles in Northern Ireland has seen an opening up of drama that confronts the ancient shibboleths of Northern Irish society. The long Troubles period saw dramatists walking tightrope razor-blades of cliche and sectarian pigeonholing, perhaps most successfully negotiated by the late Stewart Parker (*Northern Star* is a great, difficult favourite of mine), or Friel with such agonised protest plays as *Freedom of the City*, or the charged historical allegory of *Making History* — both recently revived at the Abbey.

Meanwhile, a whole cohort of straight-talking voices has emerged, thanks to the ever-wobbling ceasefires: Gary Mitchell, the ever-ready poet laureate of homicidal loyalism; Conall Morrison's blistering one-man piece, *Hard to Believe*, on Ulster's competing mantra-discourses, set against the backdrop of the Dirty War, as written about by Troubles journalist Martin Dillon; or Joe Crilly's cleverly structured *Second Hand Thunder* (rural Orange supremo rapes Southern Catholic schoolteacher under his power) and *On McQuillan's Hill* (a gay IRA man comes home from the Kesh to the mess of his former life). Daragh Carville has produced more disinterested drinkathons of Belfast young things — and what about the totem-toppling satire of the rangy sit-com on BBC Northern Ireland, *Will Ye Give My Head Peace?*

Perhaps the single most arresting convulsion of theatrical response to the edgy, post-Troublesy thaw came from Belfast's Tinderbox company in 2000, when it commissioned seven playwrights to write pieces for a ghostly promenade through the disused, notorious Crumlin Road jail and courthouse, where the most monstrous offenders of the Troubles were sent down by the Diplock Courts. The night I saw it, its resonances were intensified by a wee bit of fireworks that had broken out, a couple of hundred yards further up the Crumlin road.

The playlets threaded unrelated, like chance encounters,

through the glacial, fungal stench of the place: Nicola McCartney's coldly menacing Jury Room piece; Marie Jones's sceptical slag of officialdom's PR-spin in re-commissioning the place; Daragh Carville's satire of cynical journalism with two journos in the underground toilets; Damian Gorman's Judge's Room pisstake, in which an outrageous old m'lud suggested a Wagnerian Riverdance to commemorate the Troubles; Owen McCafferty's Kafkaesque otherworld in Court no. 1, about a haunted, re-interrogated victim who has never seen his killer brought to justice; and Gary Mitchell's piece about a loyalist nutter swinging the bars, only to burst into big-boy tears, once locked in his dark cell.

Martin Lynch's final declamatory farewell piece in the foyer got right up the noses of many critics, when his ghost character boomed at the audience: 'you pile of voyeuristic, theatre-going, fun-seeking, hedonistic, facile assholes!' — which, under the circumstances, I personally found utterly appropriate. Meanwhile, the community drama movement is sharply divided within Belfast, with the exception of CAF's astonishing production of the *Wedding Play*, which, back in 1999, shuttled audiences in buses across the burnt-out 'interface' between the nationalist Short Strand and Protestant Madrid Street in inner-city East Belfast. Devised around the notion of a mixed marriage, and then written up by Martin Lynch and Marie Jones, it was one of the most moving pieces I've ever seen about Belfast since the days of the divine Charabanc, and their affectionate howlers of community plays of cheerful, hardy Belfast women under the yoke of poverty and civil war.

Protestant community groups have been trying to forge a new sense of cultural identity with big pieces like *The Mourning Ring* — a devised piece written up by Ken Bourke and directed by Paddy McCooey — identifying the Protestant people as a community in constant flux, by juxtaposing two parallel storylines from 1995 and the Ulster plantation around 1605. Another piece of Protestant historicity from the Ballybeen group in 1999, *No Straight Lines*, was written by Moyra Donaldson.

Meanwhile, over in unrepentant West Belfast, the Pam Brighton wing of Dubbeljoint has been producing a steady stream of Republican agit prop plays, featuring former Republican prisoners, such as *Forced Upon Us* — a provocative but justifiable republican peat-shovel into the 1920s sectarian outrages, wrought by the one-party Unionist statelet. Not deemed helpful to the peace process in 1999, the subject matter of *Forced Upon Us* prompted the famous, temporary withdrawal of Dubbeljoint's Arts Council grant.

The Dubbeljoint company first embroiled itself with this kind of material in the early 1990s, by collaborating with the Just Us group of nationalist West Belfast women. Their first joint show, *Binlids* — in classic Brechtian style — took audiences by the ear into the traumatic genesis of the Troubles, including incidents such as the Ballymurphy riots in the early 1970s, which saw a number of civilians, including a priest, shot dead by the British Army. Although most Belfast and London critics found *Binlids* raucous and one-sided, the republican women had their finest hour — or at least damn good crack — when they brought *Binlids* to Amerikay.

Much of Dubbeljoint's recent material has conveniently restricted its focus to the very earliest years of the Troubles — as with its affecting one-man show, *Des*, written by former republican prisoners, Brian Campbell and Laurence McKeown. *Des* was written as the first-hand testimony of the former dioscesan priest, writer and campaigner, Des Wilson, who was continually drawn into the firing line between the British Army and republicans in his parish in Ballymurphy until his resignation in 1975. It was an oddly affectionate tribute to a man who was in the front row on opening nights in both West Belfast and Dublin's SFX.

More recently, Dubbeljoint have produced *The Laughter of our Children* about the Hunger Strikes, again scripted by Campbell and McKeown, who both edited the agonised H-Block book, *Nor Meekly Serve My Time*. Historically, McKeown followed Bobby Sands and the others into starvation for seventy days on the 1981

Hunger Strike, before being taken off by his family when he slipped into coma.

Aisling Ghear also recently produced Peter Sheridan's *Diary of a Hungerstrike* in the Culturlann on the Falls Road, and McKeown has published another book, *Out of Time*, detailing the appalling, nitty-gritty experiences of twenty-five Republican prisoners on the long H-block battle of nerves and minds, which had so much to do with impelling Sinn Féin into the political, as well as the paramilitary arena.

In drawing towards a close, one thing which must be said about theatre-creation both north and south of the border, is that it is largely a man's world, in terms of scripting and direction. There has been some notable feminist theatre in Dublin from Glasshouse, and their shows by Emma Donoghue and Trudy Hayes; also Patricia Burke Brogan's play *Eclipsed* about women in the Magdalen laundaries; and Sligo's Quare Hawks with their devised piece, *Cracked*, about women held in Loman's mental hospital in Mullingar. Tara Maria Lovett is one of a number of new women's voices whose work has appeared recently in Dublin's Project Arts Centre.

One unsettling piece I saw in Dublin's City Arts Centre was Paula Meehan's *Cell*, a well-meaning piece of advocacy, developed with inmates of the Women's Prison in Mountjoy, most of them caught within the loop of recidivism, suicide, overdose, addiction and 'the virus' — and featuring the sex-for-heroin brutality of an older lesbian character. Not a terribly comfortable Dublin to be looking at on a full stomach, and perhaps not surprising that it didn't make the leap onto the mainstage.

All of the above is a broad impression of the theatre I've had the privilege to watch over the past fifteen years or so. I have had to confine my analysis mainly to the scripts and language, and hence, I do not apportion nearly enough credit to the astonishing contribution made by many actors and performers, designers and backstage people, who have made this vast array of work possible. Neither does my account take into account the physical-theatre movement of companies such as Sligo's Blue Raincoats, who have premiered visionary new texts such as Malcolm Hamilton's *Vinegar Fog*, *Once Time* and *Still Life*, and of course, Brendan Ellis' *The Westport Murders*.

Interestingly enough, the Theatre Shop in Dublin has now embarked on the pilot of a projected Irish digitial 'playography' going back to 1950. It's an attempt to mine and define an Irish repertoire through a database, searchable under themes such as lesbianism, actors, alcoholism, domestic violence, rape, unemployment, love, emigration, journalism, drugs, memory, art, the death penalty, or whatever you're having yourself.

When these texts are all enumerated, filed, and catalogued online next year, perhaps a clearer, multi-dimensional Venn diagram may emerge of just how Irish theatre has — faithfully or otherwise, over the last five decades — represented Irish society and depredations and politics and language and popular culture. All that rich source material from which Irish theatre has constantly manufactured its perpetually anxious, but frequently uplifting magic.

Ben Barnes is currently Artistic Director of the National Theatre. He has directed extensively in theatre and opera at home and abroad. He has received national and international awards for his productions, which have been seen around the world from New York to Moscow and from Adelaide to Tokyo.

Csilla Bertha is Associate Professor at the University of Debrecen, English Department in Hungary. She has published widely on Irish literature, especially on drama, and on Irish and Hungarian literary parallels. She is author of a book-length study of Yeats' drama in Hungarian, co-author with Donald E. Morse, of *Visible and Invisible, Essays on Irish Literature* and co-editor of several volumes of essays on Irish literature.

Breandán Delap is editor of *Foinse*, the Irish language newspaper. His previous work includes *Úrscéalta Stairiúla na Gaeilge* (An Clóchomhar, 1993) and *Mad Dog Coll – an Irish Gangster* (Mercier, 1999). He also wrote the script for TG4's documentary *Mad Dog Coll*, which won an IFTA award in 2000. He is a regular theatre reviewer for *The Irish Times* in the West of Ireland. He won the Oireachtas award for journalism in 1998.

Clare Dowling is a novelist, children's writer and a scriptwriter for Fair City.

Owen Dudley Edwards was born in Dublin on 27 July 1938 and grew up in Clontarf. He was educated at Belvedere and at University College Dublin. He then studied and taught in the USA for seven years, and settled in Scotland with his wife Bonnie in 1966, teaching History at the Unviersities of Aberdeen and (since 1968) Edinburgh. He reviewed the Edinburgh Festival and Fringe for the *Irish Times* from

1974 until recently, as well as for the *Scotsman* and the BBC. His books include *The Edinburgh Fesitval* and *City of a Thousand Worlds* (a more impressionistic view of the Festival).

Emile Jean Dumay was born 1931 in France and is a former student of the Ecole Normale Supérieure de Saint-Cloud. A member of the Maison Antoine Vitez and of the Société Française d'Etudes Irlandaises, he has written a doctorate thesis on Le Théâtre de Sean O'Casey, réalité, rêve et revolution (1987). He has contributed a number of articles on contemporary Irish playwrights, and translated plays by Sebastian Barry, Tom Kilroy, Dermot Bolger and Tom Murphy.

Karen Fricker is editor in chief of *Irish Theatre Magazine* and writes and broadcasts about theatre for, among others, *The Irish Times*, RTÉ, *The Guardian*, *Variety*, and *The New York Times*. She has lectured on drama at University College Dublin and Trinity College, and is studying for a PhD at Trinity. Originally from California, she has a BA and MA from Stanford University.

Johnny Hanrahan is Meridian's Artistic Director. He is a writer and director. Recent work includes an adaptation of William Trevor's 'Reading Turgenev', 'Craving' and 'The River'. Johnny works closely with composer John Browne and in addition to these Meridian productions they collaborated on two shows for the Ark Cultural Centre in Dublin: *The Pied Piper*, a children's opera, and *The Fourth Wise Man*, a Christmas play for the millennium. Johnny recently collaborated with Olwen Fouere and Roger Doyle (Operating Theatre) on a music theatre piece entitled *Chair*, which premiered in the Peacock Theatre in October 2001.

Katy Hayes was a founder member and resident director with Glasshouse Productions from 1990 to 1995. She now works full-time as a novelist and is the mother of two small children.

Mária Kurdi is associate professor in the Department of English Literatures and Cultures at the University of Pécs, Hungary. Her main fields of teaching and research are modern Irish literature and English-speaking drama. Her publications include a book in Hungarian surveying contemporary Irish drama, and a book of essays titled *Codes and Masks: Aspects of Identity in Contemporary Irish Plays in an Intercultural Context*, published by Peter Lang in 2000. Besides these, she has published numerous articles about twentieth-century Irish, American and British authors. She is guest editor of a special issue of the *Hungarian Journal of English and American Studies*.

Ronan McDonald is the author of *Tragedy and Irish Literature: Synge, O'Casey, Beckett* and has published numerous articles and reviews on Irish culture and drama. He is co-editor of *Bullan: An Irish Studies Journal*. He studied at University College Dublin and the University of Oxford and now lectures in English at the University of Reading.

Anna McMullan is a lecturer in the School of Drama at Trinity College Dublin, and director of the M.Phil. in Irish Theatre and Film. Main areas of research include contemporary Irish theatre, gender and theatre, and the drama of Samuel Beckett. She has published several articles on women in Irish theatre and is currently co-editing with Caroline Williams the contemporary drama section of the fourth volume of the *Field Day Anthology of Irish Writing*, devoted to women's writing. She is also co-editing with Cathy Leeney a book of articles on Marina Carr to be published by Carysfort Press, in association with the Arts Council, in 2002.

Vic Merriman is the Senior Lecturer in Drama at Dublin Institute of Technology, Rathmines. Research interests include contemporary Irish theatre, post-colonialism and drama pedagogy. He was a member of the Arts Council of Ireland (1993-1998) and chaired the Council's Review of Theatre in Ireland (1995-1996).

Mic Moroney is a writer, video-maker, critic and cultural commen-tator based in Dublin.

Siân Quill is a *Fair City* scriptwriter. She is a freelance writer with *The Sunday Tribune* and the *Evening Herald* and is one of the panel of journalists on *Morning Ireland's* 'It Says in the Papers' slot. She continues to act.

Colm Tóibín was born in Enniscorthy, Co Wexford in 1955 and has lived in Dublin for many years. A former editor of *Magill* and *In Dublin*, he is the author of four novels, *The South*, *The Heather Blazing*, *The Story of the Night* and *The Blackwater Lightship* (which was shortlisted for the Booker Prize). His non-fiction works include *The Sign of the Cross: Travels in Catholic Europe* and *Homage to Barcelona*.

John Waters was born and reared in Castlerea, Co Roscommon. He is currently editor of *Magill* magazine, and a columnist with *The Irish Times*. He has published several books including *Jiving at the Crossroads* (1991); *Race of Angels* (1994) and *An Intelligent Person's Guide to Modern Ireland* (1997). His plays include *Long Black Coat* and *Easter Dues*.

Caroline Williams is currently editor of BooksIrish.com, an Irish interest internet bookshop, and has also worked as a literary researcher and editor.

NOTES

[1] The post– in this case is intended to indicate a caesura: a clean break with an unsophisticated past.

[2] D. Nowlan, 'Polemic driven to a foregone conclusion', *The Irish Times*, (15 September, 1995).

[3] Calypso Productions, Mission Statement, 1995.

[4] F. O'Toole, 'Second Opinion: A powerful gesture', *The Irish Times*, (26 September, 1995).

[5] 'Strangers in a Strange Land', *Irish Theatre Magazine*, 1.1, (Autumn 1998), p. 12.

[6] Stephen Lacey, *British Realist Theatre: The New Wave in its Context 1956 — 1965* (London, 1995).

[7] Una Chaudhuri, *Staging Place: The Geography of Modern Drama* (Ann Arbor, 1997), p. 8.

[8] Esther Beth Sullivan, 'What is "left to a woman of the house" when the Irish situation is staged', in Jeanne Colleran and Jenny S. Spencer (eds), *Staging Resistance: Essays on Political Theatre*, (Ann Arbor, 1998), p. 223.

[9] Critics of realism, including Brechtian and feminist critics, such as Elin Diamond, *Unmaking Mimesis* (London & New York, 1997), argue that it tends to present that environment as inevitably determining its inhabitants and its audiences, constraining their possibilities of rewriting history, or of reinventing identity, agency and location on an individual or communal level.

[10] A critique of the Irish political system.

[11] See Siobhán Ní Bhrádaigh, *Mairéad Ní Ghráda – Ceannródaí Dramaíochta* (Cló Iar-Chonnachta, 1996). Also a biography on the Local Ireland web site: http://www.local.ie.

[12] Mairéad Ní Ghráda, *On Trial* (Dublin, 1966), p. 60. Translation into English by Mairead Ni Ghrada, *An Triail/Breithiuntas* (Dublin, 1978).

[13] Edna O'Brien, *A Pagan Place: A Play* (London, 1973), p. 14.

[14] Ibid., p. 17.

[15] De Valera's St Patrick Day's broadcast, 1943.

[16] Edna O'Brien, *A Pagan Place: A Play*, (London, 1973), p. 33.

[17] Ibid., p. 64.

[18] Patricia Burke Brogan, *Eclipsed*, (Galway, 1994), p. 23.

[19] Ibid., p. 45.

[20] Ibid., p. 33.

[21] Ibid., p. 30.

[22] Ibid., p. 10-11.

[23] Ibid., p. 76.

[24] Marina Carr, *Plays 1* (London, 1999); Marina Carr, *On Raftery's Hill* (Meath, 2000), p. 219.

[25] In *Blue* (2000) a play by the young Clare playwright, Ursula Rani Sarma, the narrow grid of habitual routine in small town life is contrasted with a poetic evocation of the sea, which represents a different, more fluid order of space, time and identity, associated with the female and with death:

DES: 'she's a mercury blue duvet and as I step out into the air,
    she's a soft wall flying up to meet me and I'm through,
    and I'm going way down into the blue like lead,
    and I lie face down in the deep black sand and
    open my mouth and breath in the blueness,
    touch the stars that are diamond cool and smooth in my hands.
    And I see her come towards me,
    she's so beautiful and she talks to me softly
    and then moves to go,
    Can't you stay?
    Stay a while longer?
            (Unpublished manuscript)

[26] Marina Carr, *On Raftery's Hill* (Meath, 2000), p. 289.

[27] Paula Meehan, *Mrs Sweeney* in Siobhán Bourke, Ed., *Rough Magic: First Plays* (Dublin & London, 1999), p. 463.

[28] Ibid., p. 411.

[29] Ibid., p. 432.

[30] Ibid., p. 452.

[31] Ibid., p. 452.

[32] Anna Devlin, *After Easter* (London, 1995), p. 74.

[33] Ibid., p. 3.

[34] Ibid., p. 15.

[35] Ibid., p. 50.

[36] Ibid., p. 75.

[37] Ibid., p. 75.

[38] Ciarán Benson, *The Cultural Psychology of Self: Place, Morality and Art in Human Worlds* (London & New York, 2001), p. 28.

[39] Ibid., p. 60.

[40] Una Chaudhuri, *Staging Place: The Geography of Modern Drama* (Ann Arbor, 1997), p. 138.

[41] Elizabeth Kuti, *Treehouses* (London, 2000), p. 17.

[42] Christopher Murray, *Twentieth-Century Irish Drama: Mirror Up to Nation* (Manchester, 1997), p. 224.

[43] Carole Woddis, 'Review of *True Lines*', *The Guardian* (16 May 1995).

[44] Interview with author, Domnar Warehouse Theatre, London, 3 March 2000. All further quotes from Crowley are taken from this interview.

[45] Thanks to Cormac Sheridan, the lighting designer of *Alice Walking and Falling* and *True Lines*, for help in reconstructing the chronology of both productions.

[46] Crowley says it was audience response that prompted the company to change Bill's story: 'They said that the show seemed to set up the fact that he died. And there was a feeling that in a story of people of this generation, one of them wouldn't make it. When you look back, sadly there is always one missing.'

[47] Declan Kiberd, *Inventing Ireland: The Literature of the Modern Nation* (London, 1996), p. 164.

[48] Salman Rushdie, *Imaginary Homelands* (London, 1992), quoted in Kiberd, *Inventing Ireland*, p. 164.

[49] Cast member Cathy Belton provided invaluable information about the creation of *True Lines*, including this fact, in an informal interview in Dublin on 18 May 2001.

[50] Elinor Fuchs, *The Death of Character: Perspectives on Theatre after Modernism*, (Bloomington, Indiana, 1996), p. 8.

[51] Ibid., p. 10.

[52] Ibid., pp. 9-10.

[53] Fintan O'Toole, 'Second Opinion: A New World on Show', *The Irish Times* (18 October 1994).

[54] Ibid.

[55] Salman Rushdie, *Imaginary Homelands* (London, 1992), pp. 13-14.

[56] Crowley has since become associate director of the Donmar Warehouse in London and has directed acclaimed productions in Britain and America, and the *True Lines* actors, as well, have gone on to impressive careers: McElveen is a jobbing actor in Ireland, as is Belton, who has appeared in numerous high-profile productions and had a recurring role in the RTÉ soap *Glenroe*. Murphy won the 1998 Tony Award for best featured actor for his role in *The Beauty Queen of Leenane*, and Townsend recently played the title role in Gerard Stembridge's film *About Adam*.

[57] Fintan O'Toole, 'Irish Theatre: The State of the Art', in *Theatre Stuff: Critical Essays on Contemporary Irish Theatre*, ed. Eamonn Jordan (Dublin, 2000), pp. 47-49.

[58] Ibid., p. 54.

[59] Christopher Murray, 'The State of Play: Irish Theatre in the Nineties' in *The State of Play: Irish Theatre in the Nineties*, ed. Eberhard Bort Trier (Wissenschaftlicher, 1996), p. 14.

[60] Ibid., p. 14.

[61] Shaun Richards, 'Brian Friel: Seizing the Moment of Flux', *Irish University Review*, 30. 2 (Autumn-Winter 2000), 270-271.

[62] Ibid., p. 257.

[63] Brian Friel, *Wonderful Tennessee* (London, 1993), p. 42.

[64] Brian Friel, *Molly Sweeney* (Loughcrew, 1994), p. 41.

[65] Ibid., p. 67.

[66] F.C. McGrath, *Brian Friel's (Post)Colonial Drama* (Syracuse, 1999), p. 278.

[67] Shaun Richards, 'Placed Identities for Placeless Times: Brian Friel and Postcolonial Criticism', *Irish University Review*, 27. 1 (Spring-Summer 1997), p.66.

[68] Richard Pine, *The Diviner: The Art of Brian Friel* (Dublin, 1999), p.284.

[69] Seamus Heaney, '...English and Irish', *Times Literary Supplement* (October, 1980) 1199.

[70] James P. Farrelly and Mark C. 'Ireland Facing the Void: the Emergence of Meaninglessness in the Works of Brian Friel', *The Canadian Journal of Irish Studies.* 24. 1 (July,1998) 111.

[71] Brian Friel, *Molly Sweeney* (Loughcrew, 1994), p.54.

[72] William Butler Yeats, 'Among School Children' in *Collected Poems* (London, 1950), p.245.

[73] Brian Friel, *Wonderful Tennessee* (London, 1993), p. 42.

[74] Brian Friel, *Molly Sweeney* (Loughcrew, 1994), p.62.

[75] Brian Friel, *Give Me Your Answer, Do!* (London, 1997), p.79.

[76] Ibid., p.78.

[77] Ibid., pp.79–80.

[78] Ibid., p.75.

[79] Ibid., p.83.

[80] Ibid., p.52.

[81] Árpád Farkas, 'On the litter of leaves' in *Homeland in the Heights,* ed. Csilla Bertha (Budapest, 2000) transl. Len Roberts, p.217.

[82] Christopher Murray, 'The State of Play: Irish Theatre in the Nineties' in *The State of Play: Irish Theatre in the Nineties*, ed. Eberhard Bort Trier (Wissenschaftlicher, 1996), p.20.

[83] Christopher Innes, 'Introduction: Remaking Modern Classics', *Modern Drama* 43. 2 (2000), p.249.

[84] Caitríona Beaumont, 'Gender, Citizenship and the State, 1922-1990' in *Ireland in Proximity: History, Gender, Space*, eds. Scott Brewster, Virginia Crossman, Fiona Becket, and David Alderson (London, 1999), p.105.

[85] Brian Friel, *The London Vertigo* (Dublin, 1990), p.11.

[86] Ibid., p.45.

[87] Ibid., p.45.

[88] Brian Friel, *A Month in the Country: After Turgenev* (Dublin, 1992), p.18.

[89] Ibid., pp.81-82.

[90] Ibid., p.243.

[91] Shoshana Felman, 'Women and Madness: the Critical Fallacy' in *The Feminist Reader: Essays in Gender and the Politics of Literary Criticism*, eds. Catherine Belsey and Jane Moore, (London, 1989), p.134.

[92] Brian Friel, *A Month in the Country: After Turgenev* (Dublin, 1992), p. 102.

[93] Ibid., p. 103.

[94] Ibid., p. 81.

[95] Richard Pine, *The Diviner: The Art of Brian Friel* (Dublin, 1999), p. 254.

[96] Brian Friel, *A Month in the Country: After Turgenev* (Dublin, 1992), pp. 89-90.

[97] Robert Tracy, 'The Russian Connection: Friel and Chekhov' *Irish University Review*, 29. 1 (Spring-Summer, 1999), 74.

[98] Ibid., p. 70.

[99] Karl D. Kramer, '"A Subject Worthy of Ayvazovsky's Brush": Vanya's Misdirected Fury', *Modern Drama,* 42.4 (1999), p. 512.

[100] Brian Friel, *Uncle Vanya* (Dublin, 1998), p. 35.

[101] Brian Friel, 'Seven Notes for a Festival Programme' in *Brian Friel. Essays, Diaries, Interviews: 1964-1999*, ed. Christopher Murray (London, 1999), p. 179.

[102] Brian Friel, *Uncle Vanya* (Dublin, 1998), p. 23.

[103] Robert Tracy, 'The Russian Connection: Friel and Chekhov' *Irish University Review*, 29. 1 (Spring-Summer, 1999), 73.

[104] Karl D. Kramer, '"A Subject Worthy of Ayvazovsky's Brush": Vanya's Misdirected Fury', *Modern Drama*, 42. 4 (1999), p. 513.

[105] Brian Friel, *Uncle Vanya* (Dublin, 1998), p. 55.

[106] Christopher Innes, 'Introduction: Remaking Modern Classics', *Modern Drama*, 43. 2 (2000), 250.

[107] Cs. Jónás, Erzsébet. *A magyar Csehov* (The Hungarian Chekhov) (Nyíregyháza, 1995), pp. 226-227.

[108] Shaun Richards, 'Brian Friel: Seizing the Moment of Flux', *Irish University Review*, 30. 2 (Autumn-Winter, 2000), 254.

[109] Programme notes for *Tine Chnámh*.

[110] *Foinse*, September 1999.

[111] Stewart Parker, *Dramatis Personae* (Belfast,1986), p. 19.

[112] Gary Mitchell, *Tearing the Loom* (London, 1998), p. 81.

[113] Brian Friel, *Plays: 2* (London, 1999), p. 267.

[114] Ibid., p. 267.

[115] Seamus Heaney, *The Cure at Troy* (London,1990), p. 77.

[116] Ibid., p. 2.

[117] Bill Morrison, *A Love Song for Ulster: An Irish Trilogy* (London, 1994), p. xvi.

[118] Ibid., p. 4.

[119] Ibid., p. 7.

[120] Ibid., p. 7.

[121] Gary Mitchell, *In Little World of Our Own* (London, 1998), p. 51.

INDEX

A

Abbey Theatre, 9, 13, 17, 64, 75, 82, 116, 117, 161, 258, 271
   Barbaric Comedies, 13, 126–9, 171
   Edinburgh Festival productions, 165–6, 169
   Gaelic productions, 151, 218, 220–1
   managing change, 131
   and national identity, 55–7, 232
   Stage Irish, 230
   Tomas Mac Anna tribute, 121, 124–5
Ackroyd, Peter, 93, 94
Adams, Gerry, 152, 156
   Peg's Paper, 156
Ahern, Bertie, 262
Aisling Ghéar (theatre company), 222, 228–9, 274
Aisteoirí an Spidéil, 217
Aisteoirí Aon Dráma, 222
Aisteoirí Bhréanainn, 217
Aisteoirí Bulfin, 217
Aisteoirí Ghaoth Dobhair, 216
Amharclann de hÍde, 216, 217, 219, 221–4, 229–30, 254
Anderson, Lindsay, 160–1
Andrews Lane Theatre, 135, 136, 143–4
Arden, John, 74
Aron, Geraldine, 141
Arts Council of Ireland, 10, 15–16, 121, 133, 218, 221
Arts from Ireland festival (Washington), 251
Assembly Rooms (Edinburgh), 156, 161, 166–8, 172
asylum seekers, 67–70

B

Baile an Droichid, 226
ballad tradition, 30–1
Balloonatics (theatre company), 156
Barabbas (theatre company), 16, 117
Barbaric Comedies, The, 13, 126–9, 171
Barker, Howard, 135
   Gary the Thief, 167
Barnes, Ben, 13, 16, 120–31, 260, 276
Barry, Kevin, 33
Barry, Sebastian, 20, 21, 204, 206, 270–1
   Boss Grady's Boys, 202
   French performances, 196, 199–203
   Our Lady of Sligo, 199, 200, 201–3
   Prayers of Sherkin, 270
   The Adventures of Aeneas McNulty, 95
   The Steward of Christendom, 196, 199, 200–1, 202, 203, 270–1
   White Woman Street, 95
Beaumont, Caitríona, 284
Beckett, Samuel, 74, 158, 168
   Company, 167
   I'll Go On, 167–8
Bedlam Theatre, 151
Behan, Brendan, 20
   Borstal Boy, 263
   The Hostage, 172, 263
   The Quare Fella, 263
Behan, John, 125
Belfast, *see also* Northern Ireland
   Irish language drama, 227–9